P9-EES-264

ALSO BY RYSZARD KAPUŚCIŃSKI

*The Soccer War*
*The Emperor*
*Shah of Shahs*
*Another Day of Life*

# Imperium

# Imperium

RYSZARD
KAPUŚCIŃSKI

TRANSLATED FROM THE POLISH BY
KLARA GLOWCZEWSKA

ALFRED A. KNOPF • CANADA

PUBLISHED BY ALFRED A. KNOPF CANADA


*Published in Canada in 1994 by Alfred A. Knopf Canada, Toronto, and simultaneously in the United States by Alfred A. Knopf, Inc., New York. Distributed by Random House of Canada Limited, Toronto.*

*Originally published in Poland by Czytelnik, Warsaw, in 1993.*


*Grateful acknowledgment is made to the following for permission to reprint previously published material:*

Alfred A. Knopf, Inc.: *Excerpt from* The Russian Revolution *by Richard Pipes; copyright © 1990 by Richard Pipes. Reprinted by permission of Alfred A. Knopf, Inc.*

University of California Press: *Excerpt from "Prose of the Trans-Siberian and of Little Jeanne of France," from* Complete Poems *by Blaise Cendrars, translated and edited by Ron Padgett; copyright © 1947 by Editions Denoël, copyright © 1992 by Ron Padgett. Reprinted by permission of University of California Press.*

Viking Penguin: *Excerpt from Anton Chekhov letter, 1890, from* Letters of Anton Chekhov, *by Anton Chekhov, translated by Avrahm Yarmolinsky; copyright © 1973 by Avrahm Yarmolinsky, copyright © 1947, 1968 by The Viking Press, Inc. Reprinted by permission of Viking Penguin, a division of Penguin Books USA Inc.*

FIRST CANADIAN EDITION

*Canadian Cataloguing in Publication Data*
*Kapuściński, Ryszard.*
*Imperium*
*ISBN 0-394-28034-2*
*1. Soviet Union—Description and travel—1970–1991.*
*2. Soviet Union—Politics and government—1985–1991.*
*3. Soviet Union—Social conditions—1970–1991.*
*4. Kapuściński, Ryszard—Journeys—Soviet Union.*
*I. Title.*
*DK286.K36 1994 914.704'854*
*C93-094966-8*

*Printed and bound in the United States of America*

*Toronto, New York, London, Sydney, Auckland*

*. . . in other words, that these are wonders; and all of this constitutes a picture.* —ANDREI BIELY, *Imperium*

*Russia has seen many things during the one thousand years of its history. There is only one thing that Russia has not seen in one thousand years—freedom.*

—VASILY GROSSMAN

*The present is something that binds us. We create the future in our imagination. Only the past is a pure reality.*

—SIMONE WEIL

*In Russia, an artist's entire energy should be directed at showing two forces: man and nature. On the one hand, physical weakness, nervousness, early sexual maturity, a passionate desire for life and truth, a dreaming of a range of activity as wide as the steppe, analysis full of anxiety, a lack of knowledge together with high conceptual flights, and on the other hand—a boundless plain, a severe climate; a severe, gray nation with its heavy, grim history, its Tatar period, officialdom, ignorance, poverty, the humid climate of the capitals, Slavic apathy, etc. Russian life so threshes the Russian that he cannot collect himself, it threshes him like a thousand-pood stick.* —ANTON CHEKHOV

*Our dominant impression of things Russian is an impression of a vast irreparable breakdown. The great monarchy that was here in 1914 and the administrative, social, financial, and commercial systems connected with it have, under the strains of six years of incessant war, fallen down and smashed utterly. Never in all history has there been so great a* débâcle *before.*

—H. G. WELLS, 1920

*The adventure that is the Soviet Union is the greatest experiment and the most important problem of mankind.*

—EDGAR MORIN

*Russia vomited out the abomination that they were feeding it.*

—FYODOR DOSTOYEVSKY

*The system that governs us is a combination of the old nomenclatura, the sharks of finance, false democrats, and the KGB. I cannot call this democracy—it is a repugnant, historically unprecedented hybrid, and we do not know in which direction it will develop . . . [but] if this alliance will prevail, they will be exploiting us not for seventy, but for one-hundred and seventy years.*

—ALEKSANDR SOLZHENITSYN, 1992

*Something has been clarified there, but something still remains obscure.*

—VLADIMIR VOINOVICH

# CONTENTS

# PREFACE

THIS BOOK consists of three parts.

Part 1 is called "First Encounters (1939–1967)" and is a report on my long-ago sojourns in the Imperium. In it I tell about the entrance of Soviet troops into my hometown in the Polesie region of Poland (today this is Belorussia), about a journey across a snow-covered and desolate Siberia, about an expedition to Transcaucasia and to the republics of Central Asia—in other words, to the territories of the former USSR that are filled with exoticism, conflicts, and a singular atmosphere replete with emotion and sentiments.

Part 2 is called "From a Bird's-Eye View (1989–1991)"; it is an account of several of my longer wanderings over the vast lands of the Imperium, which I made in the years of its decline and final disintegration (final at least insofar as the form in which it existed in 1991 is concerned). I made these journeys alone, bypassing official institutions and routes, and the path of these expeditions led from Brest (the border between the former USSR and Poland) to Magadan on the Pacific, and from Vorkuta beyond the Arctic

Circle to Termez (the border with Afghanistan). A total of about sixty thousand kilometers.

Part 3 is called "The Sequel Continues (1992–1993)" and is a collection of reflections, observations, and notes that arose in the margins of my travels, conversations, and readings.

This book is written polyphonically, meaning that the characters, places, and themes that thread their way through its pages might reappear several times, in different years and contexts. However, in contrast to the principles of polyphony, the whole does not end with a higher and definitive synthesis, but, on the contrary, it disintegrates and falls apart, and the reason for this is that in the course of my writing the book, its main subject and theme fell apart—namely, the great Soviet superpower. In its place new states arose, among them Russia—an enormous country, inhabited by a people who for centuries were animated and unified by the imperial ambition.

This book is neither a history of Russia and the former USSR nor a history of the birth and fall of communism in this state nor a handy compendium of knowledge about the Imperium.

It is a personal report based on journeys that I took across the great expanses of this country (or, rather, of this part of the world), trying to get to whatever places time, strength, and opportunity permitted.

# First Encounters (1939–1967)

# Pińsk, '39

MY FIRST ENCOUNTER with the Imperium takes place near the bridge linking the small town of Pińsk, Poland, with the territories to the south. It is the end of September 1939. War is everywhere. Villages are burning; people are taking shelter from air raids in ditches and in forests, seeking salvation wherever they can. Dead horses lie in the road. If you want to pass, a man advises, you will have to move them to the side. How much time is lost because of this, how much sweat: dead horses are very heavy.

Crowds of refugees, fleeing in dust, dirt, panic. What do they need so many bundles for, so many suitcases? Why so many teakettles and pots? Why are they cursing? Why are they constantly asking questions? All of them are walking, riding, running somewhere—nobody knows where. But my mother knows exactly where we are going. She has taken my sister and me by the hand, and all three of us are heading to Pińsk, to our apartment near Wesola Street. We were on holiday at our uncle's near Rejowiec when the war surprised us, and so now we have to go back home. *Tutti a casa!*

After days of wandering we are near Pińsk, and in the distance we can already see the town's houses, the trees of its beautiful park, and the towers of its churches, when suddenly sailors materialize on the road right by the bridge. They have long rifles and sharp, barbed bayonets and, on their round caps, red stars. They sailed here several days ago all the way from the Black Sea, sunk our gunboats, killed our sailors, and now they don't want to let us into town. They keep us at a distance—"Don't move!" they shout, and take aim with their rifles. My mother, as well as other women and children—for they have already rounded up a group of us—is crying and begging for mercy. "Plead for mercy," the mothers, beside themselves with fear, implore us, but what more can we, the children, do—we have already been kneeling on the road, sobbing and stretching out our arms, for a long time.

Shouting, crying, rifles and bayonets, the enraged faces of the sweaty and angry sailors, some sort of fury, something dreadful and incomprehensible, it is all there by the bridge over the river Pina, in this world that I enter at seven years of age.

IN SCHOOL, starting in the first grade, we learn the Russian alphabet. We begin with the letter *s*. "What do you mean by *s*?" someone asks from the back of the classroom. "It should begin with *a*!"

"Children," says the teacher (who is a Pole) in a despondent voice, "look at the cover of our book. What is the first letter on this cover? *S!*"

Petrus, who is a Belorussian, can read the whole title: "Stalin, *Voprosy Leninizma*" (*Studies in Leninism*). It is the only book from which we learn Russian, and our only copy of this book. On the stiff cover wrapped in gray linen, large, gold letters.

"Departing from us, Comrade Lenin commanded us to . . . ," the humble and quiet Władzio reads from the first row in a faltering voice. Best not ask who Lenin was. All our mothers have already instructed us not to ask about anything. But these warnings weren't necessary anyway. I cannot explain it, I cannot say where it came from, but there was something so frightening in the air, something so tense and heavy, that the town in which we used to cavort with wild and joyful abandon had suddenly become a minefield. We were afraid even to take a deep breath, lest we set off an explosion.

All children will be members of the Pioneers! One day a car pulls into the schoolyard, and out step some gentlemen in sky-blue uniforms. Someone says that it's the NKVD. What the NKVD is isn't quite clear, but one thing is certain—when grown-ups utter this name, they lower their voice to a whisper. The NKVD must be terribly important, because its uniforms are elegant, new, spick-and-span. The army walks around in rags; instead of knapsacks they have small linen bags, most often empty, tied up with a piece of old string, and boots that look like they've never been polished, whereas if someone from the NKVD is coming, there is an azure glow for a kilometer around him.

The NKVD people brought us white shirts and red scarves. "On important holidays," says our teacher in a frightened and sad voice, "every child will come to school in this shirt and scarf." They also brought a box of stamps and distributed them to us. On each stamp was a portrait of a different gentleman. Some had mustaches, others not. One gentleman had a small beard, and two didn't have any hair. Two or three wore glasses. One of the NKVD people went from bench to bench distributing the stamps. "Children," said our teacher in a voice that resembled the sound of hollow wood, "these are your leaders." There were nine of these leaders. They were called Andreyev, Voroshilov, Zhdanov, Kaganovich, Kalinin, Mikoyan, Molotov, Khrushchev. The ninth leader was Stalin. The stamp with his portrait was twice as large as the rest. But that was understandable. The gentleman who wrote a book as thick as *Voprosy Leninizma* (from which we were learning to read) should have a stamp larger than the others.

We wore the stamps attached with a safety pin on the left side, in the place where grown-ups wear medals. But soon a problem arose—there was a shortage of stamps. It was ideal, and perhaps even obligatory, to wear all of the leaders at once, with the large Stalin stamp opening, as it were, the collection. That's what those from the NKVD also recommended: "You must wear them all!" But meantime, it turned out that somebody had Zhdanov but didn't have Mikoyan, or somebody had two Kaganovichs but didn't have Molotov. One day Janek brought in as many as four Khrushchevs, which he exchanged for one Stalin (somebody had earlier stolen his Stalin). The real Croesus among us was Petrus—he had three Stalins. He would take them out of his pocket, display them, boast about them.

One day a neighbor from a side bench, Chaim, took me aside. He wanted to exchange two Andreyevs for one Mikoyan, but I told him that Andreyev wasn't worth much (which was true, because no one could find out who this Andreyev was), and I refused. The next day Chaim took me aside again. He pulled Voroshilov out of his pocket. I trembled. Voroshilov was my dream! He wore a uniform, therefore he smelled of war, and I already knew war, which is why I felt a sort of closeness to him. In exchange I gave him Zhdanov, Kaganovich, and threw in Mikoyan for good measure. In general, Voroshilov fared well. Similarly Molotov. Molotov could be traded for three others, because grown-ups said that Molotov was important. The price was also high for Kalinin, because he resembled a Polish grandfather. He had a pale beard and—unique among the leaders—something resembling a smile.

SOMETIMES CLASSES are interrupted by gunfire. The discharge resounds nearby, violent, loud, the panes quiver, the walls tremble, and our teacher looks with terror and despair at the window. If silence follows the detonation, we go back to reading our thick book, but if the crash of iron sheets is heard, the roar of bursting walls, and the thud of falling stones, the classroom comes alive. One hears raised voices—"They hit! They hit!"—and barely has the bell rung than we are racing to the square to see what has happened. Our small, single-storied school is right by a broad square, which is called the Third of May. On this square stands a large, a truly large, church, the biggest in town. You have to raise your head high to see where the church ends and the sky begins. And it is precisely at that spot that the cannon is now firing. It is firing at the tower, to knock it down.

This is how at the time we reasoned about it in class: When the Bolsheviks were marching toward us, before they saw Poland and before they saw our town, they must have first caught a glimpse of the towers of the Pińsk church. They were that high. This apparently irritated them very much. Why? We didn't know how to answer that question. But we concluded it was irritation solely from the fact that as soon as the Russians entered the town, before they had taken a breather, before they'd had a look around to see which street is where, before they'd had a good meal and before they'd taken a few drags on their cheap tobacco, they had already set up a cannon in the square and started firing at the church.

Because all their artillery had gone to the front, they had only one cannon left. They fired it pell-mell. If they hit the mark, clouds of black dust rose from the tower; sometimes a flame burst out. People took cover in deep gateways around the square and observed this bombardment gloomily, but also with curiosity. Women knelt and said the rosary. A drunken gunner walked around the deserted square and shouted: "Look, we're firing at your God! And what does he do? Nothing! Not a peep out of him! Is he afraid, or what?" He laughed, and then got an attack of the hiccups. Our neighbor told my mother that one day when the dust had settled she saw the figure of St. Andrew Bobola on top of the ruins. St. Andrew, she said, had a terribly suffering face—they were burning him alive.

WALKING TO SCHOOL I have to cross the railroad tracks, right by the train station. I like this place; I like to look at the trains arriving and departing. Most of all I like to look at the locomotive: I would like to be a locomotive engineer. Crossing the tracks one morning, I see that the railroad workers are starting to gather freight cars. Dozens and dozens of them. Feverish motion on the shunting stations: the locomotives are moving; the brakes are screeching; the bumpers ringing out. And the place is swarming with Red Army men, with the NKVD. Finally the motion stops; for several days there is silence. Then one day I see that wooden wagons full of people and bundles are pulling up to the freight cars. Beside each wagon, several soldiers, each one holding a rifle in such a way as though he were going to fire it at any second. At whom? Those on the wagons are already half-dead with fatigue and fear. I ask my mother why they are taking these people. And she, very nervously, says that the deportations have begun. Deportations? Strange word. What does it mean? But my mother doesn't want to answer the question, doesn't want to speak to me. She is crying.

NIGHT. A knocking at the window (we live in a little house half-sunk into the ground). Father's face pressed against the window-pane, flat, melting into the darkness. I see my father entering the room, but I barely recognize him. We had said good-bye in the summer. He was in an officer's uniform; he had on tall boots, a yellow belt, and leather gloves. I walked down the street with him and listened with pride to how everything on him creaked and clattered. Now he stands before us in the clothes of a Polish peasant, thin, unshaven. He is wearing a cotton knee-length shirt tied with burlap string and straw shoes on his feet. From what my mother is saying, I understand that he fell into Soviet captivity and that he was being driven east. He says that he escaped when they were walking in a column through the forest, and in a village he exchanged his uniform with a peasant for the shirt and straw shoes.

"Children," says my mother to my sister and me, "close your eyes and go to sleep!" From the adjoining room where our parents are we can hear whispers and sudden commotions. In the morning, when I get up, Father is already gone. Walking to school, I look around in every direction—maybe I can still catch a glimpse of him? There was so much I wanted to tell him about—about myself, about school, about the cannon. And that I already know the Russian alphabet. And that I had seen a deportation. But I do not see my father, not even in the most distant reaches of Lochiszynska Street, which is so long that it probably leads all the way to the end of the earth. It is autumn. A chill wind is blowing. My eyes sting.

• • •

THE NEXT NIGHT. A pounding at the windows, at the door, so insistent, intrusive, so violent, that it seems at any moment the ceiling will cave in. Several of them burst in, Red Army men and civilians, they barge in nervously and with such lightning speed, as if enraged wolves were chasing them. Rifles immediately leveled at us. A great fear: What if they fire? And what if they kill? It's a very unpleasant sensation, seeing a dead human being. Also, seeing a dead horse. It makes one shudder.

Those holding the rifles stand like statues, without so much as budging, whereas the rest of them are chucking everything to the floor. From the wardrobes, from the chest of drawers, from the beds. Dresses, caps, our toys. Straw mattresses, shoes, Father's clothes. And to Mother: *Muz kuda?* (Where's your husband?) And Mother, pale as a sheet, spreads her trembling arms and says that she doesn't know. But they know that Father has been here, and so again: *Muz kuda?* And Mother—well, nothing, she doesn't know, doesn't know, and that's that. Why, you, says one of them, and makes a gesture as though to strike her, and she draws back her head to avoid the blow. The others are still searching and searching. Under the beds, under the cupboard, under the armchair. What are they searching for? They say that it's weapons. But what kind of weapons could we have? My toy gun, which I used to fight Indians with? Well, yes, when the gun was still good, we could always drive the Indians from our courtyard with it, but now my revolver has a broken spring, and it's good for nothing.

They want to take Mother away. Why, as punishment? They threaten her with their fists and curse terribly. *Idi!* a soldier shouts at her, and tries to push her outside into the dark night with the butt of his rifle. But just then my younger sister suddenly throws herself on him and begins pummeling, biting, and kicking him, throws herself at him in a sort of delirium, in fury, in madness. There is so much unexpected, startling determination in this, such a rapacious unyieldingness, doggedness, and finality, that one of the Red Army men, probably the eldest, probably the commander, hesitates for a moment, then puts on his cap, fastens the holster of his pistol, and says to his people, "*Pashli!*" ("Let's go!")

• • •

IN SCHOOL, during breaks, or when we are returning home in a group, the talk is of deportations. There is now no subject more interesting. Our town is full of green; gardens stretch around the houses; every open space is thick with tall grasses, weeds, bushes, and trees; therefore it is easy to hide, to see everything and yet to be invisible oneself. In the higher grades there are those who have managed to sneak away from home, conceal themselves in the underbrush, and observe an entire deportation from start to finish. We already have veritable experts on deportations. They discourse on the subject eagerly and with connoisseurship.

The deportations take place at night. The method here is surprise. The person is asleep, and suddenly shouts wake him, he sees above him the fierce faces of soldiers and of the NKVD; they pull him out of bed, shove him with rifle butts, and command him to leave the house. They order that weapons be handed over, which of course no one possesses anyway. The whole time they spew vile obscenities. The worst is when they call someone a bourgeois. "Bourgeois" is a terrible term of abuse. They turn the whole house upside down, and they take the greatest delight in this. During the time that they are conducting the house search and creating this whole indescribable mess, the wagon arrives. It is a peasant wagon pulled by a paltry little horse, for the inhabitants of the Polesie region are poor and have bad horses. When the commander sees that the wagon is there, he shouts to the ones who will be deported: You have fifteen minutes to pack and get on the wagon. If the commander has a kind heart, he gives them a half hour. Then one simply has to pounce on anything and everything and stuff it into the suitcases, whatever one can manage. Choosing anything, or deliberating about something, is out of the question. Quickly, at once, now, hurry up, hurry up! Then at a run to the wagon—literally at a run. On the wagon sits a peasant, but the peasant won't help; he is not allowed to; he is not even allowed to turn around to see who is getting into the wagon. The house is left empty, for they take the entire family—grandparents, children, everyone. They turn off the lights.

Now the wagon rolls along in the darkness, along deserted

streets, in the direction of the train station. The wagon shakes and sways, for the majority of our streets do not have asphalt, not even cobblestones. The wheels fall into deep holes or sink into mud. But everyone here is used to such inconveniences—the driver from Polesie and his horse and even these unfortunates, who are now swaying atop their bundles, dejected and terrified.

The boys who have managed to observe a deportation say that they have followed after these wagons on foot all the way to the railroad tracks. The freight cars stand there, a long transport. Every night there would be a dozen or so wagons, or several score or more. The wagons would come to a stop on the square in front of the train station. To get to the freight cars, one had to go on foot. It is difficult to board a car like that, because it is high. Those from the escort drove the deportees on, swung their rifles around, shouted, cursed. When they filled one car, they moved on to the next one. What did it mean—to fill a car? It meant to stuff these people into it using knees and rifle butts so that there would be no room left even for a pin.

ONE NEVER KNEW what night they would come, or for whom. The boys who knew a lot about the deportations attempted to discern some rules in this matter, some hierarchies, to discover the key. Alas, in vain. Because, for example, they would begin deporting from Bednarska Street, and then, suddenly, they would stop. They would go after the inhabitants of Kijowska Street, but only on the even side. All of a sudden someone from Nadbrzeżna would vanish, but that same night they would have taken people from the other side of town—from Browarna. Since the time of our house search, Mother does not let us take our clothes off at night. We can take off our shoes, but we have to have them beside us all the time. The coats lie on chairs, so they can be put on in the wink of an eye. In principle we are not permitted to sleep. My sister and I lie side by side, and we poke each other, shake each other, or pull each other by the hair. "Hey, you, don't sleep!" "You, too, don't sleep!" But, of course, in the midst of this struggling and shoving we both fall asleep. But Mother really does not sleep. She sits at the table and listens the whole time. The silence on our street rings in our ears. If someone's footsteps echo in this silence, Mother grows pale. A man at this hour is an enemy. In class we read in Stalin about enemies. An enemy is a terrifying figure. Who else would come around at this hour? Good people are afraid; they are sitting hidden in their homes.

Even if we do sleep, we're on pins and needles. We are asleep, but we hear everything. Sometimes near morning we hear the rumble of a wooden wagon. The noise swells in the darkness, and by the time the wagon passes our house, the racket is like that of some infernal machine. Mother walks to the window on tiptoe and carefully draws aside the curtain. It is possible that at this very moment other mothers on Wesola Street are doing the same thing. They see the slowly rolling wagon, on it the huddled figures, the Red Army men walking behind it, and—behind them—darkness once again. The neighbor who saw how they were burning St. Andrew Bobola alive tells Mother that it is as if these wagons are rolling over her. The next day she aches everywhere.

THE FIRST IN CLASS to disappear was Paweł. Because winter was approaching, the teacher suggested that Paweł had probably caught a cold and was staying in bed. But Paweł didn't come the next day or the next week, and in time we began to understand that he would never come. Shortly thereafter we saw that the bench in the first row, in which Janek and Zbyszek sat, was empty. We grew sad, because the two of them played the best practical jokes, which was why the teacher made them sit in the front row, so that he could keep an eye on them. In other classes children also disappeared, more and more frequently. Soon no one even asked why they didn't come or where they were. The school grew empty. After class we still played ball, hide-and-seek, stickball, but something had happened—the ball became very heavy, during hide-and-seek no one felt like running fast, and in stickball everyone waved the stick around any old way. Bizarre disputes and fierce battles erupted easily, after which everyone took off—angry, sullen, and listless.

One day our teacher disappeared. We arrived at school as usual by eight o'clock, and after the bell, when we had sat down at our benches, the principal, Mr. Lubowicki, appeared at the door. "Children," he said, "go home now and come back tomorrow, you will have a new teacher, a lady." For the first time since my father's departure I feel a cramp near my heart. Why did they take our teacher? He was constantly nervous and looked out the window frequently. He would say, "Ah, children, children," and shake his head. He was always serious and seemed very sad. He was good to us, and if a student stammered while reading Stalin, he didn't shout, and even smiled a little.

I walked home dejected. As I was crossing the tracks, I heard a familiar voice. Someone was calling me. Freight cars stood along the railway, packed with people who were about to be deported. The voice was coming from there. In the door of one of the cars I saw our teacher's face. He was waving to me. My God! I started to race in his direction. But a second later a soldier caught up with me and struck me over the head so hard that I fell. I was getting up, dizzy and with a sharp pain, when he made as if to strike me again but didn't; he only started shouting at me that I should clear out of here, go to the devil. And he called me a son of a bitch.

BEFORE LONG the hunger began. There hadn't been any frost yet, and right after school we would start prowling through the gardens. We knew well their intricate geography, because there, amid the beds and shrubs, we used to play our endless games, our wars, hide-and-seek, and Indians. Everyone knew in whose garden the large apples grew, where it was worth shaking down the pear tree, where so many plums had ripened that everything was purple, or where there had been a good crop of bulgy rutabagas. These expeditions were risky, because the owners of the gardens would fiercely drive us away. Hunger was already staring everyone in the face, and everyone was trying to lay down provisions. No one wanted to lose even one apricot, one peach or gooseberry. It was much safer to plunder the orchards of those who had been arrested and locked up in the freight cars, for no one was guarding their trees or vegetable patches.

The river market on the Pina, where peasants brought in their treasures by boat—fish, honey, kasha—was long deserted. Most of the shops were closed or had been robbed. The only hope was the countryside. Our neighbors would take a ring or a fur coat and drive to the nearby villages to buy flour, salt bacon, or poultry. It happened, however, that when these women were out of town, the NKVD would come to their houses and take their children away for deportation. Our neighbors talked about this, completely shaken, and warned my mother. But even before that she had already determined never to be more than a step away from us.

OUR LITTLE TOWN, green and sweltering in the summer, in the autumn brown and gleaming in the sun like amber, suddenly, one night, turned white. It was on the cusp between November and December. The winter of 1939–1940 was early and harsh. It was a frosty, icy hell. From the direction of Spokojna Street, from the side of the cemetery where my grandmother lay, my sister and I crawled as far as the bushes, from which we could see a transport standing on the railway siding. Inside the freight cars were people who were about to depart. Where to? The grown-ups said Siberia. I didn't know where that was, but from the way in which they pronounced this word, it was clear that even thinking about this Siberia was enough to make one shudder.

I didn't see my teacher. He had surely left long ago already, for the transports were leaving one after another. We sat hidden in the bushes, our hearts pounding from fear and curiosity. Moans and cries reached us from the direction of the siding. A moment later they grew very loud, piercing. Wagons were driving from one car to the next, collecting the bodies of those who had died that night from cold and hunger. Four NKVD men walked behind the wagons counting something, writing something. Again they counted and wrote. Counted and wrote. Afterward, they closed the doors to the cars. The doors must have been heavy, because they did this with great difficulty. The doors moved on little rollers, and the rollers screeched terribly. The men secured each door with wire, then squeezed the wire tight with pliers. Each one of the four then tested the lock to make sure no one could undo the wire. We crouched in the bushes, petrified from the cold and the emotion. The locomotive whistled several times, and the train started to move. When it was far in the distance, the four NKVD men made an about-face and went back to the station.

WE SAID NOTHING about it to Mother, so as not to make her angry. For days on end she stood at the window, motionless. She was capable of not moving for hours at a time. There was still a little bit of kasha and flour in the house. Sometimes we ate the kasha, sometimes Mother cooked flour pancakes on the stove. I noticed that she herself would not eat anything, and when we ate she would turn away so as not to watch, or she went into the other room. When we went outside, she would say, "Bring a little brushwood." We would walk around the neighborhood digging up dry stalks and sticks from beneath the snow. It's possible that she no longer had the strength to go out herself, and we had to heat the furnace, if only a little, for we were turning into icicles. In the evenings we sat in the darkness shaking from cold and from fear, waiting for deportation.

Sometimes I roamed with my friends around the town, ice-covered and sparkling in the sun. We snooped around after food, not really expecting to find anything. One could eat a bit of snow or suck on a piece of ice, but that only increased the hunger. The most tormenting thing, but at the same time the most pleasant and rare, was the smell of food cooking. "Hey, fellas!" one of us would call, and with his hand wave the others over. We would dash toward him, and he would already be standing with his nose thrust between the fence rails, staring at someone's house. Together we would begin inhaling the smell of roasting chicken or cooking sauerkraut stew that floated our way. Later, we had to pull one another away by force from such a fence.

Once, hungry and desperate, we approached the soldiers guarding the entrance to the barracks. *Tovarishch*, said Hubert, *day pokushat*, and mimed putting a piece of bread into his mouth. But the guards only shrugged their shoulders. Finally, one of the sentries reached into his pocket and instead of bread pulled out a little linen sack and handed it to us without a word. Inside were dark brown, almost black, finely chopped stems of tobacco leaves. The Red Army man also gave us a piece of newspaper, showed us how to twist it into a cone and pour into it the damp, foul-smelling tobacco gruel. Cigarettes made out of good tobacco and cigarette paper, in other words normal cigarettes, were unobtainable then.

We began to smoke. The smoke scratched our throats and stung our eyes. The world started to swirl, rock, and was turned upside down. I vomited, and my skull was splitting from pain. But the all-consuming, gnawing sensation of hunger eased, weakened. Despite the nasty taste, despite the tormenting nausea, this was more bearable than the sharp, insistent need, tearing at our guts, to fill our stomachs.

MY CLASS had dwindled by a half. Our teacher sat me on a bench with a boy whose name was Orion. We liked each other at once and began walking home together. One day Orion told me that on Zawalna Street they were supposed to be selling candy and that if I wanted to, we could go stand in line together. It was a beautiful gesture, his telling me about this candy, for we had stopped even dreaming of sweets long ago. Mother gave me permission, and we went to Zawalna Street. It was dark and snow was falling. In front of the shop, there was already a long line of children, stretching the length of several houses. The shop was closed with wooden shutters. The children standing at the head of the line said that it wouldn't open until tomorrow and that one had to stand here all night. Distressed, we returned to our place at the end of the queue. But new children were arriving continually; the line grew into infinity.

It became even colder than it had been during the day, the frost sharp, piercing, biting. As the minutes passed, then the hours, it was increasingly difficult to stand. I had had for some time very painful abscesses on my legs and hands, burning, swollen with pus. Now the icy cold made the pain unbearable. I moaned with every movement.

Meantime one fragment of the line after another would break away and scatter over the snowy, frozen street. To warm themselves the children played tag. They tussled, wrestled, rolled in the white powder. Then they returned to the line, and the next group would sally forth, yelling. In the middle of the night someone lit a fire. A delicious, luxuriant flame burst out. One by one we took turns beside it so as to warm our hands if only for a moment. The faces of the children who managed to push their way to the fire reflected a golden glow. In this glow their faces thawed, flushed with warmth. Thus warmed, they returned to their places and passed on to us, still standing in line, the rays of their heat.

Toward morning sleep overcame the line. Warnings about how one shouldn't sleep in freezing temperatures, for that means death, were of no use. No one had the strength anymore to look for firewood or play our game, the square circle. The cold pierced through to the bone, cruel, crackling. Hands and feet went numb. To save ourselves, to last the night, we stood in line huddled tightly together, one close upon the other. Despite the chain in which we locked fiercely and desperately together, all remaining warmth was escaping. The snow was burying us more and more, blanketing us with a white, soft sheepskin.

IN THE MORNING darkness, two women wrapped in thick scarves arrived and started to open the shop. The line sprang to life. We dreamed mountains of candies, magnificent chocolate palaces. We dreamed marzipan princesses and gingerbread pages. Our imagination was afire; everything in it sparkled, radiated. Finally the doors of the shop opened and the line moved. Everyone was pushing so as to warm himself and get to the front. But in the shop there was neither candy nor chocolate palaces. The women were selling empty fruit-candy tins. One for each. They were round, large cans, their sides painted with colorful, cocky roosters and an inscription in Polish—E. WEDEL.

At first we were extremely disappointed and depressed. Orion was crying. But when we began to inspect our loot more closely, we slowly cheered up. On the inside walls of these cans there remained after the candy a sweet deposit, fine, multicolored chips, a thick residue smelling of fruit. Why, our mothers could boil some water in these cans and offer us a sweet, aromatic drink!

Already appeased, contented even, instead of going straight home we turned into the park, at the place where the circus stood during the summer. The circus had departed long ago, but it had gone in a hurry and left behind the carousel. The motor from the carousel had been stolen, as had almost all the seats. But one seat remained, and if one gathered together several boys, they could get the carousel moving with a rod in such a way that it spun like mad.

It is empty and silent in the park, so we run to the carousel and start turning it. It is already stirring, creaking. I jump into the seat and buckle myself with the chain. Orion gives the orders, shouts, fires up the boys, urges them on, and they, like galley slaves, push on the rod with all their might, faster and faster and faster! Orion, all in a fever, shouts at the top of his lungs, a madness has already seized the other boys too, the carousel rushes round, I feel a stinging, frosty wind, which lashes my face, a gusting and increasingly stronger wind, on whose wings I rise like a pilot, like a bird, like a cloud.

# The Trans-Siberian, '58

THE PLACE of my second encounter with the Imperium: far away, in the steppes and snows of Asia, in a land difficult of access, whose entire geography consists of unfamiliar and extraordinary names—rivers called Argun, Unda, Chaychar; mountains, Chingan, Ilchuri, Dzagdy; and cities, Kilkok, Tungir, and Bukachacha. From these names alone one could compose sonorous, exotic poems.

The train of the Trans-Siberian Railway, which set out the previous day from Peking and is making the nine-day trip to Moscow, after Harbin, China, pulls into Zabaykal'sk, the border station of the USSR. At the approach to every border, tension rises within us; emotions heighten. People are not made to live in borderline situations; they avoid them or try to flee from them as quickly as possible. And yet man encounters them everywhere, sees and feels them everywhere. Let us take the atlas of the world: it is all borders. Borders of oceans and continents. Deserts and forests. Precipitations, monsoons, typhoons, cultivated land and fallow land, permafrost and bog, rocky soil and clay. Let us add the borders of the Quaternary deposits and volcanic flows, of basalt, chalk, and trachyte. We can also see the borders of the Patagonian plate and the Canadian plate, the zones of tropical climates and of Arctic ones, the borders of the erosion zones of the Adycha watershed and of Lake Chad. The borders demarcating the habitats of certain mammals. Certain insects. Certain reptiles and amphibians, including the extremely dangerous black cobra, as well as the frightening—although, fortunately, lazy—anaconda.

And the borders of monarchies and republics? Kingdoms remote in time and lost civilizations? Pacts, treaties, and alliances? Black tribes and red? Human migrations? The borders to which the Mongols reached. The Khazars. The Huns.

How many victims, how much blood and suffering, are connected with this business of borders! There is no end to the cemeteries of those who have been killed the world over in the defense of borders. Equally boundless are the cemeteries of the audacious who attempted to expand their borders. It is safe to assume that half of those who have ever walked upon our planet and lost their lives in the field of glory gave up the ghost in battles begun over a question of borders.

This sensitivity to the border issue, this untiring enthusiasm for constantly marking them out, widening them, or defending them, are characteristic not only of man, but all animate nature, of everything that moves on land, in water and air. Various mammals, in defense of the borders of their grazing lands, will let themselves be torn to pieces. Various beasts of prey, so as to secure new hunting grounds, will bite their adversaries to death. And even our quiet and meek kitten, how he labors, how he compresses and torments himself, to squeeze out a few drops with which to mark, here and there, the borders of his territory.

And our brains? Encoded in them, after all, is an infinite diversity of borders. Between the left and the right hemispheres, between the frontal and the temporal lobes, between the corpus callosum and the cerebellum. And the borders between ventricles, meninx, and convolutions? Between the lumbar region and the spinal cord? Notice the way in which we think. For instance, we think: That's the limit; beyond that—no. Or we say: Be careful that you don't go too far, for you will overstep the mark! Moreover, all these boundaries of thought and feeling, injunctions and interdictions, are constantly shifting, crossing and permeating one another, piling up. In our brains there is ceaseless border movement—across borders, near borders, over borders. Hence our headaches and migraines, hence the tumult in our heads; but pearls can also be produced: visions, dazzlements, flashes of inspiration, and—unfortunately more rarely—genius.

The border is stress—fear, even (significantly more rarely: liberation). The concept of the border can include a kind of finality; the doors can slam shut behind us forever: such is the border between life and death. The gods know about such anxieties, and that is why they try to win adherents by promising people that as a reward that they will enter the divine kingdom—which will have no borders. The paradise of the Christian God, the paradise of Yahweh and Allah, all have no borders. Buddhists know that the state of nirvana is the state of blissful happiness without limits. In short, that which is most desired, awaited, and longed for by everyone is precisely this unconditional, total, absolute—boundlessness.

## Zabaykal'sk—Chita

Barbed wire. Barbed-wire barriers are what you see first. They protrude out of the snow, hover over it—lines, trestles, fences of barbed wire. What extraordinary combinations, knots, billows, entire constructions of barbed wire clasping together the sky and the earth, clinging to every bit of frozen field, to the white landscape, to the icy horizon. On the face of it, this thorny, rapacious barrier stretching along the border seems like an absurd and surreal idea, for who would force his way through here? As far as the eye can see there is only a desert of snow, no roads, no people, and the snow is two meters high; taking a single step is impossible. And yet these walls of barbed wire have something to say to you, have something to communicate. They are saying: Be careful, you are crossing the border into a different world. You will not escape from here; you will not get away. It is a world of deadly seriousness, orders, and obedience. Learn to listen, learn humility, learn to occupy the least amount of space possible. Best mind your own business. Best be silent. Best not ask questions.

The barbed wire instructs you the whole time the train is rolling toward the station; it imprints upon your mind everything which you should from now on remember, and it does so relentlessly, but after all it is for your own good that it pounds into your head the long litany of limitations, prohibitions, and instructions.

Then come the dogs. German shepherds, furious, trembling, frenzied; the train has barely stopped when they throw themselves under the cars, barking, baying. But who could be riding underneath the wagon, in minus forty degrees Celsius? No matter how many sheepskin coats he had on him, he would freeze in an hour, and we have already been rolling nonstop for an entire day. The sight of the ferreting dogs is so absorbing that for a while one doesn't notice the next image—soldiers have sprung up as if from beneath the earth and have instantaneously lined up on both sides of the train. They stand in such a way that the train cars are under total surveillance, and if, for example, a passenger—a madman (or perhaps an agent, an infiltrator, a spy)—decided to jump out of any one of the cars and throw himself into the immense, snowy, ice-cold space, he would be immediately spotted and shot.

All the same, who could shoot him, just like that, instantly? Well, the sentries who stand on the lookout towers and have their rifles aimed at the doors and windows of the train cars could do so without a moment's delay (because I am looking out the window just now, one of the rifles is aimed at me—yes, directly at me!). On the other hand, however, no madman (or agent, or infiltrator, or spy) could jump out and throw himself into the snowbound space, for all the doors and windows of the cars are tightly, carefully shut.

In short, the total surveillance clearly plays the same persuasive role as those one-story-high, thick billows of barbed wire: it is simply a silent but emphatic warning, lest some preposterous idea accidentally enter your head!

But that's not the end of it. For barely has the pack of high-strung and possibly hungry German shepherds passed beneath the train, barely have the soldiers arranged themselves vigilantly along the tracks, and the sentries at the lookout posts aimed the barrels of their rifles at us, than patrols enter the cars (in one hand a flashlight, in the other a long steel skewer), throwing all the passengers out into the corridor. A search of the compartments begins, a rooting about on the shelves, under the seats, in nooks and crannies, in ashtrays. The sounding of the walls, the ceiling, the floor begins. The examining, looking, touching, smelling.

Now the passengers take everything they have—suitcases, bags, packages, bundles—and carry them to the station building, in which stand long metal tables. Everywhere, red banners joyfully welcome us to the Soviet Union. Beneath the banners, in a row, customs inspectors, men and women, without exception fierce looking, severe, almost as though they were bearing some sort of grudge, yes, very clearly a grudge. I search among them for a face with even slightly more gentle, relaxed, open features, for by this time I myself would like to relax a little, to forget for a moment that I am surrounded by barbed wire and lookouts, fierce dogs, sentries stiff as stone; I would like to establish any kind of contact, exchange a courtesy, talk a little; it's something I always need very much.

"You, what are you grinning at?" A customs inspector inquires sharply and suspiciously.

A chill goes through me. Power is seriousness: in an encounter with power, a smile is tactless, it demonstrates a lack of respect. Similarly, one must not stare too long at someone who has power. But I already know about this from the army. Our corporal, Jan Pokrywka, punished everyone who looked at him too long. "Come on over here!" he would shout. "What are you staring at me like that for?" And as punishment he would send the offender to clean the latrines.

Now it begins. The opening, the unfastening, the untying, the disemboweling. The rummaging, the plunging in, the pulling out, the shaking about. And what is this? And what is that? And what is that for? And this? And that? And this one? And that one? And which way? And what for? Worst of all are the books. What a curse to be traveling with a book! You could be carrying a suitcase of cocaine and keep a book on top of it. The cocaine wouldn't arouse the least bit of interest; all the customs inspectors would throw themselves upon the book. And what—God forbid!—if you're carrying a book in English? Then the real running, checking, paging through, reading would begin.

Nevertheless, despite the fact that I am carrying several books in English (they are mainly textbooks for studying Chinese and Japanese), I am not the worst offender. The worst offenders are positioned at a separate table, a sort of second-class table. These are the locals, citizens of the Soviet Union, thin and slight people, in torn smocks and felt boots full of holes, dark-complexioned, slit-eyed Buryats and Kamchadals, Tunguses and Aynovs, Orochans and Koryats. How they were ever allowed to go to China, I don't know. In any event, they are returning, and with them they are bringing food. I can see out of the corner of my eye that they have many little sacks of kasha.

And it is this kasha that is going to be at issue now. For clearly kasha belongs, beside books, among the products most under suspicion. Apparently there is something in kasha, some sort of ambiguity, some sort of perverse, insidious quality, some sort of deceitfulness, some sort of two-facedness; for yes, this seems to be kasha, but after all it can turn out that this is not completely kasha, that this is kasha, but not one hundred percent. That is why the customs officers are pouring all the kasha out onto the table. The table is beginning to turn gold and brown; it looks like a scale model of the Sahara spread out before them. The sifting of the kasha begins. A careful, meticulous sifting through the fingers. The fingers of the customs inspectors allow narrow little streams of kasha to pass through them, sifting, sifting, but suddenly—stop! The fingers stop and become motionless. The fingers have felt a strange grain. They felt it; they sent a signal to the customs inspector's brain; the brain responded—stop! The fingers stand still and are waiting. The brain says, Try one more time, cautiously and carefully. The fingers, delicately and imperceptibly, delicately and imperceptibly, but very carefully, very vigilantly, roll the grain about. They investigate. The experienced fingers of a Soviet customs inspector. Skilled, ready to throttle the grain instantly, catch it in a trap, imprison it. But the little grain is simply what it is—meaning, an ordinary little grain of ordinary kasha, and what has singled it out from the million other grains strewn on the table in the border station in Zabaykal'sk is an uncommon, strange shape, the result of some sort of roughness in the millstone, which turned out to be warped, uneven. So, not contraband, not a trick, concludes the customs inspector's brain, but it doesn't give up yet. On the contrary, it commands the fingers to keep on sifting, keep on examining, keep on feeling, and even at the shadow of a doubt to stop—immediately!

Let us consider, after all, that this is the 1950s, and that the mills in China are already very old and ineffectual. Let us consider what problems this creates for the customs inspectors from Zabaykal'sk. There are an infinite number of grains with atypical, suspicious shapes. Almost every second the fingers are sending a message to the brain. Almost every moment the brain raises an alarm—stop! Grain after grain, handful after handful, little sack after little sack, Buryat after Buryat.

I couldn't tear my eyes away from this spectacle. I watched fascinated, forgot about the barbed wire and the lookouts, forgot about the dogs. Why, these are fingers that should be sculpting gold, polishing diamonds! What microscopic movements, what responsive tremors, what sensitivity, what professional virtuosity!

We returned to the cars in the dark; snow was falling; ice creaked under our boots. In Zabaykal'sk I received another kind of lesson, that the border here is not a line on a map, but a school. The pupils who graduate from this school will be divided into three groups. The first group—the absolutely enraged. They will be the most miserable, for everything around them will cause them stress, will reduce them to a state of fury, to madness. Will irritate, annoy, torment. Before they even realize that they can change nothing in the reality surrounding them, that they can improve nothing, they will be felled by a heart attack or a stroke.

The second group will observe the Soviet people and imitate their way of thinking and acting. The essence of this posture is resigning oneself to the existing reality, and even being able to derive from it a certain satisfaction. There is a saying that is very helpful in this, and which it behooves one to repeat to oneself and to others every evening, regardless of how terrible the day that has just ended: "Rejoice in this day, for things will never again be as good as they were today!"

Finally, the third group. They are the ones for whom everything is above all else interesting, extraordinary, improbable, who want to get to know this different world hitherto unknown to them, examine it, plumb it. They know how to arm themselves with patience (but not superciliousness!), and to maintain distance with a calm, attentive, sober gaze.

Such are the three attitudes characteristic of foreigners who have found themselves in the Imperium.

## CHITA—ULAN-UDE

Looking through the window of the rushing train, I think: Siberia, so this is how it looks! I heard this name for the first time when I was seven years old. Stern mothers from our street cautioned: "Children, behave yourselves, or they'll deport you to the Sybir!" (They said it in Russian—Sybir—for this sounded more menacing, apocalyptic.) Gentle mothers would become indignant: "How can you frighten children this way!"

It wasn't really possible to imagine Siberia. One of my friends finally showed me a drawing in a book: in a heavy snowstorm walked a column of tattered and hunched-over men. Heavy chains with iron balls at the end were attached to their hands and legs, and they dragged these balls behind them over the ground.

Siberia, in its sinister, cruel form, is a freezing, icy space ... plus dictatorship.

In many states there exist icy territories, lands that for the greater part of the year are frozen over, dead. Such, for instance, are vast stretches of Canada. Or take Danish Greenland, or American Alaska. And yet it doesn't occur to anyone to frighten children with: "Wash your hands or they'll send you to Canada!" Or "Play nicely with that little girl or they'll deport you to America!" In those countries, quite simply, there is no dictatorship, nobody puts anyone in chains, nobody imprisons anyone in camps, dispatches him to work in hellish frost, to a certain death. In those frozen lands, man has one antagonist—the cold. Here, as many as three—the cold, hunger, and armed force.

In 1842, in Paris, the Polish poet Adam Mickiewicz delivered two speeches at the College de France about the memoirs of General Kopeć. Kopeć fought by Kościuszko's side near Maciejowice, and there was taken prisoner by the Russians and sentenced to Siberia. They drove Kopeć some ten thousand kilometers over the Russian and Siberian wilderness, to Kamchatka.

It was a real journey through hell.

They drove him, as the general writes, in a police wagon "which had the shape of a trunk, covered with skins, and inside with sheets of iron, with only a small window on one side for serving water or food.

"This trunk," Kopeć continues, "was without a seat, and because my wounds had not yet healed, they gave me a sack with straw and I was designated a secret prisoner, with a number only, no name. Such a prisoner is for them the greatest criminal, with whom no one, under pain of the greatest punishment, can converse or even know his name or the reason he was taken captive."

Driven in the police wagon, as though in a coffin with the lid slammed shut, he was able to conjecture about where he was only through sounds. Hearing the rumble of cobblestones below the wheels, he surmised that they were in a town: "On the sixth day I heard the rumble of cobblestones, it was Smolensk." From the dark police wagon they transfer him directly into a dark cell, so that Kopeć cannot tell if it is day or night: "There were two windows with iron bars, nailed up with black wooden planks so that daylight couldn't enter anywhere. One had to guess—night, or day?—the guards never wanted to say even a word to me." Exhausted by the journey, Kopeć nevertheless cannot sleep—this rest stop on the road deep into Siberia turns out to be a place of torment: "I couldn't sleep: I thought I heard beatings from beyond the walls next to me, the sounds of torture, and the clank of chains."

They drag the general to an inquest. "They ask Kopeć," Mickiewicz writes, "what was the cause of his rebellion. Love of the motherland, he answers. The commission becomes indignant at this answer and breaks off the interrogation, unable to suffer the prisoner's pride."

They drive Kopeć farther east. "From Smolensk to Irkutsk," the general reminisces, "three soldiers from my escort died, others broke their legs or arms falling off my police wagon. Drunk and careless, they would speed down mountains, and it often happened that as the horses broke into a run, the wagon would flip over and the horses would drag it for a quarter of a mile, and I, shut inside, would smash around like a herring in a barrel. The fact that I was wrapped in a sack, chaff, and straw would save me."

Despite being transported in a wagon-coffin, the general is aware of being in a certain way privileged—they are driving him; others they force to march for years on foot. "On the road I met several hundred people of both genders, being marched for deportation toward Irkutsk, under a very small guard, people they would send from settlement to settlement, and it is only at the end of the third year, if then, that they would arrive in Irkutsk from Europe. None can escape along the way, for there are no secondary settlements anywhere . . . if one of the enslaved wants to save himself by slipping away somewhere to the side, into the forest, he will be eaten by animals. . . ."

This wandering of the deportee is not only a displacement in space and in time. It is accompanied by a process of dehumanization: the one who reaches the end (if he doesn't die along the way) has already been stripped of everything that is human. He has no surname; he does not know where he is; he does not know what they will do with him. His language has been taken away: no one will speak with him. He is a consignment; he is a thing; he is a trifle.

Later, they deprive the general of even the wagon; they force him along on foot: "We always walked from morning until evening without a break."

And he adds: "No road of any kind, only through terrifying mountains and gorges."

## Ulan-Ude—Krasnoyarsk

"No road of any kind, only through terrifying mountains and gorges."

I dreamed of seeing Lake Baikal, but it was night, a black stain on the frost-covered window frame. It wasn't until morning that I caught a glimpse of mountains and gorges. Everything in snow.

Snow and snow.

It is January, the middle of the Siberian winter.

Outside the window everything appears stiff from the cold, even the firs, pines, and spruces look like great, petrified icicles, dark green stalagmites sticking out of the snow.

The immobility, the immobility of this landscape, as if the train were standing still, as if it too were a part of this region—also immobile.

And the whiteness—whiteness everywhere, blinding, unfathomable, absolute. A whiteness that draws one in, if someone lets himself be seduced by it, lets himself be caught in the trap and walks farther, deep into the whiteness—he will perish. The whiteness destroys all those who try to approach it, who try to decipher its mystery. It hurls them down from mountaintops, abandons them, frozen, on snowy plains. Siberian Buryats consider every white animal to be sacred; they believe that to kill one is to commit a sin and bring death upon oneself. They look upon white Siberia as a temple inhabited by a god. They bow to its plains, pay homage to its landscapes, continually frightened that from there, from the white depths, death will come.

Whiteness is often associated with finality, with the end, with death. In those cultures in which people live with the fear of death, mourners dress in black, to scare death away from themselves, isolate it, confine it to the deceased. But here, where death is regarded as another form, another shape of existence, mourners dress in white and dress the deceased in white: whiteness is here the color of acceptance, consent, of a surrender to fate.

There is something in this January Siberian landscape that overpowers, oppresses, stuns. Above all, it is its enormity, its boundlessness, its oceanic limitlessness. The earth has no end here; the world has no end. Man is not created for such measurelessness. For him a comfortable, palpable, serviceable measure is the measure of his village, his field, street, house. At sea, the size of the ship's deck will be such a measure. Man is created for the kind of space that he can traverse at one try, with a single effort.

## KRASNOYARSK—NOVOSIBIRSK

Beyond Krasnoyarsk (is it already the fourth day of traveling?) it begins to grow lighter. (At this time of year, darkness prevails here for the greater part of the night and the day.) I drink tea and look out the window. The same snowy plains as yesterday, as the day before yesterday (and, I am tempted to add, as last year, as centuries ago). The same endless forest. The same forests and clearings, and in the open areas high snowdrifts, sculpted by the wind into the strangest of shapes.

Suddenly I remember Blaise Cendrars and his "Prose of the Trans-Siberian and of Little Jeanne of France." In this poem, written before World War I, Cendrars describes a journey on this same railroad line, but in the opposite direction—from Moscow to Harbin. The refrain of this poem is the incessantly repeated question asked by his frightened girlfriend, Jeanne:

> "Blaise, say, are we really a long way
> from Montmartre?"

Jeanne experiences the same sensation that comes over everyone who plunges into Siberia's white boundlessness—the sensation of sinking into nonbeing, of evanescing.

The author has nothing to cheer her up with:

> A long way, Jeanne, you've been rolling along for seven
> days
> You're a long way from Montmartre . . .

Paris is the center of the world, the point of reference. How does one measure the sense of distance, remoteness? To be far from what, from what place? Where is that point on our planet from which people, as they move farther from it, would have the impression that they are closer and closer to the end of the world? Is it a point with only an emotional significance (my house as the center of the world)? Or cultural (for example, Greek civilization)? Or religious (for example, Mecca)? Most people, when asked which they consider the center of the world—Paris or Mexico—will answer: Paris. Why? After all, Mexico City is larger than Paris and also has a metro and magnificent monuments and great paintings and excellent writers. And yet they will say Paris. And what if someone declares that for him the center of the world is Cairo? It is, after all, larger than Paris and has monuments and a university and art. And yet how many people would vote for Cairo? And so it is Paris (in any event it was Paris when the frightened Jeanne was riding with her heart in her boots across Siberia). It is Europe. European civilization is the only one that has ever had global ambitions and (almost) realized them. Other civilizations either couldn't satisfy such ambitions for technical reasons (for instance, the Maya), or simply didn't have such interests (for instance, China), convinced that they themselves were the entire world.

Only European civilization proved capable of overcoming its ethnocentrism. Within it arose the desire to know other civilizations, as well as the theory (formulated by Bronislaw Malinowski) that global culture is created by a constellation of parallel cultures.

## Novosibirsk—Omsk

Day, night, and day.

The monotonous, insistent thud of the wheels, increasingly difficult to bear. It resounds the loudest at night: you are imprisoned in this thudding, as in a trembling, vibrating cage. We ran into a storm, for suddenly snow sealed up the window and you could hear the howling of the wind even inside the compartment.

"No road of any kind, only through terrifying mountains and gorges."

## Omsk—Chelyabinsk

The sixth, or maybe the eighth, day of traveling. In the great, monotonous spaces, the measures of time are lost; they cease to have any force, cease to have any meaning. The hours become formless, shapeless, elastic like the clocks in the paintings of Salvador Dalí. Moreover, the train passes through various time zones, and one should be constantly adjusting the hands of one's watch, but what for, what is there to gain by this? The perception of change (the principal determinant of time) atrophies here; so does the need for change: man lives here in something like a state of collapse, of numbness, of internal paralysis. Now, in January, the nights are very long. And for most of the day, a dark gray, persistent gloom prevails. The sun appears only occasionally: then the world becomes bright, azure, drawn with a sharp, decisive line. But later the gloom seems all the more deep and all the more pervasive.

Traveling on the Trans-Siberian, what can one see of the so-called reality of the country? Nothing, really. The greater part of the route is swathed in darkness, but even during the day little is visible beyond the snowy emptiness that unfolds in every direction. Little stations—at night, lonely, weak lights, some specters staring at the train as it rushes by in clouds of snow, and immediately vanishes, sinks from view, swallowed by the nearest forest.

I have a compartment for two, in which I ride the entire time alone. An oppressive loneliness. One cannot read, for the car lurches about in all directions, the letters jump, get blurry, and after a while the eyes hurt. There is no one to talk to. I can go out into the corridor. And then what? All the compartments are closed; I don't even know if anyone is traveling in them, for they don't have little windows to look through.

"Is anybody traveling in these compartments?" I ask the steward.

"That depends," he answers evasively, and disappears.

There is no way to start a conversation with anyone. People (even when they materialize from somewhere) either immediately skirt around me or, if I all but catch them by the sleeve, will snap something back in reply and instantly disappear. If they do answer, it is evasively, ambiguously, monosyllabically, so that nothing can really be deduced from the answer. They say, "We shall see"; they say, "Well, yes"; or they say, "Who can tell?"; or else, "Absolutely!" But most often they say something that could indicate that they have already understood everything, that they have penetrated to the very essence of the truth. They say, "Well, that's life."

If there exists such a thing as the genius of a nation, then the genius of the Russian nation is expressed in, among other things, just this saying: "Well, that's life!"

Anyone who will ponder at length the meaning of these words will understand a great deal. But I would like to learn something more—and I cannot. All around me is emptiness; all around me is scorched earth; all around me is a wall. It is no mystery why: I am a foreigner. A foreigner gives rise to mixed emotions. He gives rise to curiosity (one must quash this one!), to envy (a foreigner always has it better; it suffices to see that he is well dressed), but above all to fear. One of the pillars upon which the system rests is isolation from the world, and a foreigner, by the mere fact that he exists, undermines this pillar. For contact with a foreigner Stalin would condemn a person to five, ten, years in the camps, and often he would order him shot, so it is small wonder that people fear the foreigner as they do fire.

I too am riding in a police wagon, only it is incomparably more comfortable than the one in which they transported General Kopeć. And I have not been sentenced; I am not a deportee. But the principle of isolation is the same. This underscoring of the fact that one is a stranger here, an other, that one is an intruder, an abomination, something jarring, trouble. And that is in the best case! For a foreigner is after all something far more dangerous—he is an infiltrator and spy! Why is he staring out the window, what is he looking for? He will see nothing! The entire Trans-Siberian route is cleansed of everything that could catch the spy's attention. The train rushes on as if in a plastic tunnel—only bare walls and more walls: the wall of night, the wall of snow. And why does he try to ask questions like that? Why does this interest him? What does he need to know that for? Did he take notes? He took notes. What did he take notes of? Everything? Where does he keep those notes? With him at all times? That's not good!

And what did he ask? He asked if it's far to Sima. To Sima? But we're not stopping in Sima. Precisely. But he asked. And what did you say? Me? I said nothing. What do you mean, nothing! You had to say something. I said that it's a long way. That's not good! You should have said that we already passed Sima, that would have confused him!

There, see? It's better to avoid questions, because one doesn't ever really know how to answer them. It's easy to come out with something truly stupid. There is something about a human being that makes it difficult for him to hit it right on the button with a proper reply. And the worst of it is that anyone who has met with a foreigner and has exchanged a word with him is already suspect, already marked. One has to live in such a way, walk around town in such a way, along the streets, along the corridors of train cars, so as to prevent this from happening, so as not to bring misfortune down on one's head.

## Chelyabinsk—Kazan

It is closer and closer to old, native Russia, although it is still a long way to Moscow.

"No road of any kind, only through terrifying mountains and gorges."

While still at university I read Bierdayev's old book in which he reflected upon how the great expanses of the Imperium had influenced the Russian soul. What does a Russian think about, somewhere on the shore of the Yenisey, or deep in the Amur taiga? Every road that he takes seems to have no end. He can walk along it for days and months, and always Russia will surround him. The plains have no end, nor the forests, nor the rivers. To rule over such boundless expanses, says Bierdayev, one had to create a boundless state. And behold, the Russian fell into a contradiction—to maintain the great expanses, the Russian must maintain a great state; on the maintenance of this great state he expends his energy, of which not enough remains for anything else—for organization, for husbandry, and so on. He expends his energy on a state that then enthralls and oppresses him.

Bierdayev believes that this immensity, this limitlessness of Russia, has a negative influence on its inhabitants' way of thinking. For it does not demand of them concentration, tension, an intensification of energy, or the creation of a dynamic, vigorous culture. Everything falls apart, is diluted, drowned in this ungraspable formlessness. Russia—an expanse, on the one hand, endless, broad, and yet, on the other hand, so crushing that it takes one's breath away, and there is nothing left to breathe.

## KAZAN—MOSCOW

Fatigue, an increasingly tormenting, stifling, sleep-inducing fatigue, a sort of stickiness and numbness. During the rare surges of energy, the desire to jump out of this rushing, trembling cage. My admiration for the endurance of Kopeć and of so many thousands like him, my homage to their suffering, their torment.

FIRST, green, snow-covered woods and more woods, then woods and houses, then more and more houses, then houses and apartment buildings, finally only apartment buildings, taller and taller.

The steward removes the sheet, pillow, two blankets, and tea glass from the compartment.

The corridor fills with people.

Moscow.

# THE SOUTH, '67

NINE YEARS after my journey on the Trans-Siberian Railroad, I traveled again to the Imperium. My expedition took me across seven southern republics of the former USSR: Georgia, Armenia, Azerbaijan, Turkmenistan, Tajikistan, Kyrgystan, and Uzbekistan. The tempo of this journey was murderous—there were only several days for getting to know each of the republics. I was aware of how superficial and aleatory such encounters were. But in the case of a country so difficult of access, so closed, so steeped in mystery, one has to take advantage of even the smallest chance, of the most unexpected opportunity, so as to raise, if only slightly, the impermeable and heavy curtain.

What was most surprising in this third encounter with the Imperium? In my imagination, the USSR constituted a uniform, monolithic creation in which everything was equally gray and gloomy, monotonous, and clichéd. Nothing here could transcend the obligatory norm, distinguish itself, take on an individual character.

And then I traveled to the non-Russian republics of what was then the Imperium. What caught my eye? That despite the stiff, rigorous corset of Soviet power, the local, small, yet very ancient, nations had succeeded in preserving something of their tradition, of their history, of their, albeit, concealed pride and dignity. I discovered there, spread out in the sun, an Oriental carpet, which in many places still retained its age-old colors and the eyecatching variety of its original designs.

## GEORGIA

One should see the museum in Tbilisi. It is located in the former seat of a theological seminary, where Stalin once studied. A marble plaque at the entrance commemorates this. The building is dark but spacious and stands in the center of town, at the edge of the old downtown district. The rooms are virtually empty. A student is showing me around: Tamila Tevdoradze, a girl of a subtle, romantic beauty.

The splendor and excellence of Georgia's ancient art are overwhelming. The most fantastic are the icons! They are from a much earlier time than Russian icons; the best Georgian ones came into being long before Andrey Rublyov. According to Tamila, their originality lies in their having been executed largely in metal: only the face is painted. The most glorious period of this work spans the eighth to the thirteenth centuries. The faces of the saints, dark, but radiant in the light, dwell immobile in extremely rich gold frames studded with precious stones. There are icons that open, like the altar of Vit Stoss. Their dimensions are immense, almost monumental. There is an icon here on which several generations of masters worked for three centuries. There is a small cross, the museum's most valuable exhibit, the only remaining possession of the empress Tamara.

Then there are the frescoes in the Georgian churches. Such marvels, and yet so little is known about them outside of Georgia. Virtually nothing. The best frescoes, unfortunately, were destroyed. They covered the interior of the largest church in Georgia—Sveti Tschoveli, built in 1010 in Georgia's former capital, Meht, near Tbilisi. They were a masterpiece of the Middle Ages on a par with the stained glass of Chartres. They were painted over on the order of the czar's governor, who wanted the church whitewashed "like our peasant women whitewash stoves." No restoration efforts can return these frescoes to the world. Their brilliance is extinguished forever.

Sveti Tschoveli is the best preserved monument of eleventh-century architecture in Europe. The church looks as if it were no more than a hundred years old, even though it has never been restored. It was built by the Georgian architect Arsukizdze, whose hand the emperor later ordered cut off so that he would never erect anything that would compete. Tamerlane tried several times to blow up this church, but the walls did not so much as tremble. It is open to this day, and the head of the Georgian Church, the catholicos of Greater Georgia, Jerffrem II, celebrates services there.

I also saw, although only in photographs, Vardzya. It is one of those incomprehensible wonders that contemporary man cannot explain. Vardzya is a Georgian town of the twelfth century, carved completely out of rock. It is laid out not horizontally but vertically, as if in stories. It is important to understand that this is not some collection of caverns or ruins, but an entire town, with a plan, with streets, with original architecture, only all of this is cut into living rock, embedded in an enormous mountain. But how, with the aid of what tools? Carving out such a town must have been more difficult than building an Egyptian pyramid. Vardzya was once a practical creation. Today, like the pyramids, it is dead. What remains is the wall of rock, sculpted into a melancholy, surrealistic composition.

At the end Tamila led me to the Niko Pirosmanashvili room so I could see the paintings that soon would be going to Paris for an exhibition. Tamila claims that Niko Pirosmanashvili is all the rage in Paris these days. Niko died in 1916. He was a Georgian Nikifor or Rousseau.

A great naive.

Niko lived in Nachalovce, the Tbilisi neighborhood of the

lumpen and the poor. He never had anything. He made his own brushes. The predominant color in Niko's paintings is black—he always used mostly black because he got his paint from coffin makers. He collected old tin signboards so he would have something to paint on. That is why lettering sometimes shows through in the background of his paintings, an incompletely covered over "Magaz" or "Tabak." The advertisement in gold and red and, on top of that, Niko's black-and-white visions. Georgian naive art laid over Russian commercial art nouveau. Niko painted in taverns, in stuffy Nachalovce bars. Sometimes onlookers would buy him wine. Perhaps he had tuberculosis? Perhaps epilepsy? Little is known about him. Many of Niko's works perished, a portion survived. The main subject of his paintings is the supper.

Niko painted suppers like Veronese.

Only Niko's suppers are Georgian and secular. Against a background of the Georgian landscape, a richly laid table; at this table Georgians are drinking and eating. The table is in the foreground. It is the most important thing. The culinary fascinated Niko. What will there be to eat, what will man gorge himself on? All this Niko would paint. He depicted what he would like to eat and what he would not eat, not today, or maybe not ever. Tables piled high. Roasted lambs. Greasy piglets. Wines red and heavy like calves' blood. Juicy watermelons. Fragrant pomegranates. There is a kind of masochism in this painting, a sticking the knife into one's own stomach, although Niko's art is cheerful, even humorous.

Niko's Georgia is sated, always feasting, well nourished. The land flows with milk. Manna pours from the sky. All the days are fat. The residents of Nachalovce dreamed at night of such a Georgia.

Niko painted Nachalovce's dreams.

Painting did not bring him happiness. He had a girl called Margerita. No one knows what sort of girl she was. Niko loved her and painted her portrait. Margerita's face is done according to the conventions of the great naives, by which everything is too big and out of proportion. Oversized lips, bulging eyeballs, enormous ears. Niko gave this portrait to Margerita. The girl shrieked in indignation. Enraged, full of hatred, she left him. His talent condemned him to solitude.

From then on he lived in lonely abandonment.

Over and over again he painted his feasts, with that table against a mountainous landscape. He was fifty-four when he died, in Tbilisi, in some room, of unknown causes, hungry, maybe mad.

VACHTANG INASHVILI showed me his place of work: a great hall filled to the ceiling with barrels. The barrels lie on wooden horses, huge, heavy, still.

In the barrels cognac is maturing.

Not everyone knows how cognac comes into being. To make cognac, you need four things: wine, sun, oak, and time. And in addition to these, as in every art, you must have taste. The rest is as follows.

In the fall, after the vintage, a grape alcohol is made. This alcohol is poured into barrels. The barrels must be of oak. The entire secret of cognac is hidden in the rings of the oak tree. The oak grows and gathers sun into itself. The sun settles into the rings of the oak as amber settles at the bottom of the sea. It is a long process, lasting decades. A barrel made from a young oak would not produce good cognac. The oak grows; its trunk begins to turn silver. The oak swells; its wood gathers strength, color, and fragrance. Not every oak will give good cognac. The best cognac is given by solitary oaks, which grow in quiet places, on dry ground. Such oaks have basked in the sun. There is as much sun in them as there is honey in a honeycomb. Wet ground is acidic, and then the oak will be too bitter. One senses that immediately in a cognac. A tree that was wounded when it was young will also not give a good cognac. In a wounded trunk the juices do not circulate properly, and the wood no longer has that taste.

Then the coopers make the barrels. Such a cooper has to know what he is doing. If he cuts the wood badly, it will not yield its aroma. It will yield color, but the aroma it will withhold. The oak is a lazy tree, and with cognac the oak must work. A cooper should have the touch of a violin maker. A good barrel can last one hundred years. And there are barrels that are two hundred years old and more. Not every barrel is a success. There are barrels without taste, and then others that give cognac like gold. After several years one knows which barrels are which.

Into the barrels one pours the grape alcohol. Five hundred, a thousand liters, it depends. One lays the barrel on a wooden horse and leaves it like that. One does not need to do anything more; one must wait. The right time will come for everything. The alcohol now enters the oak, and then the wood yields everything it has. It yields sun; it yields fragrance; it yields color. The wood squeezes the juices out of itself; it works.

That is why it needs calm.

There must be a cross breeze, because the wood breathes. And the air must be dry. Humidity will spoil the color, will give a heavy color, without light. Wine likes humidity, but cognac will not tolerate it. Cognac is more capricious. One gets the first cognac after three years. Three years, three stars. The starred cognacs are the youngest, of poorest quality. The best cognacs are those that have been given a name, without stars. Those are the cognacs that matured over ten, twenty, up to one hundred years. But in fact a cognac's age is even greater. One must add the age of the oak tree from which the barrel was made. At this time, oaks are being worked on that shot up during the French Revolution.

One can tell by the taste whether a cognac is young or old. A young cognac is sharp, fast, impulsive. Its taste will be sour, harsh. An old one, on the other hand, enters gently, softly. Only later does it begin to radiate. There is a lot of warmth in an old cognac, a lot of sun. It will go to one's head calmly, without hurry.

And it will do what it is supposed to do.

## ARMENIA

Vanik Santrian leads me around various back alleys of Yerevan, because that is what I've asked him to do: take us off the beaten path. In this way we happen upon the backyard of Benik Petrusyan. This backyard, enclosed on four sides by the walls of apartment buildings, is the site of a permanent exhibition of Benik's works. Benik is twenty-eight years old, has graduated from the Academy of Yerevan, and is a sculptor. Slight of build, shy, he lives in his cramped studio, whose door opens on this backyard showroom. In the studio hang magnificent Armenian stone crosses, called *hachkars*, which Armenians once carved in cliffs. You encounter these *hachkars* all over Armenia, for they were the symbols of Armenian existence, or else boundary markers, and also, sometimes, signposts. You can find old *hachkars* in the most inaccessible places, sometimes high up on the tops of sheer cliffs, and today it is impossible to imagine how their sculptors, most often monks, managed to climb up there.

Benik treated us to wine. We were sitting on a plank bed, among stones that he had been working on for several years. He turned on a tape player so that we could hear *patarks*. *Patarks* are a kind of Armenian psalm, haunting, beautiful. Benik had a new French recording of *patarks* sung in Paris by an Armenian choir. You can also hear *patarks* in Armenia if you go outside of Yerevan, to Echmiadzin, which is the Vatican of the Armenian Church.

Benik sculpts in stone and also practices *chekanka*, a kind of metallic bas-relief. He has a remarkable talent. The subject of his sculpture and of the *chekankas* is always love—more precisely, the amorous embrace. But there is little joy in these gestures: only lovers who in a moment must part forever hold each other in this way. One of Benik's cycles is the parting of Adam and Eve.

His sculptures seldom find their way to exhibitions. Most often they stand, as they do now, in his backyard, under trees or leaning against a wall, or lying directly on the ground. Benik sculpts for the residents of the four buildings that enclose his backyard. He sculpts for the superintendent and the mailman. For the garbagemen who come to clean up the piles of refuse. For the children who wash these sculptures for the fun of it or in the hope that they will get a piece of candy. For the bill collector from the electrical company. And also for the policeman, should he come around here on some business.

In the same neighborhood where Benik lives, Amayak Bdeyan

has his studio. Bdeyan makes enormous amphoras, vases, and water jugs, which he exhibits in the squares of Yerevan. It is a monumental ceramics, just right for showing on the lawns of Yerevan's wide avenues. Bdeyan likes bright, cheerful colors, but the texture of his forms is rough, lumpy. He covers the tips of these bumpy protuberances with a light, luminous enamel, so that the vases and water jugs glitter from afar. Bdeyan's amphoras can be seen all over the city. Bdeyan is a professor at the Armenian Institute of Art and has founded a movement that aims to turn Yerevan not only into a work of architecture but also into an artistic showplace. The municipal authorities bestow their full support upon these ambitions. Thus, Bdeyan has designed the interior of the Dramatic Theater in Yerevan—one of the most interesting achievements of contemporary interior art. The interior of the Café Araks is also his work, as is the splendid interior of the Ararat restaurant. Ararat is situated underground and is an example of modern design executed with taste and restraint. There are already many such places in Yerevan. Armenia's capital is becoming, piece by piece, a museum of the latest art.

There was a heavy downpour when we arrived at Bdeyan's, and his studio, which lies below street level, was flooding. Bdeyan, like an antique potter, was molding a slender vat out of clay. He showed me photographs of his exhibitions—from Canada, Switzerland, Italy, Syria. He is forty-two years old, a massive man, silent, hard driven. Unfortunately, Bdeyan's most interesting works can be seen only in Yerevan, because what he creates first and foremost is the city.

We also visited a young composer—Emin Aristakesyan. Vanik took me there so that I could hear the great Komitas sing. Komitas is to Armenians what Chopin is to Poles: their musical genius. His real name was Soomo Soomonyan, but as a monk he assumed the monastic name Komitas, and that is what they call him here. He was born in Turkey in 1869. At that time the majority of Armenians lived in Turkey. Estimates differ: two, three million. He studied composition in Berlin. He dedicated his entire life to Armenian music. He wandered around villages collecting songs. He established tens, others say hundreds, of

Armenian choirs. He was a wandering balladeer; he improvised epics; he sang. He created hundreds of compositions, magnificent, great, known to all the Philharmonic orchestras of the world. He wrote masses, sung to this day in Armenian churches.

In 1915 the massacre of Armenians began in Turkey. Until the time of Hitler, it was the greatest massacre in world history: 1.5 million Armenians perished. Turkish soldiers dragged Komitas up on a cliff from which they were going to push him. At the last minute his pupil, the sultan of Istanbul's daughter, saved him. But he had already seen the abyss, and this made him lose his mind.

He was forty-five years old then. Someone took him to Paris. He did not know that he was in Paris. He lived on for twenty more years. He did not make a sound. Twenty years in an institution for the mentally ill. He hardly walked, said nothing, but he watched. One can assume that he could see; those who visited him say that he observed faces.

Questioned, he did not answer.

They tried various things. They sat him down at the organ. He got up and walked away. They played records for him. He gave the impression that he did not hear. Someone placed a folk instrument on his knees, the tar. He carefully laid it aside. No one knows for certain whether he was ill. What if he chose silence?

Perhaps that was his freedom.

He had not died, but he no longer lived.

He existed-did-not-exist in that limbo between life and death, the purgatory of the insane. Those who visited him say that he grew more and more tired. He became stooped, gaunt; his skin blackened. Sometimes he tapped his finger along the table, in silence, for the table emitted no sound. He was calm, always serious.

He died in 1935: and so only after twenty years did he fall into the abyss from which his pupil, the sultan of Istanbul's daughter, had once saved him.

IN MATENADARAN one can see the ancient books of the Armenians. To me they are doubly inaccessible: they lie in cabinets behind glass, and I do not know how to read them. I ask Vanik if he understands them. Yes and no, for he can read the letters but cannot discern the meaning. The alphabet has remained the same for fifteen centuries, but the language has changed. The Armenian walks into Matenadaran like a Muslim into Mecca. It is the end of his pilgrimage; he is moved, overwhelmed. In Armenian history, the book was the national relic. The comrade who is our guide (so beautiful!) says in a hushed voice that many of the manuscripts that we see were saved at the cost of human life. There are pages stained with blood here. There are books that for years lay hidden in the ground, in the crevices of rocks. Armenians buried them in the same way defeated armies bury their banners. They were recovered without difficulty: information about their hiding places had been handed down from generation to generation.

A nation that does not have a state seeks salvation in symbols. The protection of the symbol is as important to it as the protection of borders is to other states. The cult of the symbol becomes a form of the cult of country. Protection of the symbol is an act of patriotism. Not that the Armenians never had a state. They had one, but it was destroyed in antiquity. It was then reborn in the ninth century, and after 160 years it perished—in that earlier form—forever. It is not just a question of statehood. For at least two thousand years Armenians were in danger of complete extermination. They were still threatened with it as recently as this century, right up until 1920.

The history of Armenians is measured in millennia. We are in that part of the world that is customarily called the cradle of civilization. We are moving among the oldest traces of man's existence. In the valley of the Razdan River, near Yerevan, stone tools from half a million years ago have been unearthed. The first mention of Armenia is four thousand years old, but by then, as the stone inscription proclaims, there had already existed on Armenian territory "sixty empires" and "hundreds of cities." Armenia therefore is the contemporary of the world's oldest civilizations. Babylon and Assyria were its neighbors. The biblical rivers Tigris and Euphrates have their sources within its borders.

Armenians have a measure of time different from ours. They

experienced their first partition 2,500 years ago. Their renaissance occurred in the fourth century of our era. They accepted Christianity seven centuries earlier than we. Ten centuries before us they started to write in their own language. But Armenia shared with ancient Egypt, Sumer, and Byzantium a drama typical of this part of the world—its essence was a lack of historical continuity, that sudden appearance of empty chapters in the history book of one's own state.

A magnificent ascent, and then a dispiriting fall.

Gradually, the nations living in this cradle of mankind, having created great, monumental civilizations, as if exhausted by the superhuman effort, or perhaps even crushed by the immensity of what they had brought forth and no longer capable of further developing it, handed over the reins to younger peoples, bursting with energy and eager to live. Europe will come on the scene and, later, America.

The source of all of Armenia's misfortunes was its disastrous geographic location. One has to look at the map, not from our vantage point, from the center of Europe, but from an entirely different place, from the south of Asia, the way those who sealed Armenia's fate looked at it. Historically, Armenia occupied the Armenian Highland. Periodically (and these periods lasted centuries) Armenia reached farther, was a state of three seas—the Mediterranean, the Black, and the Caspian. But let us remain within the borders of the Highland. It is this area upon which the Armenians' historical memory draws. After the eleventh century, the Armenians never succeeded in rebuilding Armenia within those borders.

The map, looked at from the south of Asia, explains the tragedy of the Armenians. Fate could not have placed their country in a more unfortunate spot. In the south of the Highland it borders upon two of the past's most formidable powers—Persia and Turkey. Let's add to that the Arabian caliphate. And even Byzantium. Four political colossi, ambitious, extremely expansionist, fanatical, voracious. And now—what does the ruler of each of these four powers see when he looks at the map? He sees that if he takes Armenia, then his empire will be enclosed by an ideal natural border in the north. Because from the north the

Armenian Highland is magnificently protected, guarded by two seas (the Black and the Caspian) and by the gigantic barrier of the Caucasus. And the north is dangerous for Persia and for Turkey, for the Arabs and Byzantium. Because in those days from the north an unsubdued Mongolian fury loomed.

And so Armenia gives all the pashas and emperors sleepless nights. Each one of them would like his realm to have a nicely rounded border. So that in his realm, as in King Philip's, the sun should never set. A border that does not dissipate itself amid flatlands, but which leans against a proper mountain, against the edge of the sea. The consequence of these ambitions is continual invasions of Armenia; someone is always conquering and destroying it, always subjugating it.

That is the political sphere. But there is also the matter of religion. In the year 301, during the reign of the emperor of the Armenians Tiridates III Arashakuni, Armenia adopts Christianity. It is the first country in the world in which Christianity attains the rank of a state religion. Conflict hangs in the air: neighboring Persia professes Zoroastrianism, hostile to Christianity, and from the south Islam will soon draw near, hostile to both. The epoch of unleashed fanaticisms begins, of religious massacres, sectarianism, schisms, medieval madness. And Armenia enters this epoch.

Armenians have their church, which is called the Holy Apostolic Armenian Church. In the centuries-long feud between the Vatican and Byzantium, they occupied a middle ground—somewhat closer, however, to the Vatican. That is why, although they belonged to the group of churches practicing the Greek rite, in Constantinople they were counted among those who had severed themselves—among the heretics even. "Their rite," Runciman reports, "diverged in many particulars from the Greek. They readily offered bloody animal sacrifices, they began the great fast on the Septuagesima, fasted on Saturdays, and above all used unleavened bread in the Eucharist." Because of this bread, on which they heretically insisted, they were contemptuously called "the unleavened."

The head of the Armenian Church is the catholicos, who

traditionally always resides in Echmiadzin, near Yerevan. The catholicoses have counted among their number several distinguished poets, philosophers, musicians, and grammarians. During those periods when the Armenian state did not exist—an almost permanent condition in feudal and more recent times—it was the catholicoses who represented the Armenian cause in the international arena. They performed the function of the unofficial head of a nonexistent state. From this they derived additional prestige.

A certain monk named Mashtots creates the Armenian alphabet. Mashtots's life bears the mark of the anonymous monastic existence. He is entirely hidden by his work. Armenians always say of him "the genius Mashtots." For this alphabet, the church makes Mashtots a saint, an act that in this case can be considered a kind of state honor. It is astonishing that the invention of a then-little-known monk could be so immediately and generally espoused. And yet it is a fact! Already, then, there must have existed among Armenians a strong need for identity and individuation. They were a lonely Christian island in a sea of alien Asiatic elements. The mountains could not save them: at approximately the same time as Mashtots's alphabet is proclaimed, Armenia loses its independence.

From then on foreign armies—Persian, Mongolian, Arab, Turkish—will blow across this country like ill winds. A curse will grip this land. Whatever is built will be destroyed. The rivers will flow with blood. The chronicles are full of dismal images. "Armenian roses and violets have died," despairs a medieval Armenian historian, Leo. "Armenia has become the motherland of pain. The fugitive Armenian either wanders in foreign climes or strays, hungry, over a corpse-strewn native ground."

Vanquished in the field of arms, Armenia seeks salvation in the scriptoria. It is a retreat, but in this withdrawal there is dignity and a will to live. What is a scriptorium? It can be a cell, sometimes a room in a clay cottage, even a cave in the rocks. In such a scriptorium is a writing desk, and behind it stands a copyist, writing. Armenian consciousness was always infused with a sense of impending ruin. And by the fervent concomitant desire for rescue. The desire to save one's world. Since it cannot be saved with the sword, let its memory be preserved. The ship will sink, but let the captain's log remain.

So comes into being that phenomenon unique in world culture: the Armenian book. Having their alphabet, Armenians immediately go about writing books. Mashtots himself sets the example. He had barely produced the alphabet, and already we find him translating the Bible. He is assisted by another luminary of Armenian culture, Catholicos Saak Partef, and a whole pleiad of translators recruited throughout the dioceses. Mashtots initiates the great movement of the medieval copyists, which among the Armenians will develop to an extent unknown anywhere else.

Already by the sixth century, they had translated into Armenian all of Aristotle. By the tenth century, they had translated the majority of the Greek and Roman philosophers, hundreds of titles of ancient literature. Armenians have an open, assimilative intellect. They translated everything that was within reach. They remind me in this of the Japanese, who translate wholesale whatever comes their way. Many works of ancient literature survived owing entirely to the fact that they were preserved in Armenian translations. The copyists threw themselves upon every novelty and immediately placed it on the writing table. When the Arabs conquered Armenia, the Armenians translated all the Arabs. When the Persians invaded Armenia, the Armenians translated the Persians! They were in conflict with Byzantium, but whatever appeared on the market there, they would take and translate that as well.

Entire libraries start coming into being. These must have been enormous collections: in 1170 the Seljuks destroy a library in Syunik consisting of ten thousand volumes. They are all Armenian manuscripts. To this day, twenty-five thousand Armenian manuscripts have survived. Of these, more than ten thousand are in Yerevan, in Matenadaran. Whoever would like to see the rest will have to make a journey around the world. The largest collections are in the Library of St. Jacob in Jerusalem, in the Library of St.

Lazarus in Venice, and in the Library of the Mekitarians in Vienna. Paris and Los Angeles have beautiful collections. Poland also once had a large collection, in Lvov, where, incidentally, there was a large Armenian printing press.

At first they wrote on skins, then on paper. They once made a book that weighed thirty-two kilograms. Seven hundred calves went into it. But they also have trifles, books small as May flies. Whoever could read and write, copied, but there were also professional copyists whose entire lives were spent behind the writing desk. In the fifteenth century Ovanes Mankasharence transcribed 132 books. "For seventy-two years," notes his pupil Zachariash, "winter and summer, day and night, Ovanes copied books. When he reached his later years, his sight dimmed, and his hand shook and writing caused him great suffering. He died in Panu at the age of eighty-six, and now I, Zachariash, pupil of Ovanes, am completing his unfinished manuscript." These were titans of painstaking labor, martyrs of their passion. Another copyist describes how, while going hungry, he would spend his last penny on resinous chips to illuminate the pages he was transcribing. Many of these books are masterpieces of the calligraphic art. Golden armies of small Armenian letters crawl over hundreds of pages. The copyists were also accomplished painters. The art of the miniature attains world-class heights in the Armenian book. The names of two miniaturists in particular—Toros Roslin and Sarkis Picak—shine with an immortal light. The miniatures with which Roslin decorated manuscripts in the thirteenth century have retained the full intensity of their original color, and to this day they dazzle from the pages of the books of Matenadaran.

The fate of these books is the history of the Armenians. Armenians, persecuted and exterminated, reacted to their situation in one of two ways: some went up into the mountains, taking refuge in caverns, and some emigrated, scattering over all the continents. Both groups took Armenian books with them. Because the wanderers left Armenia on foot, certain manuscripts, those that were too heavy, were divided in half. These halves often roamed to different ends of the earth.

## AZERBAIJAN

On Oilmen Boulevard, Gulnara Guseinova heals people with the smell of flowers. Those who are afflicted with senility are made to sniff laurel leaves. Those with high blood pressure—geraniums. For asthma, rosemary is best. People come to Gulnara with a piece of paper from Professor Gasanov. On it the professor has prescribed the name of a flower and the length of time it should be sniffed. You sniff sitting down, most often for ten minutes. Gulnara sees to it that everybody sniffs that which they are supposed to; that some senile old fellow, for instance, doesn't start sniffing rosemary. The flowers stand in rows in a glass house that is called the office of phytotherapy, which resembles a greenhouse. Gulnara tells me to sit down and sniff something too. Do I detect the fragrance? I detect nothing. Well, now—that's because the flower does not smell in and of itself. One has to gently move the stem, and then the flower feels that someone is interested in it. And it begins to release its scent. Flowers do not smell for themselves, only for someone else. To every touch the flower will respond with fragrance—it is naive and frivolous; it wants to please everyone. "Comrades, move the flowers!" Gulnara admonishes the old men sitting in the office, who begin shaking the twigs as if they were brushing ants off them.

I ask Gulnara, who is a student of medicine, if she believes that a flower can cure a man. I don't mean heal someone psychically, for that has been proven possible, but heal physically—for instance restore elasticity to a calcifying joint. Gulnara smiles. She offers only that people come to her for healing from all over the world. She emphasizes: "Even from America." Professor Gasanov's method—this healing with the scent of flowers—is already renowned.

I think that the enchanting thing about this method, for Gulnara, as for me, is its aesthetic aspect, as well as the cheerfulness and kindliness of its wisdom. For what can the professor do with a seventy-year-old man who forgets the date of his birth? He could, of course, place him in a crowded hospital room, with the odor of chloroform and iodine. But what for? Is a twilight fragrant with flowers not more beautiful than one reeking of chloroform? So when someone who must look at his identification card to give his date of birth comes to Gasanov complaining that something is muddying his head, the professor listens to him attentively and then writes down for him on a piece of paper: "Rx: Laurel leaves. Ten minutes a day. For three weeks." And look, says Gulnara, crowds are pouring in to see the professor. You have to wait months for an appointment.

I am sitting with Gulnara on Oilmen Boulevard, at the edge of the sea. From here Baku rises up gently in stone terraces. The city lies on a bay, has the shape of an amphitheater, and so is completely visible. Gulnara asks if I like Baku. I answer that I do, yes, very much. Its buildings parade one next to another in a great revue of architectural styles and epochs. Everything is here! Pseudo-Gothic and pseudobaroque and post-Moorish and Corbusier's school and twenties' constructivism and edifices in the grand style and pretty modern constructions. It is a one-of-a-kind spectacle. Everything is in one place, each style displayed right next to the other, as in the window of the London office of Mr. Cox, Estate Agent, which offers everyone exactly what he desires.

Furthermore, there are several Bakus.

The oldest Baku is the smallest. It is not only tiny, but so tightly packed, so compressed, so cluttered, that when I walk into it I involuntarily take a deep breath to make sure I will have enough air to breathe. If one were to stop here in the middle of the street and stretch out one's arms, then one could with one hand stroke a child sleeping in a cradle in the apartment on the left and with the other treat oneself to a pear lying on the table in the apartment on the right. One walks single file here, because a couple walking side by side immediately creates a bottleneck. And Baku's old town has no plan—or maybe it has one, but it is so surrealistic that no normal mind can grasp it. One never knows how to find one's way out of here. I came with Valery, who was born and raised in Baku; we tried various alternatives, this way, and that way, but nothing worked. We were at the end of our rope when some kids finally saved us.

This part of Baku is called Ichen-Shereh, which means "Inner City." It is steeped in legend and extolled in many backyard ballads. For residents of the larger Baku, Ichen-Shereh has always been utterly exotic, a place where people speak their own language and live as if under one roof, without secrets. Today Ichen-Shereh is gradually being pulled down; there will be a new neighborhood here.

Around the Inner City stretches Baku proper, large and slightly snobbish. For this large Baku is a city custom-built, built for privateers, for parvenus, for the kings of Baku oil. Baku always made a career of oil. As far back as the tenth century Arab writers refer to Baku as the place from which oil is brought. According to *Adjaib ad-Dunia*, a twelfth-century Persian treatise, "Baku blazes like a fire all night. They stand a cauldron on the ground and boil water in it." A Turkish traveler, Eveli Chelebi, describes this boiling in 1666: "There are various barren places in Baku. If a man or a horse should put his foot down there and stand a while, his foot will start to burn. Caravan guides dig up the earth in those places, set kettles in it, and the food starts to boil immediately. Prodigious is God's wisdom!"

Caravans transported the oil over all of Asia. Marco Polo writes that it was first and foremost an invaluable cure for the skin diseases of camels. And so, in a certain sense, the transportation network of medieval Asia depended on Baku oil. Because of the burning ground, Baku was also the Mecca for Hindu fire worshipers, who journeyed here from India to warm themselves near their flaming gods. Their temple, Ateshga, has been preserved, with four extinguished chimneys.

One hundred years ago the first derrick goes up in Baku. The city's vertiginous career begins. A Pole came here—an elegant man, I am told, with dash. He hired a droshky and had himself driven around. At a certain moment he took off his top hat and threw it on the ground. He indicated to the astonished driver the place where the hat had fallen. "We are going to drill here," he said. He was a rich man later. More than two hundred foreign firms exploit Baku oil. "In 1873," writes Harvey O'Connor,

> the first oil spouts in Baku from an automatic shaft. During the next decade Baku grew to the level of the world's wealthiest city, and Armenian and Tatar oil millionaires started to rival millionaires from Texas. The city became the largest refining center in the world. Russia assumed the position of a great exporter of crude oil, and for a few years would overshadow the United States. The Nobel brothers, who arrived in Baku quite by accident in 1875, built their first refinery here a year later, and in 1878 formed the Nobel Brothers Naphtha Company, which by 1883 already controlled 51 percent of crude oil production. They built the first oil pipeline in the Baku region, brought in drillers from Pennsylvania, and applied the latest scientific advances to the organization of this chaotically developing industry. In the course of a few years the Nobels acquired a fleet of enormous ocean-going steam-powered tankers and smaller river tankers for the transport of oil on the Volga. This was happening at a time when sailing ships still transported oil from America in barrels and cans. The Nobels were to be the exception to the rule which held that whoever lived even a year among the oil magnates in Baku could never again become a civilized man. The "Black City" of Baku became one of the most hideous, crowded, and rough corners of the world. Tatars, Armenians, Persians, and Jews created, together with the Russians, an ethnic mosaic which from time to time exploded in violent massacres. Quite a few oil-rich fields were given as presents by the czar to various court favorites. Speculation was unleashed, fortunes were made from one day to the next. The world had never before seen anything like it, not even in western Pennsylvania. Because there was no way to catch all the streams of gushing crude, the wells were ringed with dikes, creating

lakes. Nevertheless entire rivers of crude frequently flowed from the wells straight into the sea.

"PLEASE FORGIVE ME, but I will speak a bit nationalistically." She is very amusing, this pugnacious Azerbaijani girl, who on the one hand knows that nationalism is a forbidden fruit and on the other cannot resist the temptation. We are standing over a relief map of Central Asia, and she wants to show me how great Azerbaijan once was (this is what she regards as a bit of nationalism). I tell her that her desire to present to me the Great Yesterday is a universal impulse in today's world. Wherever one goes, in each country people will boast about how far their ancestors had once reached. People seem to need this awareness, perhaps more and more as time goes on. I tell her that there must be some law of compensation at work here. The world once used to be roomy, and if some nation suddenly felt that it had to expand, it could go quite far in this expansion. Consider the impressive expansion of the Romans. Look at how magnificently the Mongols expanded themselves. How the Turks did. Can one fail to marvel at how the Spaniards expanded themselves? Even Venice, so small, after all, but what successes in expansion.

Today expansion is difficult and risky, as a rule broadening ends in narrowing, and that is why nations must satisfy the instinct for breadth with a feeling of depth, which means reaching into the depths of history to demonstrate their strength and significance. It is the situation in which all small nations that value peace find themselves. Fortunately, if one looks at the history of humanity, it turns out that every nation, in one epoch or another, has had its period of swelling and broadening, at least one patriotic spurt, which today allows it to preserve a certain—admittedly relative—psychic balance among the rest of mankind.

I don't even know this Azerbaijani's name. Girls' names always mean something here, and parents attach great importance to the choice of a name. Gulnara means "Flower"; Nargis is "Narcissus"; Bahar is "Spring"; Aydyn is "Light." Sevil is a girl with whom someone is in love. After the Revolution, Valery tells me, they started giving girls' names that celebrate the modern inventions now making their way to the countryside. So there are girls with the names Tractor, Chauffeur. One father, apparently counting on tax reductions, called his daughter Finotdiel, which is an abbreviation of the name of the Office of Finance (Finansovyj Otdiel).

So I stand with the nameless Azerbaijani over the map of Asia and look at how great Azerbaijan once was. It stretched from the Caucasus to Tehran and from the Caspian Sea to Turkey. Soviet Azerbaijan represents only the smaller part of that other, earlier Azerbaijan. The rest lies in Iran. The majority of Azerbaijanis, around 4 million live there, and in the Soviet Union around 3.5 million.

In the past Azerbaijan was more of a geographic and cultural concept than a political one. There never really was a centralized state of Azerbaijan, and in this its history differs from that of Georgia and Armenia. It differs in other respects, as well. By way of the Black Sea and Anatolia, Georgia and Armenia maintained contact with ancient Europe, and later with Byzantium. They received Christianity from there, which created within their territories a resistance to the spread of Islam. In Azerbaijan the influence of Europe was weak from the onset, at best secondary. Between Europe and Azerbaijan rise the barriers of the Caucasus and the Armenian Highland, whereas in the east Azerbaijan turns into lowlands, is easily accessible, open.

Azerbaijan is the threshold of Central Asia.

The dominant religions are, first, Zoroastrianism, then Islam, but when I read *Sketches from the History and Philosophy of Azerbaijan* by the Eight Authors, I am astonished at how many heretics, apostates, atheists, sectarians, dissenters, mystics, pit dwellers, and hermits found shelter and a pulpit here. For Azerbaijan had Matazalites, Batists, Ismailis, Mazdakites, Manichaeans, as well as Monophysites, fire worshipers, Bedtashites, Nugdavites, also Sufis, Hurramites, the Pure Brethern, and Hurufites—known as mystics of the numeral—Serbedites, Kadirites, and Sunnis. In relation to the cosmopolitan centers of the East, this region must have been considered part of the deep provinces, a place of asylum and survival, although this was not always true: in 1417 the heretical philosopher Imadeddin Nezimi is skinned alive here, and several years before that, the leader of the Hurufites, Shichabedin Fazlullach Naimi Tebrizi Azterabadi al-Hurufi, dies in Azerbaijan at the hands of the Muslim inquisition.

The disciples of this martyr, the Hurufites—mystics of the numeral, cabalists, and diviners—believed that the origins of the universe could be comprehended in terms of the figures 28 and 32. Using these numerals one can explain the mystery of each thing. It was the Hurufites' belief that God expressed himself through beauty: the more beautiful something was, the more God manifested himself in it. Beauty was their criterion for valuating the phenomenal world.

They searched for God in the human face.

Although Muslims, they saw God in the faces of beautiful women.

There was in the twelfth century an Azerbaijani poet of world renown named Nezāmī. Like Kant, Nezāmī never left his native city, which was Gandzha, today's Kirovabad. Hegel said of Nezāmī's poetry that it is "soft and sweet." "At nights," Nezāmī writes, "I extract shining pearls of verses, scorching my brain in a hundred fires." His remark that "the surface of the word should be vast" is wise. Nezāmī was an epic poet and a philosopher who occupied himself with logic and grammar, even cosmogony.

From one side pressed upon by Turkey, from the other by Persia, Azerbaijan was unable to secure its autonomy. A series of principalities did in fact exist here, but their significance was local. For many centuries Azerbaijan was a province of Persia. In the years 1502–1736, Persia was ruled by the Safavid dynasty, which is of Azerbaijani descent. Under this dynasty Persia experienced years of glory. But the Azerbaijan language belongs not to the Persian group, but to the Turkic. Few realize that the Turkic constitutes the largest language group in the Soviet Union. Uzbeks, Tatars, Kazakhs, Azerbaijanis, Chuvashes, Turkmen, Bashkirs, Kirghiz, Yakuts, Dolganes, Karakalpaks, Kumites, Haguzites, Tuvinians, Uighurs, Karachai, Chakasites, Chulites, Altays, Balashites, Nogai, Turks, Shirtes, Karaites, Crimean Jews, and Tofals are all Turkic speakers. An Uzbek and a Tatar, a Kirghiz and a

Bashkir, can speak to one another, each in his own language, and understand one another well.

IN THE EVENING, Nik-Nik orders me to climb high up in a tower.

From the tower I will be able to see how the Oil Rocks shine, and Nik-Nik says that I cannot leave until I have seen this. The tower stands in the middle of the sea, the sea is black, although it is called Caspian, and I am climbing up to heaven on stairs that creak because they are made of wood, the whole tower is made of wood nailed together, it reaches to the stars, and although the wind rocks it like a stalk, it stands, *gniotsa nie lamiotsa* (it will bend but it won't break), so on this tower I am climbing up to heaven, it is dark here, actually it is black like the sea, we are walking into tar, I prefer not to look anymore, I would like to stop, enough is enough, but I can hear Nik-Nik going farther, so I go too, into the darkness, into the abyss, into the chasm. Everything is becoming unreal, because I can no longer see anything, meaning that I can see only this thing of wood around me, rough, unplaned, as if hairy, a piece of raw wood wedged into the sky, in an utterly gratuitous place, jutting out in the darkness, improbable, abstract.

"Nik-Nik!" I cry.

Because, you understand, I was left alone with this piece of wood, in some strange situation, incomprehensible, really, suspended in an indefinable place, for beyond this piece of wood was darkness, no point of reference whatsoever by which to determine my coordinates, no chance of taking a few steps, lighting a cigarette, calmly considering what next; above all I didn't know what to do with this piece of wood, and in this way I remained, stuck in the dark, idiotic and senseless, until I heard Nik-Nik's voice, somewhere above me, in another region of the galaxy.

"Did you see it?" panted Nik-Nik, who was long ago lost from sight. Only now did I look down, although with great trepidation because I have a fear of heights.

I saw the city.

It is nothing strange to see a city, even country people are accustomed to the sight today, but I saw a city on the open sea, on a stormy, turbulent, vast sea; it was one hundred kilometers from this city to the nearest land.

I saw the city's lights, its streets, which disappeared over the horizon, the bustle downtown, people seemed to be coming out of the movies, I myself had gone there the previous day to see the Polish film *Boomerang*, in the center of the city neon lights flickered, buses were running, a café shone brightly, shops and apartment windows glowed. A tanker stood in the harbor, for there is also a port here, two ports even, and an airport. Very far away I could see the derricks over the oil wells, buzzing like beehives, although this was barely audible from here, the night shift was at work up in those towers. This city never really sleeps, not even toward morning.

Below, underneath the city, the sea surges.

The sea pounds against the rows of steel piles upon which the city stands, pours itself into the labyrinth of metal constructions that keep its streets, squares, and houses above water. But the city stands motionless, resting on mighty pillars planted firmly in the seafloor. Let's put it another way: it is a city built on mountaintops, only these mountains lie underwater.

An underwater mountain range connects the eastern and western shores of the Caspian Sea. The mountains stretch from Baku to Krasnovodsk in Turkmenistan. In these mountains, along their entire length, are rich deposits of oil and gas. When the sea is calm one can see in certain places the peaks of this underwater chain. From crevices, from under rocks, here and there oil is leaking. That is why these rocks were called the Oil Rocks, and it is from this that the city built in the middle of the sea got its name.

## TURKMENISTAN

Ashkhabad, a peaceful city. Now and then a Volga passes along the street. Now and then a donkey's hooves tap against the asphalt. They are selling hot tea in the Russian market. One potful—twenty kopecks. But can the value of tea be measured in this way?

Here, tea is life. An old Turkman takes the teapot and pours two small bowls—one for himself, the other he passes to the little yellow-haired boy. "*Nu*," he says to the boy. "*Oy, Diadia*," the little one answers, "I'm always telling you that you're supposed to say *na*, not *nu*." Diadia laughs, perhaps at the same thought that occurs to me: that he can no longer be taught anything. A Turkman that has lived long enough to have a gray beard knows everything. His head is full of wisdom; his eyes have read the book of life. When he got his first camel, he learned what wealth was. When a herd of his sheep died, he learned the unhappiness of poverty. He has seen dry wells, and so he knows what despair is, and he has seen wells full of water, and so he knows what joy is. He knows that the sun brings life, but he also knows that the sun brings death, which no European really understands.

He knows what thirst is and how it feels to have one's thirst quenched.

He knows that when it is hot one must dress warmly, in smock and sheepskin, and not strip down to the bare skin, as some men do. A dressed man is thinking, an undressed one—no. A naked man is capable of committing every stupidity. Those who created great things were always dressed. In Sumeria and Mesopotamia, in Samarkand and Baghdad, despite the diabolical heat, people walked about dressed. Great civilizations arose there, which neither Australia nor the African equator, where people walked naked in the sun, can boast of. All you need do is read the history of the world.

It could be that this old man knows the answers to Shakespeare's great question.

He has seen the desert, and he has seen the oasis, and in the final analysis it comes down to this one division. There are more and more people in the world; the oases are becoming overcrowded, even the large oasis that is Europe, not to mention those of the Ganges and of the Nile. Will not mankind, which was born in the desert, as all the sources attest, have to return there to its cradle? And then to whom will he turn for advice, this sweaty urbanite, with his broken-down Fiat, with his refrigerator and no place to plug it in? Will he not start searching for the Turkman with the gray beard, the Tuareg wrapped in a turban? They know where the wells are, which means that they know the secret of survival and salvation. Their knowledge, devoid of scholasticism and doctrinairism, is great, because it serves life. In Europe they have the habit of writing that people of the desert are backward, even extremely backward. And it doesn't occur to anyone that this is no way to judge a people who have been able to survive millennia under the most dire conditions, producing a culture that is most valuable because it is practical, a culture that allowed entire nations to exist and develop while during that very same time many sedentary civilizations fell and disappeared forever from the face of the earth.

Some think that man went into the desert out of poverty, because he had no other choice. But it was exactly the opposite. In Turkmenistan only those who had herds could go into the desert, and thus only the rich; nomadism was a privilege of the wealthy. "A sojourn in the desert," says Professor Gabriel, "is an honor, the desert is the chosen ground." The transition to a sedentary life was for the nomad always a last resort, a sign of failure in life, a degradation. One can settle a nomad only by force, by economic or political coercion. For him, the freedom that the desert gives has no price.

Can one even begin to imagine human civilization without the contribution of the nomads? Take the Golden Horde and the state of the Timurids. They were the greatest empires of the Middle Ages. The longest epic in world literature, which is called *Manas* and numbers forty volumes, is the national epic of a nomadic people—the Kirghiz. Take the flowering of Indian art under the rule of the nomadic dynasty of the Great Mogul. And one must not forget Islam, a phenomenon that has influenced world events for thirteen centuries, a religion whose following is still growing, with members across the great sweep of the globe, from Senegal to Indonesia, from Mongolia to Zanzibar.

But above all, in the course of those millennia that did not know the airplane, and still earlier did not know the steamship, the nomads were the only people who had mastered the magnificent and dangerous art of conquering dead space; simply in the course of their continual wanderings, they created what was truly the world's first global system of mass communication, carrying from city to city, from continent to continent, from one extremity to another, not only gold, spices, and dates, but books and letters, political news and reports of discoveries, originals and copies of great works of learning and of imagination—which made possible, in those ages of dispersion and isolation, the exchange of accomplishments and the development of culture.

Next to where the old Turkman, the boy, and I are drinking our tea stands a flower vendor. "*Gradzanki*," she calls, "*nev zabyvajtie roz*." Ashkhabadian roses, heavy, languorous. But no one is buying flowers; the marketplace is empty at this time of day; it is noon in the desert. Ashkhabad, crushed by the heat, lies in the sun, numbed, silent. It is one hundred meters from this place to my hotel. From here to the Iranian border—one hour's drive. But it is far to Moscow—4,300 kilometers. To Warsaw—more than five thousand. In 1935 a group of Turkmen set off on horseback for Moscow. They rode day in and day out for three months, a total of eighty-three days, and this record has been noted down in *The History of the Turkmen SSR*.

In the marketplace there are vegetable vendors, meaning kolkhoz members come here to sell the produce from their private gardens and plots, vendors of medicines, which one can buy here from stalls, nationalized booksellers, and barbers. Many barbers, but only for men. Turkmen women braid their hair, and you don't need a barber for that. There is a vendor of pencils and notebooks, so fantastically wet, sweaty, positively dripping, he looks as if he were standing under a continuous shower. "*Uzbek*!" he calls to the tea vendor. "*Day chayu*!" And he pumps the hot beverage into himself, bowl after bowl. "*Grazdanie*!" he calls after a moment, "support culture! Buy notebooks!"

The entire marketplace is covered in asphalt, the streets too. On the streets run trolley cars, hot as furnaces. Both sides of the streets are planted with trees; there are many lawns and flower beds; one can see a great concern for greenery; the city is well cared for, clean and groomed. The trees give shade, but they also serve another function, this one psychological. The presence of greenery eases the exhausting sense of claustrophobia, which torments the resident of the oasis. A sedentary man fears the desert; the desert fills him with dread. And all he has to do is go to the edge of town, often just to the end of his own backyard: desert all around. The desert forces its way into the city, buries squares and streets. I was in Nuakshott, which lies in the Sahara, where heaps of sand that have drifted over the asphalt are regularly removed, just as snow is removed from the streets at home during winter. In the Atar oasis I saw peasants whose continual task it was to dig out date palms that were being buried up to their tops in sand. The desert attacks houses, which is why there are no windows except those that are kept permanently closed. In such a climate! And yet in this way man protects himself from the dust, which ruins homes, provisions, possessions.

Trees create the soothing impression that the oasis is not an island endlessly under attack by the elements of the desert, but a fragment of a greater earth propitious to people and to plants.

Ashkhabad is a young city in two senses. It started to come into being only in 1881, when the Russian army, after breaking the Turkmen's resistance, built a fort here. The fort started to sprout little streets, a small town grew around it. In 1948, during an earthquake, one of the most severe in modern history, in the space of fifteen seconds the town disappeared from the face of the earth. There had been one cemetery in the town, Misha recalls, and after the quake there were sixteen. Of all the city's structures, only the statue of Lenin survived.

The Ashkhabad you see today is the city that came into being after the disaster, essentially new from the foundations up. There is nothing here for the lover of antiquities to visit.

RASHYD SHOWED ME on the map where the Uzboj flowed.

It drew its waters from the Amu Darya River, cut across the Kara Kum Desert, and plunged into the Caspian Sea. It was a beautiful river, said Rashyd, as long as the Seine. This river died, he said, and its death became the beginning of war. He added that the archaeologist Yusupov studied the history of the Uzboj. According to Yusupov, the river appeared on the desert suddenly and relatively recently, perhaps five thousand years ago. Together with the water, fish and birds arrived in the desert. Later, people came. They belonged to the tribes of Ali-ili, Chyzr, and Tivedzij. Turkmen at the time were divided into 110 tribes, perhaps even more. The people of Ali-ili, Chyzr, and Tivedzij divided the Uzboj into three segments, a third of the river's length falling to each tribe. The banks of the Uzboj were transformed into a flowering and populous oasis. Villages and centers of manufacture, gardens and plantations, arose. In the very heart of the desert it became crowded and noisy. That is what water can bring. Water is the beginning of everything. It is the first nourishment. It is the blood of the earth. People represented water with three wavy lines. Above the lines they drew a fish. The fish was the symbol of happiness. Three lines plus a fish signified—life.

Merchant ships sailed on the river. Goods passed through here on their way from India to Anatolia, from Khorez to Persia. The Uzboj was renowned the world over. In countries where people were literate, various references to it have survived. We find references among the Greeks and Persians, and also references among the Arabs. On the banks of the Uzboj stood hospitable caravansaries where rowers could rest, get a place to sleep and a meal. There were bazaars in Dov-Kala, Orta-Kuy, and Talaychan where everyone could buy goods of the highest quality from all over the world.

The people of the Uzboj worshiped sacred stones. This is typical of inhabitants of deserts, who revere everything they have at hand—stones, gorges, wells, and trees. Fighting was forbidden in the place where a sacred stone stood. The stone protected one from death. A concentrated force dwelled inside it, imprisoned in an immutable form, bestowed upon it for all eternity. Kissing the stone gave people an almost sensual pleasure. Rashyd calls my attention to a fragment of *The Voyage* in which Abū 'Abd Allāh Mohammad ibn 'Abd Allāh al-Lawātī aṭ-Ṭandzi, otherwise known as Ibn Baṭṭūṭah, writes that "the lips feel an immense sweetness when kissing stone, so that one wants to go on kissing it forever." To the people of the Uzboj, a stone was a divine being.

Human thought during those times revolved around such matters as the distribution of water. We can ascertain this through deductive reasoning. Even after the Revolution, until reforms were instituted, the division of water was for the Turkmen an event as important as the outbreak of war or the signing of peace. Virtually everything depended on it. Water reached the fields through canals called *aryks*. The distribution of water took place at the main *aryk*. If the spring was good, the distribution of water became a celebration. But good springs occur rarely here. In the course of an entire year there can be as little rainfall as one shower brings in Europe. And it can also happen that the entire yearly rainfall pours down from the sky in the course of only two days, and after that there is only drought. The distribution of water would then turn into war. Cemeteries stretch on both sides of the *aryks*, at the bottom of the canals lie human bones.

The rich had large *aryks* and the poor small ones. The poor man tried to open the valves on the sly to let more water into his *aryk*. The rich man suppressed such practices. That is how the class struggle looked. Water was an object of speculation; it was a commodity on the black market. There was a water exchange, a water boom, a water crash. People made fortunes on water, or lost everything. Various customs arose that only the Revolution would abolish. A woman did not have the right to a water allotment. Only married men received water. A man to whom a son was born married the infant to a grown girl; the infant, being married, received a water allotment. Water was the road to riches for those people to whom many sons were born. It was not until 1925 that the First Congress of the Councils of Turkmenistan ratified the revolutionary decree that forbids the marrying of infants and grants women the right to water.

Everyone tried to live as close to the Uzboj as possible. The river carried water; it carried life. Along its banks ran the trails of caravans. In the currents of the Uzboj the army of Genghis Khan watered its horses. To its shores journeyed the merchants of Samarkand and the Yomud—slave traders.

The river's agony, said Rashyd, began four hundred years ago. Having appeared suddenly on the desert, the river now just as suddenly began to vanish. The Uzboj had created a civilization in the very heart of the desert, had sustained three tribes, linked the west with the east; on the banks of the Uzboj stood dozens of cities and settlements, which Yusupov would excavate. Now the sands were swallowing up the river. Its energy began to weaken, its current to wane. It is not known who first noticed this. The Ali-ili, Chyzr, and Tivedzij gathered on the banks to watch the river, the source of life, departing; they sat and they watched, because people like to observe their own misfortune. The water level fell from one day to the next; an abyss was yawning before them. The whole class struggle over the opening and shutting of the valves lost all its meaning. It made no difference who had what *aryk*—there was no water in any of them. People ran to the mullahs, ran to the *ishans*, embraced every stone they came across. Nothing helped. The fields were drying up and the trees withering. For a skin of water one could buy a Karakul sheep. Caravans, which before stopped here and there, now passed by in a hurry, as if an epidemic had befallen this land. The bazaars grew deserted; merchants closed their shops.

Yusupov, who excavated in the former oases of the Uzboj, claims that there is a great disorder among the objects found there. People just abandoned everything they had. Children abandoned their toys; women abandoned their pots. They must have been seized with panic, hysteria, fear. No doubt the most fantastic rumors circulated. Perhaps prophets and fortune-tellers appeared. People felt the band of the desert tightening around them; the sand was whistling at their door.

A great exodus began. The people of the Ali-ili tribe, of the tribes of Chyzr and Tivedzij (the latter also called the camel drivers) set off toward the south, for in the south lay the then-renowned oases of Mar and Tedzhen. The exiles walked across the Kara Kum Desert, which means Black Sand, the largest desert of Turkmenistan and of all of Central Asia. Behind them was a dead river, which lay in the sands like a broken pitcher. The sand buried *aryks*, fields, and houses.

Rashyd says that the tribes of the dead river encountered resistance from the populations of the southern oases, the tribes of Tekke and Sariq. They were all Turkmen, the newcomers and the natives; it was one nation torn apart by the struggle for water. Rashyd says that in oases an ideal proportion reigns between the amount of water and the number of inhabitants, and that is why an oasis cannot absorb new people. An oasis can absorb a guest, it can absorb a merchant, but it will not absorb an entire tribe, for that would immediately disturb the balance upon which its very existence depends. That is why there must be war between the desert and the oasis. Man finds himself in a much more dramatic situation in these climes than does his brother living in a temperate zone, and for this reason the causes of wars are deeper here and, one would like to say, more humane than in Europe, where history records wars started over such petty affairs as lèse-majesté, a dynastic feud, or a ruler's persecution mania. In the desert the cause of war is the desire to live, man is born already entangled in that contradiction, and therein lies the drama. That is why Turkmen never knew unity; the empty *aryk* divided them.

The death of the Uzboj, which drove its tribes to the south, set off the fratricidal wars of the Turkmen. The wars went on for centuries, until right after the Revolution, although these postrevolutionary struggles were already more politicized. Rashyd said that today the ministry apportions water. He said that in 1954 bulldozers arrived in Bosaga. Bosaga lies in Turkmenistan on the Amu Darya River, not far from the border with Afghanistan. They started to dig a canal from there. In this way the river, which at one time appeared all by itself and then went away, was again brought into the desert, this time by man. Such is the circle history describes. And as before, together with the water, fish and birds were drawn to the desert. The banks of the canal were transformed into a flowering and populous oasis. The canal is now eight hundred kilometers in length, and when it is completed it will have twice as many and will reach the Caspian Sea, as the Uzboj once did.

The water in the canal is sweet, said Rashyd. He filled a pitcher and ordered me to drink. It was cool and tasty. A pontoon swayed near the bank, and all around was desert. On this pontoon, in a large cabin wallpapered with photographs of actresses and naked pinup girls, lived the crew of Yaroslav Shchaviey, four

Ukrainians. Rashyd and I were their guests, although by accident, for our motorboat had broken down, and we had to stop. The brigade is digging a branch of the canal so that water can reach a nearby kolkhoz. Enormous trucks, with wheels as high as a man, transport sand from one place to another. On the mountain of sand stands a blue-eyed girl, keeping a record of each run a driver makes. And how does she keep this record? In such a way as to ensure that the drivers meet their quotas. Her name is Palina, and she came here from somewhere near Char'kov. If a driver is nice, Palina will give him as many pencil marks as he needs to become a superquota worker. When it gets very hot, Palina puts down the notebook, jumps into the canal, swims to the other side, returns, and again makes her pencil marks. Shchaviey is after her to fry some fish. He himself sent one of those gigantic trucks off somewhere, to the kolkhoz, for vodka. They gave us a lavish banquet. We left in the evening. The lights of ships were reflected in the water of the canal.

RETURN TO MARY and the last day in Turkmenistan. Mary is the capital of the Murgab oasis and the second largest city after Ashkhabad, with a population of sixty thousand. The population of Turkmenistan (less than two million) lives in five oases, and the rest of the Republic, ninety percent of its surface, is desert. The center of Mary is old, single storied, painted blue and yellow. Once there were hundreds of little stores here, Uzbek, Russian, and Armenian, now nationalized or converted into workshops and warehouses. It is hot, airless; in the middle of the day it turns gray. A sandstorm is approaching from the desert. A sharp wind and clouds of dust, which fill all the space between the earth and the sky. Dust that blinds and chokes; there is nothing to breathe. All life stops; machines grind to a halt. Now Palina, Shchaviey, and everyone else hide in corners, sink into crannies, draw sheets over their heads, blankets, whatever happens to be at hand, so as not to suffocate; the sandstorm buries everything; the deluge drowns men and herds (for in the desert there *are* deluges!), chokes, suffocates, gags to death. Particles of dust, these bits of near nothingness (they are stones ground to powder by wind and water), suspended in the air, grow warm in the sun, and thus comes into being a dry mist, the terror of all desert people, a dry and hot mist, clouds of powder as hot as burning coals; that is what the desert commands one to breathe in the hour of its fury. I am in a hotel, in my room; there is no light, and more important there is no water; the wind must have torn down the wires, the sand stopped up the pipes; I still have a sip of warm liquid in the pitcher, but what will happen later? The city has no water; the telephones are down; there is only radio communication. I am lying on the bed, but everything is damp, dusty; the pillow gives off heat like a furnace; in the desert, during a storm, people are seized by a water madness, all of a sudden they drink their entire water supply, greedily, thoughtlessly, it is really a kind of madness, they drink not because at that moment they are suffering from thirst, they drink from fear, obsessed by the thought that there will be no more water, they drink to beat the inevitable to the punch. Deserted streets, quiet in the hotel, empty corridor, I go downstairs. Empty restaurant. The barmaid is sitting, staring out the window. A Russian comes in from the street, dusty, the wind has pulled his shirt out of his pants, on his head he wears a warm cap with earmuffs, buckled beneath his chin. "Give us two hundred grams," he says to the barmaid. She gets up, pours him a glass of vodka. He drinks it and utters an ahhhhhhhhh! "Now that's better," he says, and walks out into the street with this fire in his belly—into the fire of the desert. For a moment the barmaid follows him with her eyes. "He's one of us," she says, "that sort will endure everything." Then she looks at me, kindly, but also with a touch of irony, and without a word hands me a bottle of lemonade.

## TAJIKISTAN

We are going to the Komintern kolkhoz. It is near Dushanbe and encompasses fifteen villages. It is a large kolkhoz, but there are larger ones still. The director of Komintern is called Abdulkarin

Sharipov. A large, heavy man without one leg. He lost it in the war, defending the Ukraine. He got hit by German shrapnel; they took him to the hospital; from there he returned home. He never saw a German, neither during the war nor later.

Sharipov cannot walk; he drives us everywhere in his small director's pickup. Along the way he recites what a kolkhoz member can own: three cows, twelve sheep, and as many donkeys and horses as he wants. A good sheep costs 150 rubles, and a new house costs 15 sheep. In addition to raising animals, kolkhoz members farm the land. They collect eight hundred pounds of wheat from one hectar. It should come as no surprise that the harvest is so small and yet lasts several months, since the fields are high up in the mountains and situated at various altitudes, with the low fields ripening early and the high ones late. It is like this in all of Tajikistan, where they sow and gather year-round. In June in the valley of Vahsh it is already harvesttime, while in the Pamirs peasants are just then going out to sow. Apricots are ripening in Leninabad, while in Isfar the apricot trees have just started to flower.

We pass through a village. Tajik women stop, turn their backs to the car, and hide their faces with their hands. The Revolution liberated these faces from their coverings, women took off the veil, but the reflex has remained. At the university in Dushanbe I met Rochat Nabijeva, who in 1963 became the first Tajik woman to receive an academic degree. The subject of her thesis was the struggle to abolish the veil. The struggle had cost many lives. Hundreds of women who had bared their faces were killed. The Basmachis publicly executed these women. It is curious that mankind, whose essential nature is so determined and invariable, should produce at various latitudes such contradictory customs. For in some civilizations it is man's ambition to expose his woman's face as much as possible, and, in others, to conceal it as much as possible.

Sharipov drove us to the edge of the village, into the shade of a spreading tree. Here he threw a party. There were cherries, apricots, and apples. Immense bowls of steaming meat. Stacks of wheat pancakes. Various soups, national dishes, salads. Mountains of all kinds of food. Cases of vodka. Sharipov wouldn't drink, saying that Muslims are forbidden to drink. But in the end he did drink something. Then he got up, stripped, detached his prosthesis, and stepped into the stream that flowed nearby. The peasants stared at the naked director. What is he doing? I asked. He is lowering his blood pressure, one of them answered.

The feast continued without the director. Many people had gathered. One of them started to tell a story, and now and then all the others would burst out laughing. I asked what they were talking about. Then a teacher translated for me the story about a young Tajik who returned from the war to the Komintern kolkhoz and had forgotten his own language. He spoke to everyone in Russian. Few people in the village know Russian. "Speak in Tajik," his father told him, but the young Tajik pretended he didn't understand what his father was saying. People started to gather in front of his father's house, wanting to see what a Tajik who has forgotten his native tongue looks like. First the neighbors came, then the entire village. The crowd stood and watched the young Tajik who had returned from the war. Somebody started to laugh, and the laughter spread. The whole village laughed, roared with laughter; people were holding their stomachs, rolling on the ground. Finally the young Tajik couldn't stand it any longer; he came out of the house and shouted to the people: "Enough!" He shouted in Tajik and then started to laugh himself. That day on which the young Tajik remembered his native tongue, a sheep was slaughtered in the village, and everyone feasted all night.

"It is good to know Russian," the teacher concluded, "but a Tajik must also know his own language." We drank a toast to all the languages of the world.

In the morning I was flying to Kyrgystan. Turan took me to the airport. In each direction a different landscape. To the north—gentle, green hills. To the south—high, snow-covered mountains. To the east—desert mountains, scorched by the sun. And then—buried in greenery—Dushanbe. Beyond the snow-covered mountains—India. Beyond the desert mountains—China.

## KYRGYSTAN

In Kyrgystan I am accompanied by Rustam Umralin. Rustam is a man of few words; in the course of an entire day he utters only a couple. "I don't really like talking," he told me on the first day we met. As a result we spent our time in silence. On Sunday we went out on the town. Frunze resembles Ashkhabad and Dushanbe, only it has a better climate, and Russians who for one reason or another have to live in Asia try to settle in Frunze. In appearance and atmosphere the city is European, Russian. The main street, which is called Twenty-second Congress of the CPSU, serves as a promenade. One can see many young people on it, strolling in groups or in couples—a Russian couple, an Uzbek couple, a Kirghiz couple. On Twenty-second Congress of the CPSU Street one can buy ice cream and pierogi with meat; one can look at modern shop windows. One can sit on a bench.

In front of the old post office African students congregate, extremely elegant, bored, without girls. It is hard to figure out where to go. There is a bar, but there is a line in front of it. We look in on the sports stadium. Junior teams are playing; the bleachers are empty. We walk farther, but where are we going, what for? I sense that Rustam doesn't know what to do with me. Rustam has to walk with me because that is in the program of my visit. I don't know how to behave. Stop this walk? "Maybe we should stop walking?" I ask Rustam, but he protests. "How can we? No, no, we will walk," he says. He falls silent again, keeps walking; I trail behind; he's edgy and I'm edgy; we cannot find a comfortable fit, get close, get friendly; we cannot come to an understanding even on what would appear to be the simplest of matters—whether or not to stop walking.

From Twenty-second Congress of the CPSU Street we turn into Sovieckaya Street. There are little cottages here, cozy, well cared for, with mallows and raspberries growing beneath the windows. A landscape transported straight from Smolensk to here, to the foot of the Tien Shan range. On the porches sit Russian grandmothers, wrapped up despite the heat in checkered kerchiefs, in warm lambskin jerkins, in ankle-length skirts. The grandmothers ply their trade cautiously, holding in plain view only one or two glasses of cherries, ten kopecks for a glass. The old women sit in solitude, one on each porch, along the entire length of Sovieckaya Street, which stretches for kilometers.

I SPENT THE EVENING in the yurt of Dzhumal Smanov, in the Tien Shan, in the Susamyr Valley, two hundred kilometers from Frunze. Dzhumal herds the sheep of the Panfilov kolkhoz, and because he distinguished himself in this work, he was awarded by government decree the title of Outstanding Shepherd of the Kirghiz Soviet Socialist Republic. The flock Dzhumal herds numbers six hundred head of sheep. If one inquires carefully, it will turn out that in this kolkhoz flock only half the sheep are kolkhoz sheep. The rest are Dzhumal's, his brother's, his uncle's, his neighbor's, and so on. Dzhumal finished the seventh grade, is forty-one years old, and has nine children. Here families are large, with many children. Dzhumal spends the entire summer in his yurt and returns for the winter to the kolkhoz. He lives in the yurt with his wife, with other shepherds, and with a large troop of his own and others' children. The hospitality of these people is extraordinary; for my arrival, which was completely unexpected, Dzhumal slaughtered a ram and hosted a feast. The entire yurt filled up with people, who, notified by a mounted messenger, arrived here from other pastures. We squatted on felt rugs, gnawing on sheep bones and drinking vodka. In the drinking of vodka the Kirghiz surpass the Russians, not to mention the Poles. Women also drink. As a rule, during the feast they remain outside the yurt. Every now and then the host pours a glass of Stolichnaya and calls out a woman's name. She comes in, squats, and tosses back the entire glass in one gulp. Then, without a word, without a bite of anything to eat, she gets up and disappears in the darkness outside.

During the feast they serve the guest the sheep's boiled head on a plate. The guest must eat the brain. Then he must pluck out and eat one of the eyes. The host eats the other eye. In this way the knots of brotherhood are tied. It is an experience one does not quickly forget.

## UZBEKISTAN

Erkin said that he had business in town and left, leaving me alone in the fortress of the emir of Bukhara. There is a museum inside the fortress. One can view the emir's gold robe; one can view the executioner's knife, so worn through use that not much of the blade is left. Elderly American women are running around the courtyard, around the emir's bedroom, snapping photographs, peering into the depths of the dungeons. They are thrilled by the robe, by the sight of the knife. "And now look here," says a teacher to a group of schoolchildren. They crowd around the entrance to the dungeon, sealed off by iron bars. Inside, in the semidarkness, are figures representing the emir's prisoners. One is hanging from a halter; another is awash in blood. Several figures are sitting on the ground, chained to the wall. The teacher explains what a cruel ruler the emir was and that all this—this fortress, these robes, that one in the halter—is called feudalism.

It is noon. I go out of the fortress onto a large, dusty square. On the opposite side is a *chaykhana*. At this time of day the *chaykhanas* are full of Uzbeks. They squat, colorful skullcaps on their heads, drinking green tea. They drink like this for hours, often all day. It's a pleasant life, spent in the shadow of a tree, on a little carpet, among close friends. I sat down on the grass and ordered a pot of tea. On one side I had a view of the fortress, as big as Kraków's Vavel Castle, only made of clay. But on the other side I had an even better view.

On the other side stood a glorious mosque.

The mosque caught my attention because it was made of wood, which is extremely rare in Muslim architecture, whose materials are typically stone and clay. Furthermore, in the hot, numb silence of the desert at noon, one could hear a knocking inside the mosque. I put aside my teapot and went to investigate the matter.

It was billiard balls knocking.

The mosque is called Bolo-Khauz. It is a unique example of eighteenth-century Central Asian architecture, virtually the only structure from that period to have survived. The portal and exterior walls of Bolo-Khauz are decorated with a wooden ornamentation whose beauty and precision have no equal. One cannot help but be enraptured.

I looked inside. There were six green tables, and at each one young boys with tousled blond hair were playing billiards. A crowd of onlookers rooted for the various competitors. It cost eighty kopecks to rent a table for an hour, so it was cheap, and there were so many willing customers that there was a line in front of the entrance. I didn't feel like standing in it and so couldn't get a good look at the interior. I returned to the *chaykhana*.

Blinding sun fell on the square. Dogs wandered about. Tour groups were coming out of the fortress, first the American women, then the children. Between the fortress-turned-museum and the mosque-turned-billiards hall sat Uzbeks drinking tea. They sat in silence, facing the mosque, in accordance with the ways of the fathers. There was a kind of dignity in the silent presence of these people, and despite their worn gray smocks, they looked distinguished. I had the urge to walk up to them and shake their hands. I wanted to express my respect in some way, but I didn't know how. In these men, in their bearing, in their wise calm, was something that aroused my spontaneous and genuine admiration. They have sat for generations in this *chaykhana*, which is old, perhaps older than the fortress and the mosque. Many things are different now—many, but not all. One can say that the world is changing, but it is not changing completely; in any case it is not changing to the degree that an Uzbek cannot sit in a *chaykhana* and drink tea even during working hours.

In Bukhara I also saw the crowded and colorful bazaars. These bazaars are old, dating back more than a thousand years, and yet still alive, teeming with humanity. Erkin showed me the bazaar in which Avicenna liked to stroll. He showed me the bazaar where

Ibn Baṭṭūṭah would buy dates. Small stores, booths, stands, each one with a number, because they have been nationalized. Erkin said that an Uzbek prefers to overpay and buy in the bazaar than to spend less in a store. The bazaar is tradition, the place of meetings and conversation, a second home.

I went to the courtyard of the Mir-Arab Madrasa. A madrasa is a Muslim university. Mir-Arab is an imposing architectural complex built in 1503 and now undergoing assiduous restoration. The university was closed after the Revolution, but is now open once again. Its new name is Theological Seminary of the Muslims of Central Asia and Kazakhstan.

It is the only university of its kind in the Soviet Union. The first class was admitted in 1966. There were sixteen candidates for each place.

BUKHARA IS BROWNISH; it is the color of clay baked in the sun. Samarkand is intensely blue; it is the color of sky and water.

Bukhara is commercial, noisy, concrete, and material; it is a city of merchandise and marketplaces; it is an enormous warehouse, a desert port, Asia's belly. Samarkand is inspired, abstract, lofty, and beautiful; it is a city of concentration and reflection; it is a musical note and a painting; it is turned toward the stars. Erkin told me that one must look at Samarkand on a moonlit night, during a full moon. The ground remains dark; the walls and the towers catch all the light; the city starts to shimmer, then it floats upward, like a lantern.

H. Papworth, in his book *The Legend of Timur*, questions whether the miracle that is Samarkand is in fact the work of Timur, also known as Tamerlane. There is something incomprehensible—he writes—in the notion that this city, which with all its beauty and composition directs man's thoughts toward mysticism and contemplation, was created by such a cruel demon, marauder, and despot as was Timur.

But there is no denying the fact that the basis of Samarkand's fame was born at the turn of the fourteenth and fifteenth centuries and hence during Timur's reign. Timur is an astonishing historical phenomenon. His name aroused terror for decades. He was a great ruler who kept Asia under his heel, but his might did not stop him from concerning himself with details. Timur devoted much attention to details. His armies were famed for their cruelty. Wherever Timur appeared, writes the Arab historian Zaid Vosifi, "blood poured from people as from vessels," and "the sky was the color of a field of tulips." Timur himself would stand at the head of each and every expedition, overseeing everything himself. Those whom he conquered he ordered beheaded. He ordered towers built from their skulls, and walls and roads. He supervised the progress of the work himself. He ordered the stomachs of merchants ripped open and searched for gold. He himself supervised the process to ensure they were being searched diligently. He ordered his adversaries and opponents poisoned. He prepared the potions himself. He carried the standard of death, and this mission absorbed him for half the day. During the second half of the day, art absorbed him. Timur devoted himself to the dissemination of art with the same zeal he sustained for the spread of death. In Timur's consciousness, an extremely narrow line separated art and death, and it is precisely this fact that Papworth cannot comprehend. It is true that Timur killed. But it is also true that he did not kill all. He spared people with creative qualifications. In Timur's Imperium, the best sanctuary was talent. Timur drew talent to Samarkand; he courted every artist. He did not allow anyone who carried within him the divine spark to be touched. Artists bloomed, and Samarkand bloomed. The city was his pride. On one of its gates Timur ordered inscribed the sentence: IF YOU DOUBT OUR MIGHT—LOOK AT OUR BUILDINGS! and that sentence has outlived Timur by many centuries. Today Samarkand still stuns us with its peerless beauty, its excellence of form, its artistic genius. Timur supervised each construction himself. That which was unsuccessful he ordered removed, and his taste was excellent. He deliberated about the various alternatives in ornamentation; he judged the delicacy of design, the purity of line. And then he threw himself again into the whirl of a new military expedition, into carnage, into blood, into flames, into cries.

Papworth does not understand that Timur was playing a game that few people have the means to play. Timur was sounding the limits of man's possibilities. Timur demonstrated that which Dostoyevsky later described—that man is capable of everything. One can define Timur's creation through a sentence of Saint-Exupéry's: "That which I have done no animal would ever do." Both the good and the bad. Timur's scissors had two blades—the blade of creation and the blade of destruction. These two blades define the limits of every man's activity. Ordinarily, though, the scissors are barely open. Sometimes they are open a little more. In Timur's case they were open as far as they could go.

Erkin showed me Timur's grave in Samarkand, made of green nephrite. Before the entrance to the mausoleum there is an inscription, whose author is Timur: HAPPY IS HE WHO RENOUNCED THE WORLD BEFORE THE WORLD RENOUNCED HIM.

He died at the age of sixty-nine, in 1405, during an expedition to China.

# From a Bird's-Eye View

## 1989–1991

# The Third Rome

WHEN IN THE FALL of 1989 I began the cycle of my travels over the territories of the Imperium, my contacts with this power, although sporadic and individually brief, already had their long history. I thought that they would now be of great help to me. I was mistaken. This last series of journeys was for me a great revelation for two reasons. First, I had never taken a close interest in this country; I was not a specialist; I was not a Russicist, a Sovietologist, Kremlinologist, and so on. The Third World absorbed me, the colorful continents of Asia, Africa, and Latin America—it was to these that I had almost exclusively devoted myself. My actual familiarity with the Imperium was therefore negligible, haphazard, superficial. Second, as the epoch of Stalin and Brezhnev recedes more and more, our knowledge about this system and country grows geometrically. Not only does each year and each month bring new materials and information, but each week and each day! Someone newly interested in communism as an ideology and in the Imperium as its worldly political incarnation might not realize that ninety percent, if not more, of the materials now available to him had still not seen the light of day just a few years ago!

Just as Columbus lived in the epoch of great geographic discoveries, when every sailing expedition altered the picture of the world, so we live today in the epoch of great political discoveries in which ever newer and newer revelations continuously change the picture of our contemporaneity.

IN THE SPRING of 1989, reading the news arriving from Moscow, I thought: It would be worth going there. It was a time when everyone felt a sense of curiosity about and anticipation of something extraordinary. It seemed then, at the end of the eighties, that the world was entering a period of great metamorphosis, of a transformation so profound and fundamental that it would not bypass anyone, no country or state, and so certainly not the last imperium on earth—the Soviet Union.

A climate conducive to democracy and freedom prevailed increasingly across the world. On every continent, dictatorships fell one after the other: Obote's in Uganda, Marcos's in the Philippines, Pinochet's in Chile. In Latin America, despotic military regimes lost power in favor of more moderate civilian ones, and in Africa the one-party systems that had been nearly ubiquitous (and as a rule grotesque and thoroughly corrupt) were disintegrating and exiting the political stage.

Against this new and promising global panorama the Stalinist-Brezhnevian system of the USSR looked more and more anachronistic, like a decaying and ineffectual relic. But it was an anachronism with a still-powerful and dangerous force. The crisis that the Imperium was undergoing was followed throughout the world with attention, but with anxious attention—everyone was aware that this was a power equipped with weapons of mass destruction that could blow up our planet. Yet the possibility of this gloomy and alarming scenario nevertheless did not mask the satisfaction and universal relief that communism was ending and that there was in this fact some sort of irreversible finality.

Germans say Zeitgeist, the spirit of the times. It is a fascinating moment, fraught with promise, when this spirit of the times, dozing pitifully and apathetically, like a huge wet bird on a branch, suddenly and without a clear reason (or at any rate without a reason allowing of an entirely rational explanation) unexpectedly takes off in bold and joyful flight. We all hear the *shush* of this flight. It stirs our imagination and gives us energy: we begin to act.

IF I COULD—I am planning in the year 1989—I would like to traverse the entire Soviet Union, its fifteen federal republics. (I am not thinking, however, of making my way to all the forty-four republics, districts, and autonomous regions, for I would simply not live long enough to do that.) The most far-flung points of my itinerary would be:

In the west—Brest (the border with Poland)
In the east—the Pacific (Vladivostok, Kamchatka, or Magadan)
In the north—Vorkuta or Inovaya Zemlya
In the south—Astara (the border with Iran) or Termez (the border with Afghanistan)

A huge area of the world. But then the surface of the Imperium measures more than twenty-two million square kilometers, and its continental borders are longer than the equator and stretch for forty-two thousand kilometers.

Keeping in mind that wherever it is technically possible, these borders were and are marked with thick coils of barbed wire (I saw such barriers on the borders with Poland, China, and Iran) and that this wire, because of the dreadful climate, quickly deteriorates and therefore must often be replaced across hundreds, no, thousands, of kilometers, one can assume that a significant portion of the Soviet metallurgical industry is devoted to producing barbed wire.

For the matter does not end with the wiring of borders! How many thousands of kilometers of wire were used to fence in the gulag archipelago? Those hundreds of camps, staging points, and prisons scattered throughout the territory of the entire Imperium!

How many thousands more kilometers were swallowed up for the wiring of artillery, tank, and atomic ranges? And the wiring of barracks? And various warehouses?

If one were to multiply all this by the number of years the Soviet government has been in existence, it would be easy to see why, in the shops of Smolensk or Omsk, one can buy neither a hoe nor a hammer, never mind a knife or a spoon: such things could simply not be produced, since the necessary raw materials were used up in the manufacture of barbed wire. And that is still not the end of it! After all, tons of this wire had to be transported by ships, railroad, helicopters, camels, dog teams, to the farthest, most inaccessible corners of the Imperium, and then it all had to be unloaded, uncoiled, cut, fastened. It is easy to imagine those unending telephone, telegraphic, and postal reminders issued by the commanders of the border guards, the commanders of the gulag camps, and prison directors following up on their requisitions for more tons of barbed wire, the pains they would take to build up a reserve supply of this wire in case of a shortage in the central warehouses. And it is equally easy to imagine those thousands of commissions and control teams dispatched across the entire territory of the Imperium to make certain that everything is properly enclosed, that the fences are high and thick enough, so meticulously entangled and woven that even a mouse cannot squeeze through. It is also easy to imagine telephone calls from officials in Moscow to their subordinates in the field, telephone calls characterized by a constant and vigilant concern expressed in the question "Are you all really properly wired in?" And so instead of building themselves houses and hospitals, instead of repairing the continually failing sewage and electrical systems, people were for years occupied (although fortunately not everyone!) with the internal and external, local and national, wiring of their Imperium.

THE IDEA of a great journey was born in the course of reading the news about perestroika. Almost all of it originated from Moscow. Even if it concerned events in a place as distant as Chabarovsk, it was still datelined "Moscow." My reporter's soul would rebel. In such moments I was drawn to Chabarovsk; I wanted to see for myself what was going on there. It was a temptation all the stronger because, even with my slight knowledge of the Imperium, I was aware how much Moscow differs from the rest of the country (although not in everything), and that enormous areas of this superpower are an immeasurable terra incognita (even for the inhabitants of Moscow).

But doubts at once assailed me—was I really right to search for perestroika outside Moscow? I had just read a new book, published in early 1989, by the eminent historian Nathan Ejdelman, *Revolution from the Top in Russia.* The author regards perestroika as just one more in a series of turning points in Russian history and reminds us that all such turning points, revolutions, convulsions, and breakthroughs in this country came about because they were the will of the czar, the will of the secretary-general, or the will of the Kremlin (or of Petersburg). The energy of the Russian nation, says Ejdelman, has always been spent not on independent grass-roots initiatives, but on carrying out the will of the ruling elite.

The message between the lines: perestroika will last as long as the Kremlin will allow it to.

So, if one wished to know the direction and strength of the wind, perhaps it would be better to be in Moscow, near the Kremlin, and to observe the seismographs, thermometers, barometers, and weather vanes that are situated around its walls? For Kremlinology more often reminded me of meteorology than of knowledge such as one gathers at the crossroads of history and philosophy.

IT IS AUTUMN 1989. My first encounter with the Imperium in years. I was last here more than twenty years ago, at the start of the Brezhnev era. The era of Stalin, the era of Khrushchev, the era of Brezhnev. And before that: the era of Peter I, Catherine II, Alexander III. In what other country does the persona of the ruler, his character traits, his manias and phobias, leave such a profound stamp on the national history, its course, its ascents and downfalls? Hence the rapt attention with which the moods, depressions, and caprices of successive czars and secretaries-general were always followed in Russia and around the world—how much depended on this! (Mickiewicz on Nicholas I: "The Czar is surprised—the inhabitants of Petersburg tremble with fear, / The Czar is angry—his courtiers die of fear; armies are marching, whose God and faith / is the Czar. The Czar is angry: let us die, we will cheer up the Czar!")

The czar has been considered a god, literally, for centuries, for Russia's entire history. Not until the nineteenth century was there a czarist decree to remove the portraits of the czar from the Orthodox churches. A czarist decree! Without it no one would have been so bold as to touch such a portrait, or rather, icon. Even Bakunin, that anarchist and subversive, Jacobin and dynamiter, calls the czar "the Russian Christ." And just as the czars are the vicars of God, so Lenin and Stalin are the vicars of world communism. Only after Stalin's death does the slow process of secularizing the rule of the Almighty begin. Secularization—and with it the gradual erosion of omnipotence. Brezhnev complained about this. In the fall of 1968, criticizing Dubček and his people, who wanted to reform the system in Czechoslovakia and as a result drew Soviet tanks down upon their heads, Brezhnev lamented: "You thought that because you are in power, you can do whatever you please. But that is a great mistake! Even I cannot do what I would like—of all the things I would like to have come true, I can perhaps realize barely a third" (Zdenek Mlynar, *The Frost from the East*).

SO, THE AIRPORT, passport control. In the little window a young soldier from the border guards. The checking of the passport begins. Looking, reading, but, first and foremost, searching for the photograph. There it is! The soldier looks at the photograph, and then at me, at the photograph and immediately at me, at the photograph and at me. Something does not seem quite right to him. "Take off your glasses!" he orders. At the photograph and at me, at the photograph and at me. But I can see that now, without the glasses, it seems even less right. I can see concentration in his pale eyes and sense that his mind is starting to work feverishly. I think I know what this mind is working on at this moment—it is searching for the enemy. The enemy doesn't have his credentials stamped on his forehead; quite the contrary—the enemy is masked. So the trick is to unmask him. It is precisely in this skill that they school my soldier and thousands of his colleagues. Here you have a hundred photographs, says the sergeant, among them one is of a spy. Whoever guesses correctly which one it is will receive a week's vacation. The boys stare and stare; sweat breaks out on their foreheads. A week's vacation!

This one? Or maybe this one?! No, not this one, this one looks like a decent man. So you think that a spy has horns on his head? A spy can look normal; he can even have a good-natured smile! Of course they don't guess correctly, for there wasn't a single spy among the hundred choices. There are no more spies now. There aren't? Can one imagine a world without spies? The soldier's mind works, searches, penetrates. One thing is certain—the spy wants to get in here at all costs, to slip through, break in. The only question is, Which one is he from among the dozens of people, each of them patiently waiting for the moment when the vigilant pair of pale eyes will come to rest upon his face? Some say that there is no more cold war. But it exists there, it is in this back-and-forth gaze between the photograph and the face, in this insistent and piercing stare, in this scrutiny and suspicious glance, in this pensiveness, hesitation, and uncertainty about what, finally, to do with us.

THE SIGHT of Moscow enraptured Chateaubriand. The author of *Memoirs from Beyond the Tomb* accompanied Bonaparte on the expedition to Moscow. On September 6, 1812, the French army reached the great city:

> Napoleon appeared on horseback near the advance guard. One more rise had to be crossed; it bordered Moscow the way Montmartre borders Paris and was called the Hill of Homage, for Russians prayed here at

> the sight of the holy city like pilgrims at the sight of Jerusalem. Moscow of the golden domes, as Slavic poets say, blazed in the sun: two hundred and ninety-five churches, one thousand five hundred palaces, houses out of decoratively sculpted wood, yellow, green, pink, all that was lacking was cypresses and the Bosphorus. The Kremlin, covered in burnished or painted sheets of iron, was a part of this ensemble. Among the exquisite villas made of brick and marble flowed the River Moscow, surrounded by parks of pines—the palms of this sky. Venice in the days of its glory on the waters of the Adriatic was not more splendid. . . . Moscow! Moscow!, our soldiers shouted and started to applaud.

"...FOR RUSSIANS prayed here at the sight of the holy city like pilgrims at the sight of Jerusalem."

Yes, because Moscow was for them a holy city, the capital of the world—a Third Rome. This last notion was put forth in the sixteenth century by the Pskov sage and visionary, the monk Philotheus. "Two Romes have already fallen (Peter's and Byzantium)," he writes in a letter to the contemporary Muscovite prince Vasily III. "The Third Rome (Moscow) stands. There will not be a fourth," he categorically assures the prince. Moscow: it is the end of history, the end of mankind's earthly wanderings, the open gateway to the heavens.

Russians were capable of believing in such things profoundly, with conviction, fanatically.

The Moscow Napoleon saw on that sunny September afternoon of 1812 no longer exists. The Russians burned it down the next day so as to force the French to turn around. Later, Moscow burned several more times. "Our cities," Turgenev writes somewhere, "burn every five years." It is understandable: Russia's building material was timber. Timber was cheap; there were forests everywhere. One could raise a building out of timber quickly, and, moreover, a wooden wall retains heat well. But then if a fire breaks out, everything burns, the whole city. Thousands upon thousands of Russian townspeople went to their deaths in flames.

• • •

ONLY THOSE CHURCHES and palaces of the aristocracy that were built out of bricks and stone had a chance of surviving. But that kind of construction was a rarity in Russia, a luxury. Therefore, the demolishing of Orthodox churches by the Bolsheviks was not only a battle with religion, but also the destruction of the only remaining vestiges of the past, of all of history. A desert remained, a black hole.

IT WAS STALIN who tried once and for all to destroy the old Moscow, the one that today can be seen only in the illustrations of Mikhail Pilayev.

All dictators, irrespective of epoch or country, have one common trait: they know everything, are experts on everything. The thoughts of Qadaffi and Ceauşescu, Idi Amin and Alfredo Stroessner—there is no end to the profundities and wisdom. Stalin was expert on history, economics, poetry, and linguistics. As it turned out, he was also expert on architecture. In 1934—which means between one ghastly purge and the next, even more horrifying, one—he commissioned a plan for the rebuilding of Moscow. He devoted to it, as was piously written, much time and attention. The new Moscow was to manifest in its appearance the following traits of the epoch: triumph, power, monumentality, might, seriousness, massiveness, invincibility (according to E. V. Sidorin, *Voprosy Filosofii*, 12/1988). They set energetically to work. Explosives, pickaxes, and bulldozers went into motion. Entire neighborhoods were razed, churches and palaces blown up. Tens of thousands of people were expelled from beautiful, bourgeois apartments—into tents, into slums. Old Moscow vanished from the face of the earth, and in its place arose heavy and monotonous, although powerful, edifices—symbols of the new authority. Fortunately, as was often the case under real socialism, disorder, laziness, and a lack of tools saved a part of the city from final destruction.

AS I SAID, a few old streets, houses, and small apartment buildings were preserved; neglected, yes, shabby and lichen covered, yes, but there they are, they are still standing. With some effort it is possible to imagine that this was once a moderately cozy city. One could sit down on a little porch, catch one's breath on a bench under a tree, walk into an inn, a tavern, or a bar, to relax, warm oneself, drink some tea or cognac. There is nothing like it in today's Moscow! I have been walking around the city for several hours now, and we have no place to go. The few restaurants are either closed, or old KGB types are standing around in front of them, just waiting to grab you by the collar and throw you into the middle of the street, under the speeding traffic. Moreover, the socks in my boots have gotten twisted in such a fashion that I cannot walk any farther; I must fix them, but where is there to sit down, where is there to sit down in Moscow in the late autumn in the rain and the snow, when one is out on the street, when one has neither a home nor a hotel (the home or the hotel are far away) and the only place left is a frozen puddle of mud?

AS I WALKED this way through the streets of old Moscow, it suddenly struck me that I was beginning to understand the meaning of the October Revolution—the great event of the twentieth century, which (as we all know) changed the course of human history. I noticed that the ground floors of these houses and small apartment buildings were built—long, long ago—as accommodations for stores, for artisans' workshops, for little restaurants and cafés. This is evident from the display windows, the type of stairs, doors, and spacious interiors. Here beats the heart of the old, commercial, bustling, and enterprising Moscow. Throngs of people passed through these streets. It was colorful and noisy, crowded, exotic. Today, walking through these same, although now-empty and lifeless, streets, I instinctively look into the display windows. Desks stand in all of them. There are no counters or shelves here, no grocery items or textiles. Only more or less shabby desks. Desks, moreover, tightly jammed together, crammed, stuffed in as if by force, arranged practically in layers, like bunk beds in military barracks. How much discussion must go on about this, how many conferences, how much deliberation on such a vital subject as—where is there room to fit in one more desk? On those desks (visible through the display windows), piles of inquiries, forms, and questionnaires. And—this too is everywhere—tea glasses.

Cunning often reveals itself in the simplest things. The streets through which I now walk confirm this truth. The maneuver that brought victory to the Bolsheviks consisted of expelling and expropriating the merchants (independent people who guided themselves by the laws of the marketplace) and placing clerks in their stores—meek and obedient instruments of the authorities. The man behind the counter was replaced by the man behind the desk: the Revolution triumphed.

MOSCOW, even old Moscow, is so vast that no end of houses, streets, even entire settlements could be built in it, and it would still remain spacious and uncluttered. It is this spaciousness that is one of the city's striking features, and as in each of the world's urban giants, one must walk endlessly to get anywhere, or ride for hours on the metro, the bus, in a taxi. This is especially troublesome for those who live in the huge new neighborhoods that now surround the center of the metropolis. But these problems do not discourage anyone. Everyone wants to live in Moscow. The city numbers around ten million people, and another ten million arrive here daily to work and shop. The Moscow writer Vladimir Sorokin calls his neighbors (and actually the inhabitants of Russian cities in general) the urban peasantry. These people are a sociological phenomenon. Once upon a time they left the village, and now they cannot return: the village no longer exists, destroyed and replaced as it was by kolkhozes. But a kind of memory has endured among these people, certain habits and reflexes. Paradoxically, the spirit of the Russian village survived, not in the vast fields of the Volga Valley, but in the skyscrapers, each dozens of stories high, of Moscow's new neighborhoods: Bielayev, Miedviedkov, Golianov. It is difficult to find one's way to any of them, and at night, if someone doesn't know the place well, it is impossible to find one's way at all. One of the humorous ditties of Moscow taxi drivers addresses this:

I will take you to the tundra
Even to Ivonov
I will take you wherever you desire
Only not to Golianov [Miedviedkov, Boberov, et
cetera].

TO FLY INTO Moscow at the end of 1989 is to enter a world dominated by the proliferating, unbridled word. After years of the gag, of silence, and of censorship, the dams are bursting, and stormy, powerful, ubiquitous torrents of words are flooding over everything. The Russian intelligentsia is once again (or, rather, for the first time) in its element—endless, indefatigable, fierce, frantic discussion. How they love this, how good this makes them feel! Wherever someone announces some discussion, immeasurable crowds immediately gather. The subject of the discussion can be anything, but of course the preferred theme is the past. So, what about Lenin, what about Trotsky, what about Bucharin? And the poets are as important as the politicians. Did Mandelshtam die in the camps of hunger or as a result of an epidemic? Who is responsible for the suicide of Cvietayev? These matters are debated for hours on end, till dawn.

But even more time is spent in front of television sets, watching broadcasts of the sessions of the Supreme Soviet that go on night and day. Several factors contributed simultaneously to this explosion of political passions. First, politics at the highest rungs of power was surrounded here for centuries by an airtight, almost mystical secrecy. The rulers decided about the life or death of people, and yet these people were never able to see the rulers with their own eyes. And then, suddenly, here they are, the rulers, getting angry, their ties askew waving their arms around, picking their ears. Second, as they follow the deliberations of their highest popular assembly, Russians for the first time have the sense of participating in something important.

And finally—perestroika coincided with the explosion of television in this country. Television gave to perestroika a dimension that no other event in the history of the Imperium had ever had.

# The Temple and the Palace

NO MATTER how many times I pass that way, I cannot tear my eyes away from the place. I stare intently, as if I'm looking for something, through the mist, through time, although of course there is nothing to see.

To get there, driving along Leninski Prospekt (where I'm staying) toward the center of town, one must pass Kammenyj Most ("Stone Bridge" in Russian) and immediately turn downhill to the right, then right again, emerging on the boulevard that runs along the river and is called Nabereznaja. The spot is right there, just after the traffic lights, directly beyond the high viaduct, enclosed by a fence.

IN THE WINTER, clouds of white steam rise into the air. The steam comes from a large swimming pool that remains open year-round because the water is heated. When the cold reaches minus thirty degrees Celsius, the swimming pool becomes a paradise for a special category of people, whose greatest satisfaction in life comes from being able to bathe in such a terrible cold in an open-air pool. And nothing happens! They live! We can see that they are truly satisfied with themselves because of the manner in which they get out of the water and strut along the edge of the pool: their movements are energetic, their silhouettes firm, chests thrust forward, heads held high.

THE FALL OF 1812. Napoleon, leading his crushed and decimated army, has abandoned Moscow and is fleeing Russia. He has suffered a shattering defeat. The Russians are broadening their offensive, they are triumphing. To express gratitude to Providence for having "rescued Russia from the ruin threatening her," the czar, Alexander I, decides to construct in Moscow a temple "in the name of the one who saved Russia"—in the name of Christ the Savior.

The temple is to be as large as is the czar's gratitude to the Son of God—therefore it is to be immense, gigantic.

But because the czar was busy with the conquest of Azerbaijan and Bessarabia, and also because of disorder and, perhaps, ordinary forgetfulness as well, the temple was not erected during his lifetime. It was not until the fifth year of the reign of Alexander I's successor and brother, Nicholas I, in other words in 1830, that the idea of constructing the temple of gratitude was taken up anew. Two years later Nicholas I approved a design presented to him by the architect Konstantin Ton. And then for six years he deliberated over where to build this temple. He finally made up his mind and chose precisely this place, where today a special category of people, swimming in an open-air pool during severe frosts, offer proof of their courage and grit. This place had two advantages: first, it was near the Kremlin, and, second, nearby flowed the river in which the Orthodox People of God could perform their traditional religious ablutions.

BEFORE LONG the czar formed the Committee for the Construction of the Temple of Christ the Savior, and work began on a grand scale.

Construction went on uninterrupted for forty-five years.

Nicholas I was in charge, but he died, under mysterious circumstances, in 1855. The father's work was carried on by the son, Czar Alexander II, although he died in a bombing incident in March 1881. Fortunately the next czar, Alexander III, the son of Alexander II, also displayed an abiding and fervent solicitude for the project. Each imperator lavished upon this ambitious (and, it would seem, immortal) effort endless time and money. Not only Moscow, not only Russia, but also the entire world watched the construction with astonishment and speechless admiration. Czars came and went, old generations died off and new ones populated the earth, Russia threw herself into the chaos of consecutive wars and conquests or suffered recurring waves of famine and epidemic, and yet nothing could interrupt, or even delay, the labor on this unique and extraordinary structure.

THE CONSECRATION of the temple takes place in the presence of Czar Alexander III on the twenty-sixth of May 1883. Although the exterior of the building, arising for years before everyone's eyes, is after all well known, those now entering the interior utter a cry of rapture and admiration. The figures cited by the architects heighten still further this mood of transport and ecstasy.

And indeed. The Temple of Christ the Savior is more than thirty stories tall. Its walls are 3.2 meters thick; they were built out of forty million bricks. These walls—on the outside and on the inside—are covered with slabs of Altaic and Podolia marble as well as Finnish granite. The slabs are attached to the bricks along the entire surface of the temple with the help of special lead grips. The shrine is crowned by a gigantic cupola covered with sheets of bronze that weigh 176 tons. On the summit stands a cross three stories high. The cupola is surrounded by four belfries in each of which hang fourteen bells with a combined weight of 65 tons. The main bell weighs 24 tons. (The largest bell in Poland—the Zygmunt on Wawel Castle—weighs 8 tons.) Twelve gates sculpted in bronze lead into the interior of the church. Their combined weight is 140 tons.

The interior is the most impressive. It is lit up by candles placed in three thousand candleholders. Furthermore, because the faithful enter the church and light their own candles in accordance with the Orthodox custom—and this building can hold more than ten thousand worshipers at a time—its windows glow for a great distance.

After entering one sees before him a gigantic and dazzling iconostasis, for which 422 kilograms of gold were used. The iconostasis reflects the shimmering light of the thousands of tallow candles, and its intense and commanding brilliance puts us imperceptibly into an inspired and humble state of mind.

The lower portions of the walls are covered with 177 marble plaques on which the following particulars have been engraved:

- The dates and places of the battles of Russian armies
- The names of the regiments and divisions fighting there
- The last names of their commanders
- The numbers of dead and wounded
- Who received what decoration, and in particular who was awarded the Cross of Saint George

Higher up, above the marble plaques, up to the summit of the cupola, the surface of the walls is covered with frescoes, painted using a special technique on white plaster. There are portraits of the saints there, scenes from the life of Christ and the apostles, biblical motifs. The authors of these works are the most famous Russian painters of the epoch—Bruni and Viereshchagin, Kramskoy and Litovchenko, Siedov and Surikov.*

THIS IMPRESSIVE and magnificent shrine, unique as an architectural specimen, and in its élan, the true glory of Russian art, existed for forty-eight years—until the middle of 1931, when Stalin decided to raze it. This he did not do in an excessively coarse manner, he did not announce to one and all, "And now we will raze the Temple of Christ the Savior!"

No! Of course not!

*The facts for this text come from various sources, mainly from the article by Irina Ilovanska-Alberti included in the book *Razrushenie chrama christa spasitiela* (London, 1988).

No such pronouncements or declarations! Quite simply, on July 18, 1931, there appeared in *Pravda* a news item to the effect that the authorities of the USSR had decided to build a Palace of the Soviets in Moscow. The item also included information about where this palace was to be erected. The address mentioned signified nothing to outsiders, but to the inhabitants of Moscow it signified everything—the palace was to be built in the spot where the temple stood. Why precisely in this place? Moscow is after all an enormous city; there were many empty areas in it; there were even empty lots, near the Kremlin, so one could have chosen any number of truly excellent locations. But no, no, what is wanted is precisely that patch of ground on which stands the Temple of Christ the Savior!

Stalin orders the largest sacral object in Moscow to be razed. Let us for a moment give free reign to our imagination. It is 1931. Let us imagine that Mussolini, who at that time rules Italy, orders the Basilica of St. Peter in Rome to be razed. Let us imagine that Paul Doumer, who is at that time president of France, orders the Cathedral of Notre-Dame in Paris to be razed. Let us imagine that Poland's Marshall Józef Piłsudski orders the Jasnogórski Monastery in Czestochowa to be razed.

Can we imagine such a thing?

No.

IN THE COURSE of one night they enclose the enormous site of the temple with a fence, and by dawn they have already set to work. One could divide the labor of demolishing thc temple in acoustical terms into (a) the quiet stage, (b) the noisy stage. During the quiet stage, the regime robs the temple. We know what treasures were in this church. Almost half a ton of gold alone. And how many tons of silver, brass, enamel, amethysts! How many diamonds and emeralds, turquoises and topazes! How many priceless icons and ornate gospels, how many croziers and censers! And the collections of liturgical vestments woven with gold and silver, those chasubles, belts, slippers set with precious stones!

All this now had to be taken down from the walls and altars, taken out of closets and chests of drawers, frames and hinges. All this had to be carried away and hidden—some in the warehouses of the Kremlin, some in the safes of the NKVD. Taking down the marbles was the most work. The marble, fastened with lead to the brick walls, did not want to give, could not be torn away. Its removal lasted weeks, and we do not know whether the delay irritated Stalin. If it did—it would be small wonder. For during this time Stalin had dozens of things on his mind. First and foremost, he was directing the campaign of killing ten million people in the Ukraine by starvation. The killing of ten million people given the current state of technology was no easy matter. They did not yet know about gas chambers; they did not know about weapons of mass destruction. Facts bespeak that the course of this campaign was of special interest to him. Stalin was a suspicious man, did not trust anyone, read the dispatches from the Ukraine himself, scolded the sluggish, issued new instructions and decrees, and all this must have cost him much in time and nerves.

Simultaneously, the secretary-general was keeping close watch on the ambitious expansion of the network of labor camps—an immense task in such a huge country, and all the more different if one considers the intemperate climate, the enormity of the transportation difficulties, and the shortage of all building materials. And time was pressing—the Leader was already plotting his first purge and needed somewhere to put up the millions of condemned. Under the circumstances it would be difficult to blame Stalin if, for example, he relaxed somewhat his supervision of and interest in the destruction of the Temple of Christ the Savior. He was already over fifty, after all, and must have felt weary to his bones from the years of murderous struggle for power.

And yet—no!

Everything indicates that Stalin did not neglect the matter for even a moment. He must have been aware of how tremendous was the challenge confronting him and his people. The goal was after all to destroy, using only very backward and primitive techniques, in barely four months (such was the deadline set for this horrifying operation) that which was built with uncommon effort and extraordinary sacrifice over the course of forty-five years.

But even this proved possible! And when finally the temple

was stripped of everything that could be carried off from its dazzlingly sumptuous interior, from its treasury and dressing room, from its closets and secret receptacles, altars and belfries, stripped of everything that could be torn from the iconostasis, from the walls and gates, of everything that could be hammered off, chopped away, screwed off, pulled out, forced out, gouged out, and broken off, when, as I say, the dexterous brigades, working day and night, finally accomplished their feat—the wreckers saw before them an overwhelming sight: there they were, standing inside a gigantic, gloomy, and repellent shell of bricks, to which here and there, like insects to the skin of a monstrous beast, clung the figures of workmen on scaffoldings.

THE ANALOGY with the shattering vision of Giovanni Battista Piranesi comes to mind.

THE SECOND ACT of the drama of the Temple of Christ the Savior begins. Until now the point has been to rob and ruin it; now it is to raze it to the ground. But here a real technical problem arises: how to tear down such a gigantic structure standing in the center of the city. It would be simplest to bomb it, but this is out of the question, since near the church are situated various embassies, and most important the Kremlin is not far away. What if the pilot were to miss?

They try hammers. But a hammer is useless here. How can one demolish with a hammer walls one hundred meters high, whose thickness exceeds three meters? There are of course sufficient stores of dynamite in the warehouses of the Red Army to place charges under the temple and blow up the entire structure. Yes, but what if one miscalculates and half the city is blown up, and—worst of all—the Kremlin?

In the end they decide (with great presence of mind) to go the route of experiment and experience. They drill a hole and put in a stick of explosives. A bang, a flash, dust rises. When the cloud settles, they gather round, look, measure how much was torn out. Now they drill a larger hole and put in two sticks. A correspondingly larger bang, a brighter flash, more dust. And so on, step after step, stick after stick, meter after meter. Now they knock down a piece of the cupola; now they blow up the summit of the belfry; now they crumble a fragment of a wall. They are counting on these shocks so rocking the entire edifice, so loosening and weakening its structure, that later one strong charge will suffice and the great temple will lie in ruins.

And what do the inhabitants of Moscow say about this? (There are three million of them at the time.) After all, it is their Basilica of St. Peter that is being torn down, their Cathedral of Notre-Dame, their Jasnogórski Monastery.

What do they say?

They say nothing.

Life goes on. In the morning adults hurry to work; children go to school; grandmothers go stand in lines. More and more frequently a family member is taken away, now a friend from work, now a neighbor.

Why, that's life.

Only the residents of houses in the vicinity of the temple display a certain activity. In spare moments they walk out onto their balconies or clamber up to the roofs of their buildings and observe the work of the wreckers—the dynamiters and those who with hammers smash the statues of saints, the portals, and the cornices.

They look, watch, and remain silent, for what is there to say?

No one protests, demonstrates, pickets. And anyway, Koba* would not tolerate such things.

THE DEATH of the temple takes place on December 5, 1931.

Since morning the city has been rocked by powerful detonations. In the afternoon, a tall, smoking mountain of rubble lies where the church had stood. "A terrifying silence reigned in this place," notes one of the witnesses of the event. A heavy cloud of smoke and dust hangs above Moscow. The only photograph that has survived from that day is so incompetent, so old and faded,

* One of the pseudonyms of Iosif Dzhugashvili (Stalin).

that it is difficult even to see that it was already winter and whether or not there was snow.

A COMPETITION was immediately announced for the design of the Palace of the Soviets, which (as we recall) was to be erected precisely on the site of the Temple of Christ the Savior. From among the projects submitted Stalin at once selected the work of two architects—Yofon and Shchusev. It is impossible to determine today whether Stalin had earlier told them what he had in mind or whether Yofon and Shchusev themselves had simply surmised the secretary-general's greatest ambition and fondest dream. In any case, the greatest ambition and fondest dream of Stalin was precisely the same as the greatest ambition and fondest dream of all Soviet leaders—namely, to catch up with and surpass the United States!

Of course, England is important, and France, and Germany, and Italy, but if one looks at the map of the world, these are all small countries, even very small ones. Only America is large. What sort of honor is it, for a power like the USSR, to surpass France? Surpassing America, on the other hand—yes, that is truly something!

Naturally Stalin understands that he cannot surpass America in something like highway construction or automobile production. But he believes that it is possible to identify areas in which, if one gathers all one's resources, one can manage to catch up with the United States and then leave it behind! Following this thought, cleverly surmised by Yofon and Shchusev, he arrives at the conclusion that he could tweak America's nose by the construction of a building larger than the largest edifice in the United States (which at the time is the Empire State Building in New York City) and—so as to bury America completely—he resolves to place atop this building a sculpture taller than the Statue of Liberty.

And so on June 4, 1933, he signs the go-ahead on Yofon and Shchusev's design, thus launching his bold challenge to America. So: the Palace of the Soviets will be six times more massive than the Empire State Building, and crowning it will be a statue of Lenin three times higher (more than one hundred meters) and two and a half times heavier than the Statue of Liberty. Other impressive and head-spinning specifications also accepted by Koba:

- The height of the palace, together with the statue of Lenin at its top—415 meters (around 150 floors)
- The weight of the palace—1.5 million tons
- The capacity of the palace—7 million cubic meters, which equals the combined capacities of New York's then six largest skyscrapers

The statue of Lenin:

- The length of the index finger of Vladimir Ilyich—6 meters
- The length of the foot—14 meters
- The width of the shoulders—32 meters
- The weight of the statue—6,000 tons

The plan included among other things the importation of faience sheets from Spain and majolica from Florence. In general a significant number of fittings were to be imported from abroad.

Let us remember the date, for it is relevant: June 1933.

June 1933 was one of those months when the fields and roads of the Ukraine were strewn with tens of thousands of corpses of people who had perished from hunger, and when there were incidents (today coming to light) of women, crazed with hunger and no longer cognizant of their actions, eating their own children. Moreover, they were dying of hunger not only in the Ukraine. They were dying also in the Volga region and in Siberia, in the Urals and by the White Sea.

Yes, all this was taking place simultaneously—the demolishing of the temple, the millions of people starving to death, the palace that was to eclipse America, and the cannibalism of those unfortunate mothers.

The construction of the Palace of the Soviets gives rise to two questions: First, why was it to be quite so enormous? Second, why was it to be erected precisely there, where the Temple of Christ the Savior had stood?

Why so enormous, we already know—the point was to catch up with and overshadow. But why this location? (Let us add that the temple stood on extremely poor ground, shifting, unstable, porous, constantly underrun by water. It was treacherous soil for building on, unreliable, and meant doubling the costs of every investment, although costs, it is true, were of no significance.)

The explanation that atheism now ruled, that a struggle was being waged with religion, that churches and monasteries were being closed, was of course correct, but it didn't account for everything. After all, there are countless churches in Moscow; there are even churches in the Kremlin, and yet the Leader's finger came to rest on just this one place, where there towered the spectacular silhouette of the temple built by the czars of Greater Russia to thank God for forcing Napoleon to retreat and saving their Imperium.

The czar is man and God—in this dual nature of Russia's Highest Authority lay its stability, longevity, and strength. This authority is omnipotent, since it is sanctioned by the heavens. The czar is the messenger and the anointed of the Almighty—more than that, he is his personification, his earthly reflection. Only hc who maintains (and has somehow proven) that his authority has a human and divine nature can rule here, can lead the people and count on their obedience and devotion. Hencc the preponderance in Russian history of pretender czars, false prophets, haunted and fanatical holy men—they claim the power to rule souls and that they are touched by the hand of God. The hand of God is in this case the sole legitimation of power.

The Bolsheviks attempt to fit into this tradition, to draw from its proven life-giving springs. Bolshevism is of course yet another pretender, but a pretender that goes a step further: it is not only the earthly reflection of God, it is God. To achieve this status, to transform oneself into the new God, one must demolish the Houses of the former God (demolish them or strip them of their holiness, converting them into fuel dumps or furniture warehouses) and on their foundations raise new temples, new objects of admiration and worship—Houses of the Party, Palaces of the Soviets, Committees. In this transformation—or, more precisely, in this revolution—one effects a simple but radical exchange of symbols. In this place (a church stood here) where, consumed with burning faith, you paid homage to the Almighty (who is in heaven), you will now (the House of the Party stands here) pay homage to the Almighty (who is on earth). In short, the background scenery changes, but the main principle of history, which continues to operate in the foreground, remains unchanged—the principle of the cult. Thus it is no coincidence that after Stalin's death the critics of his rule reached for terminology from the theological dictionary—the cult of personality.

The author of a critical biography of Stalin—Roy Medvedev—writes:

> In the first decades of the twentieth century there existed even among the Marxists a current of "god-creators," then represented by Anatoly Lunacherski, Vadim Bazarov, and even Maxim Gorky. They considered it their task to create on the foundation of Marxism-Leninism some sort of "proletarian religion without God." In point of fact Stalin took over and even accomplished this assignment, but with significant improvements. He helped create on the foundation of Marxism something akin to religion, but with a God, and the almighty, all-knowing, and dangerous God of the new religion was proclaimed to be Stalin himself.

STALIN'S PLANS for the construction of the Palace of the Soviets were complicated by an uneasy and unfavorable turn of events. For just at the time when the secretary-general thinks he will be able to concentrate on the building of the palace, the remains of a shy and weak, yet nevertheless anti-Stalinist, opposition come to life (for completely unrelated reasons). Even the slightest opposition is, under the conditions of that system, extremely dangerous, and Stalin must occupy himself fully with the struggle against this nightmare that sleep banishes. Several months after the approval of the Yofon-Shchusev design, the chief of the GPU, Mienzhinsky, dies, and Stalin nominates as his successor a bloodthirsty hangman and, incidentally, a pharmacist from Lódź—Henryk Jagoda. Before long, and at Stalin's inspiration, his principal competitor, Kirov, dies, and this death moves the secretary-general to undertake his first great massacre, which goes down in history under the gentler term of "purge." Then there are the so-called great Moscow trials in which Stalin disposes of his closest collaborators; then comes the next massacre, in 1937; and then he occupies himself with the annexation of Poland, Lithuania, Latvia, and Estonia, with the war in Finland, and, finally, the Second World War. Immediately after the war he must uproot and transplant the various nations that he suspects of treason (the Crimean Tatars, the Chechen, the Ingush, and so on), he must oversee the deportation to Siberia and to Kazakhstan of entire conveyances of Poles, Lithuanians, Germans, Ukrainians; he must organize new trials and massacres, and then by that time he is old, has a stroke, and dies.

In the face of such an overwhelming press of duties, it is too much to expect that he could calmly attend to the construction of the palace. And because he rarely left the Kremlin during the last years, it is almost certain that he did not even look in on the future construction site to see what was happening.

And nothing good was happening.

Water accumulated in the deep excavation, and neighborhood boys tried to catch fish in it. Whether or not there were any fish there, I do not know. In time a multitude of frogs propagated there. The water became covered with green duckweed. In the summer the site was overgrown with a thick carpet of weeds—burdock, origan, nettles. Here and there clumps of bushes grew. The bushes gave shelter to local drunks and prostitutes. What was happening on the building site was increasingly visible from the street, because people were dismantling the fence, stealing the wood for fuel, until finally nothing concealed the sorry-looking garbage dump right near the Kremlin.

In the end it was Khrushchev who ordered that an outdoor swimming pool be built there, utilizing the foundations of the Temple of Christ the Savior—thus giving so much pleasure to those proud-looking hulks, who in temperatures of minus thirty degrees Celsius strut along the edge of the pool, thrusting out their naked chests. Sometimes they disappear in clouds of thick steam, which in the winter rises high above this extraordinary place.

THE CHAIRMAN of the committee formed by Stalin for the purpose of demolishing and erasing from the map of Moscow and of Russia the Temple of Christ the Savior was Vyacheslav Molotov. The same one who several years later signed (with Ribbentrop) the pact to erase Poland from the map of the world.

# We Look, We Cry

I AM FLYING SOUTH, to Transcaucasia, into familiar territory although I haven't seen it for a long time (more than twenty years). At first I thought that I would go the old route, Tbilisi-Yerevan-Baku, but times have changed; there is no travel between Yerevan and Baku, and so I choose another option: first Yerevan, then Tbilisi, and from there Baku.

ON THE PLANE, my neighbor to the right is Leonid P., a Moscow democrat. Moscow democrats are a new breed of people—products of perestroika. They are not dissidents. Dissidents (there were never many of them; in 1968 six people protested in Moscow's Red Square against the armed intervention in Czechoslovakia) either emigrated or—like Marchenko—are sitting in prisons. The democrats come from the intelligentsia, most frequently from academic or literary circles, and they struggle against the ruling nomenclatura and communism.

The Western democrat and the Moscow democrat are possessed of two entirely different mindsets. The mind of the Western democrat roams freely among the problems of the contemporary world, reflects upon how to live well and happily, how modern technology might serve man better, and how to ensure that each one of us produces more and more material goods and attains greater and greater spiritual well-being. Yet these are all matters beyond the Moscow democrat's field of vision. Only one thing interests him: how to defeat communism. On this subject he can discourse with energy and passion for hours, concoct schemes, present proposals and plans, unaware that as he does so he becomes for a second time communism's victim: the first time he was a victim by force, imprisoned by the system, and now he has become a victim voluntarily, for he has allowed himself to be imprisoned in the web of communism's problems. For such is the demonic nature of great evil—that without our knowledge and consent, it manages to blind us and force us into its strait-jacket.

I observed audiences in London and Toronto, in Rotterdam and Santander, when Moscow democrats would make appearances. It was a collision of free minds (the listeners) with minds obsessed (the speakers). The audience listened with polite attention, but also with a growing conviction that the two sides—despite the fact that both consider themselves democrats—move in different worlds, that the listeners are pondering how to increase their comfort and satisfaction in life, whereas the speakers are preoccupied with seeking an answer to the question posed by Solzhenitsyn: How did we get into this quagmire (that is, into communism)?

During the first half of the trip, Leonid P. tries to persuade me that if Trotsky had listened more to his advisers, he would have had a chance of winning against Stalin. Unfortunately, Trotsky was very conceited, sure of himself, petulant even. This turned people against him, even though there were still many who were prepared to lay down their life for him. Let us suppose for a moment that Trotsky had won. What would have happened then? I say that I don't know. "You don't know?" He becomes animated. "This is something worth discussing!"

• • •

DURING THE SECOND HALF of the trip my neighbor wonders about whether or not Armenia will secede from the Imperium. As a democrat he approves of separation; as a Muscovite he would prefer that it did not come to that. It would be best, he says, if one could succeed in driving out the Communists and thoroughly democratizing everything. He waxes enthusiastic over this idea, but just in case asks what I think of it.

I reply that, honestly, I do not believe one can democratize an imperium that was created through hundreds of years of conquest and annexation. It is not the time to reach back to examples as distant as those of Rome or even Turkey. Let us take a more recent case, one with which I am familiar from personal experience—Iran in the seventies. The revolution against the shah was a democratic movement, a liberal movement, directed against a police dictatorship. But Iran was a multinational state, governed by the Persians, who ruled over the Arab, Azeri, Baluchi, Kurdish, and other minorities living within its borders. Now these oppressed nations, hearing that someone is talking about democracy in Tehran, immediately translated that slogan into their slogan of independence, immediately wanted to detach themselves and create their own states! Iran is in danger of disintegrating, of losing several important provinces, of being reduced to the status of an amputee state. And it is just then that Greater Persian nationalism finds its voice; its custodians—the Shiite clergy with Ayatollah Khomeini at the forefront—assume full power; the word "democracy" vanishes from banners; and the revolution ends with a series of bloody anti-Azeri, anti-Kurdish, et cetera, expeditions and with the victory of authoritarian rule. Iran's borders remain unchanged. Finally—I am winding up to the finish, for we are already starting our descent—there exists an insurmountable contradiction between the rigid and peremptory nature of imperium and the elastic and tolerant nature of democracy. The ethnic minorities inhabiting an imperium will take advantage of the slightest whiff of democracy to tear themselves away, make themselves independent, make themselves autonomous. For them, there is one response to the slogan "Democracy"—freedom. Freedom understood as detachment. This of course provokes objections on the part of the ruling majority, which, in order to maintain its privileged position, is ready to resort to the use of force, to authoritarian solutions.

NO SOONER do the wheels of the plane touch the ground than the three hundred passengers aboard the large, heavy AN-86, as though they have been administered an electrical shock, bolt from their seats and amid bellows of joy, elbowing and pushing one another, rush to the exit! But we are only at the start of the runway; the airplane is still careering forward; the fuselage is swaying and rocking; the wheels are bouncing; the shock absorbers are thudding; the stewardesses are shouting, pleading, and threatening; they are trying to push people back into their seats by force, but it's useless; their efforts are in vain; no one can restrain this crowd any longer; an elemental force has stirred them and seized control of the situation.

Happily we somehow manage to reach the terminal, the steps are rolled up, and then—a new attack of madness, for my fellow passengers, skipping steps, do not so much walk down as fall to the asphalt, and then, loaded down with bags, baskets, bundles, run to the airport building, where a dense, tightly packed, feverish crowd is already waiting for them, and now both of these fired up, vibrating, quivering human throngs throw themselves upon each other with such force, fury, and demonic possession that I observe the scene spellbound. There is no end to the pulling, the hugging, the tussling, the cheering.

Armenians! They must be together. They search for one another the world over, and—the tragic paradox of their fate—the more their diaspora expands and dissipates away, the greater their mutual longing for one another, their desire and need to be together. Only after one understands this characteristic of Armenian nature can one appreciate how painful a thorn for them is the matter of Nagorno-Karabakh—to live a dozen or so kilometers from one another and yet not to be able to be together! An eternal splinter, an eternal wound, an eternal stigma.

• • •

MY ARMENIAN guardian angel, Valery Vartanian, extracts me by some miracle from this crowd and drives me to town, to an apartment full of people (they live in large families here) gathered around a large, spacious table set with all types of food—meats, breads, cheeses, onions, *pili-pili*, greens of all sorts, and also cakes, sweets, bottles of wine and cognac. But it was always this way here. Is there anything new? What's new is that children now enter the room and with great emotion, even a sort of dogged determination, sing a song about the fedayeen. The young fedayeen are the heroes of the day, the young men who, without regard for their own lives, will go fight for the freedom of Nagorno-Karabakh.

Yes, now I understand that I have arrived in another Armenia, in an Armenia with fedayeen. This otherness, moreover, has many aspects and forms, as anyone, like me, visiting Yerevan after many years away, will notice.

First—from a small and sleepy one-horse town it has grown into a large city. A busy, noisy, colorful city, very Oriental. It is as if we were in Damascus, in Istanbul, in Tehran. The bazaars are crowded, the streets teem with cars that go where they please, and only one traffic ordinance is in force: the one responsible is the one who hits. A cacophony of horns: everyone, absolutely everyone, is honking, as if to confirm in this way that they are in fact driving. Here and there new bars are opening up, places selling shish kebabs, little restaurants. Shouts, calls, quarrels, haggling, gesticulating. Chaos. Countries such as this react to any political thaw with increased chaos (which is often irritating, but also gives a flavor to life). An odor, difficult to define, of an Eastern city, clouds of dust, malarial dogs in the squares, heat, airlessness—and, here and there, on the sidewalks, against walls, inside gateways, under trees, shreds of restorative, cool shade.

Second—almost all Russian and Soviet symbolism has vanished from the streets. Russian signs, posters, portraits—it is all gone. The city is undergoing a period of intense and scrupulous de-Russification. Many Russians are leaving; Russian schools are closing, as are Russian theaters. There are no Russian newspapers or books. They have also stopped teaching Russian in Armenian schools. But because there is a shortage of English and French teachers, Armenians are increasingly sequestering themselves within their extremely difficult language, increasingly isolating themselves from the world. Already I can communicate with the children only through the mediation of the grown-ups, who know Russian.

Third—the fedayeen. They walk the streets in groups, drive around in trucks, have set up their guard posts at various points in the city. For someone who knew the customs of the old Imperium, the sight of these fedayeen is perhaps the most extraordinary thing. At one time, only a Red Army soldier could carry weapons here. Only several years ago, possession of arms entailed the risk of being imprisoned in a labor camp—or, more frequently, of being executed. And now there are, they say, as many as thirty-seven private national armies. They are dressed most outlandishly, fantastically, in whatever they happen to possess, just so long as whatever it is at least brings to mind a uniform or an improvisation of a partisan's attire. How do they recognize one another, tell who is from what army? I think it must be by faces alone. It seems to me that in this small country everybody knows everybody else.

HERE, opposite the hotel in which I am staying, they are demolishing an old Yerevan neighborhood. They are tearing down the old houses, porches, bowers, hanging gardens, flower beds and vegetable patches, miniature streams and waterfalls, little roofs strewn with carpets of flowers, fences overgrown with thick vines; they are demolishing wooden stairs, destroying little benches standing beneath walls, tearing down woodsheds and chicken coops, arches and gateways. All this is disappearing from view. People watch as the bulldozers press down upon this landscape sculpted over the course of countless years (in its place will be erected concrete boxes made of large slabs), as they trample and turn these quiet, green, and cozy streets, alleys, and crannies into a heap of garbage. People are standing and crying. And I too stand among them and cry.

Everything has passed—the USSR, and the Armenian Soviet

Socialist Republic, and communism, but the habit of mind, the habit of mind whose first principle, first and foremost, is to destroy what one can, this habit of mind has survived; it feels fine; it is thriving.

HRANT MATEVOSIAN, their distinguished writer. Born in 1935. Thin, tall, slightly bent. He has an endlessly careworn expression, and his thoughts are endlessly careworn. They concern the future of Armenians. There are ten million of them in the world. Do they have a chance of surviving? Most important—of surviving in Armenia, where there are only three million of them and thousands upon thousands are constantly emigrating? Doesn't the fate of the Jews await them: they will exist, but only in a diaspora, only as exiles, condemned to their ghettos scattered on all the continents?

With Armenians one must typically expect to talk only about Armenians. One finds out which countries they live in, what their last names and addresses are. One can ask, for example: "And are there any Armenians in Senegal?" A moment of reflection, then the answer: "There was one Armenian woman, the wife of a French doctor, but she has now left and is living in Marseille."

Everywhere, Armenians are trying to perform good deeds. Did I know that the doctor attempting to bring Mickiewicz back to life after the Turks had poisoned him was an Armenian? I didn't know? But it is a historical fact!

But with Matevosian we speak neither about Senegal nor about Mickiewicz. We talk about the past. Is it possible to leave the past behind? The Armenian past is a tragic tree that continues to cast a shadow. Were it not for the past and the massacre of a million Armenians in 1915, one could reach an understanding with the Turks, reach an understanding with Islam, and live peacefully. But there is the past. In the course of the conversation we cannot reach a conclusion about anything or find an answer to any question. I am reminded of the view of the French philosopher Antoine Cournot, that we do not resolve difficulties, we only displace them. "The art of clarification," says Cournot, "like the art of negotiation, is often simply the art of displacing difficulties.

There is, one might say, a kind of untouchable reserve of incomprehensibility in certain things that the calculations of human intelligence are capable neither of removing nor of diminishing, but only of arranging this way or that, sometimes leaving everything in a half-light, at another time illuminating certain points at the expense of others, which are then submerged by a darkness even deeper than before."

When we say our farewells, Matevosian tells me: "Call me, call and shout—Hrant, I want tea!"

I am returning to the hotel. It is an early autumn evening, warm, mild. Crowds of strolling people. There is a kind of friendliness to these streets, to this town. In one of the back alleys, in the depths of darkness, live embers are glowing. A small boy is sitting by an iron stove. He is broiling shish kebabs. His large black eyes stare at the fire. A fascinated, almost unconscious gaze, as if beyond place, beyond time.

TIGRAN MANSURIAN, composer. His concertos for cello were played by the symphonies of Boston and London. Recently he composed "Le tombeau" to commemorate the twelve-year-old violinist Siranus Matosian, who died during the earthquake in Spitak.

"Here?" He repeats the question. "This part of the world is a cultural desert. We have a great singer, Araks Davtian, one of the ten best sopranos in the world. But no one here knows her, no one has heard of her. She would have to sing to an empty hall. Here? Here they know how to pull the trigger—that's easy. When the year is ending, they say to themselves—what good fortune, another year has gone by!" Mansurian—animated, nervous, sensitivity incarnate. He doesn't have his own record, not yet. No one cares about that here.

He gazes out the window. He lives on the fourth floor of one of those dreadful apartment towers from the Brezhnev era, which are so shoddily constructed, so crooked, lopsided, and squalid, that they should have been torn down before they were ever turned over to the tenants. It is hard to believe, but in the place of elevators they built cages like the ones for miners, and the bundles of electrical wiring, instead of being inside the walls, hang outside or lie along the edge of the stairs. Because there are no attics, and only the elite have washing machines and dryers, people hang their wash out on ropes and wires stretched between balconies, between buildings, between streets. On those miraculous days when there is soap in the stores, the washing and hanging out of clothes and linens take place everywhere. If the wind is blowing, the wash billows, undulates, and flutters, and the towns of Armenia resemble fleets of powerful sailing ships, riding upon a turbulent sea toward distant shores.

In front of Mansurian's building grows a clump of tall poplar trees. One can see from the window their trembling leaves, gleaming silver in the sun. "My world," Mansurian tells me as we sit in his cramped, neat apartment, "is Debussy and these leaves. I can listen nonstop to their music." He falls silent, tilts his head, points with his finger in the direction of the window. "Do you hear?" he asks, and smiles. Against the rich musical background created by the recurring, rhythmic sough of the trees, one can hear, scattered into a delicate and mobile tonal motif, the rustle of the crisp, restless leaves, permeated, interlaced with the high, vibrating twitter of birds.

Valery also drives me thirty kilometers east of Yerevan—to Gari. I have absolutely no time, but it turns out that going to Gari is something categorically, radically, obligatory! You are a slave here—you must be humble, compliant, obedient, or else you will not see anything, will not learn anything.

As far as the eye can see, bare, rocky hills, rounded, smoothed by the wind for millions of years, not a sign of a tree anywhere. And suddenly—at the top of one of these hills—a cow. Motionless, rooted to the earth like a stone. What does this poor animal feed on? There is nothing here, no grass, no leaves. A cow abandoned, as if forgotten by everyone. Forced to rely on herself, on her own patience, on her own luck. Here finally one can understand Yesenin, who, sitting in Paris, dreamed of throwing his arms around a cow's neck!

Along the way Valery stopped to show me the place where Egishe Harenc liked to spend time. Harenc—their greatest poet, murdered by Stalin in 1937. "So when you step through your fragrant field / And spring walks at your side . . ."

The view from this place is expansive, high. Mountains and more mountains, mist, light, a pastel brightness—impressionism.

Gari is a temple built more than two thousand years ago in honor of the beautiful sun god Helios. I must see Gari, for what if I should have some doubts about whether Armenia really belongs to the Mediterranean world, the world of ancient Greece and Rome? Here you go—proof. And moreover, all around lie the ruins of a fortress—a fortress that for centuries held back various Mongols, Tatars, all of brutish Asia. That's what colonization meant in the time of Gari. It meant building roads that are still used today, it meant building factories, constructing magnificent Ionic temples. And what does it mean today? It means placing *kalashnikovs* in the hands of barefoot, hungry people mad with hatred!

NOW BY BUS from Yerevan to Georgia, to Tbilisi. At the city limits, a road sign:

Tbilisi—253 km.
Moscow—1971 km.

The highway runs along Lake Sevan. In the spot where it almost touches the water, a group of boys stop the bus—they are selling fish. The passengers rush toward the exit, and, as always happens in the Imperium wherever some merchandise appears, immediately a breathless and shrieking human throng forms, immediately a struggle begins. Now they are grabbing fish away from one another, but this combat is difficult, for the fish are slippery and, furthermore, still alive, agile, strong, and so they escape; some passengers try to hide them inside their coats or in their pockets, but the beasts either slither out, or some greedy and skillful fellow passenger snatches them for himself.

The fish-human war ends at an impasse. Half the passengers are left with wet, slimy, but empty, hands. The rest are stuffing their still-jumping, but now-dying, prizes wherever they can. The bus stinks like a fish market, but we are driving on.

I took with me for the road *The Book of History*—the work of the late medieval Armenian historian Arakelian from Tebryz. In chapter 53 the author introduces us to the mysterious and colorful world of precious stones:

> Kayc, or korund. Its attributes are as follows: if a man puts it in his mouth, his thirst will disappear; and if one melts gold and throws a korund into the melted gold, the korund will not burn and its color as well as its luster will remain intact. And it is also said: whoever carries a korund on his person, he is pleasing to others; and also, a korund is good for apoplexy.

We are driving along precipices, streams down below, masses of snow above, and then, suddenly, a turn, and—the border patrol. The army. Russians. They enter the bus, looking around, searching for something. It is obvious for what—weapons. Suddenly an Armenian or Georgian starts shouting at them that they are delaying the bus, taking up our time, and so on. He shouts and shouts. Now, I think, this Red Army man will shoot him on the spot. But nothing of the sort happens—these are different times! The soldier starts to explain, apologizes, says that they were acting on orders—the whole patrol quickly disappears, and we crawl on over the mountains.

> Agate, or ayn-ul-hurr. It possesses all the characteristics of the korund. Whoever wears it will not fall ill with leprosy, the itch mite, or similar diseases. His wealth and property will not diminish, his person and his words will be pleasing to others. It is advisable to wear an agate in order to increase one's good judgment. And no matter how much wine he should drink, a man who wears an agate does not lose his reason. That's what they say, but I do not believe this, for wine is a lion's milk and whoever

drinks it greedily deprives himself of fame, reason, and property.

WE ARE IN GEORGIA. There is no need for the signs, already in a different, Georgian alphabet. It is enough to take a look around. In comparison with Armenia, Georgia is wealth; it is better, more affluent houses, large vineyards, good-looking herds of sheep and cows, big tobacco plantations, green, succulent meadows.

The road continues through mountains, winding, plastered to the steep slopes. The forests already autumnal, multicolored, patterned. Fish, a smell like the one at a fish market.

> Diamond. And if you inquire about the attributes of a diamond, they are as follows: if a man has a spotted complexion, a diamond will drive away the spots. He who wears a diamond is pleasing to kings, his words arouse respect, he is not afraid of evil, he will not suffer from stomach pains or the itch mite, his memory will not fail him, and he will live eternally. If one were to pound a diamond on an anvil and serve it to a man, one could kill him with it as with poison.

Higher still, up to the mountain peaks, and suddenly, from here, one can see the whole city.

This is Tbilisi.

# The Man on the Asphalt Mountain

ONCE UPON A TIME Tbilisi was a city of only one street—Rustaveli Boulevard, which stretched for kilometers along the bottom of a winding valley. By its location alone, amid green mountains warmed by the sun, Tbilisi brought to mind one of those quiet and popular health resorts so prevalent in the Swiss and Italian Alps. Throughout the Imperium one had to stand in line to buy a bottle of mineral water, but here one could drink this same water straight from the springs, in which the city abounded.

The western end of Rustaveli Boulevard ended at the neighborhood of Sololaki, spread out on small and gentle hills, a neighborhood of latticework pastel houses, verandas, balconies, and gardens. Even today, Sololaki has retained in places a touch of its former charm. The eastern end of the avenue, on the other hand, until recently, when a new neighborhood arose there, disappeared into the forest surrounding the city.

Tbilisi has changed greatly in recent years. Georgia, like the rest of the southern territories of the Imperium, assumed a model of development typical of the entire Third World: a rapid, unnatural buildup of the capital paid for by the neglect and further impoverishment of the countryside. A monstrous disproportion was thus created between the capital and the rest of the country.

Today one-quarter of the citizens of Georgia live in Tbilisi, one-third of the citizens of Armenia in Yerevan. Applying the same proportions, it is as if more than fifty million people were living in Washington, D.C., eight to ten million in Warsaw.

Life in the provinces means stagnation, poverty, hopelessness. Hence the rush to live in a large town, and, above all else, in the capital. Here there is the possibility of a better existence, of advancement, of a career. As a result, old Tbilisi, Yerevan, Baku, et cetera, are overgrown with gigantic neighborhoods of shoddy housing projects, constructed without any care, cheaply and sloppily. Nothing in these apartment buildings shuts properly, screws tight. Nothing matches anything else. Even so, the quality of these houses varies greatly throughout the Imperium. They build the best in Moscow. Worse in the other European parts of the Imperium. The lowest standards befall the houses of Georgians, Uzbeks, Yakuts, Buryats.

DO YOU REMEMBER *Wind, Sand and Stars*, by Saint-Exupéry? It is 1926. The author, a pilot in training, is to make the flight from Toulouse, across Spain, to Dakar. Aviation technology is in its infancy; airplanes break down; the pilot must be prepared for a landing at any time, in any place. Saint-Exupéry studies the map of his route, but it tells him nothing; it is abstract, general, "vapid." He decides to consult his older colleague, Henry Guillaumet, who knows this route by heart. "But what a strange lesson in geography I was given!" the author recalled. ". . . Instead of telling me about Guadix [Cádiz], he spoke of three orange-trees on the edge of town. 'Beware of those trees. Better mark them on the map.' " And those three orange-trees seemed to me thenceforth higher than the Sierra Nevada." Guillaumet draws his attention to a stream flowing somewhere far away, hidden among the grasses. " 'Careful of that brook: it breaks up the whole field. Mark it on your map . . .' Meandering among the grasses in this blessed paradise of a field where I might have sought salvation, it lies in wait for me two thousand kilometers from here. It would transform me at the first opportunity into a ball of fire. . . . I also assumed a defensive posture vis-à-vis the thirty sheep scattered as in a loose battle formation on the slope of a hill. . . . 'You think the meadow empty, and suddenly bang! there are thirty sheep in your wheels. . . .' "

I think that every Georgian, every inhabitant of the Caucasus, has such a map encoded in his memory. He has studied its particulars from childhood—in his home, in his village, on his street. It is a map-memento, a map of dangers. Only the map of the inhabitant of the Caucasus does not caution him about orange trees, a stream, or a herd of sheep, but about someone from another clan, from another tribe, of another nationality. "Be careful, this is the house in which a man from Ossetia lives. . . ." "This is an Abkhaz village, try to avoid it. . . ." "Don't walk along this path, because you are not a Georgian. The Georgians will not forgive you. . . ."

When one talks with these people, one is struck by the fact that each one of them has an excellent, intricate knowledge of their region. Who lives where, from what tribe, how many of them there are, what the relations between them were once upon a time, yesterday, what they are today. This improbably detailed knowledge of others extends only to those in the most immediate neighborhood. What is beyond its borders (which, moreover, are extremely difficult to define), this nobody knows or—more important—cares to know. The world of the inhabitant of the Caucasus is closed, cramped, confined to his village, to his valley. One's native country is that which one can embrace with a single glance, that which one can cross in a single day. The Caucasus is an extremely rich ethnic mosaic, woven from an infinite number of little, sometimes downright miniature, groups, clans, tribes, and, rarely, nations (although on account of the prestige and respect of the term "nation," it is in common usage here, even if the talk is of small communities).

The second thing that is immediately noticeable is the immemoriality of prevailing judgments, the tyranny of stereotypes.

Here everything was fixed, determined, defined in times that have receded into the obscure mists of history. No one is really able to explain why Armenians and Azerbaijanis hate each other. They hate each other and that's that! Everyone knows this; everyone imbibed this with his mother's milk. This immutability of judgments was fostered by mutual isolation (mountains!) and by the fact that the entire region of the Caucasus was squeezed in between very backward countries—Iran, Russia, and Turkey. Contact with the liberal and democratic thinking of the West was impossible, and existing neighbors did not provide constructive examples; there wasn't anyone to learn from.

The people living here are also characterized by a startling and incomprehensible emotional seesaw, unpredictable, sudden changes of mood. In general they are friendly, hospitable; after all, they have been living together, relatively peacefully, for years. And then suddenly, suddenly, something happens. What? They don't even ask; they don't even listen; they just grab daggers and swords (these days it's machine guns and bazookas) and, in a trembling fury, rush at the enemy and do not rest until they see blood. But each one of them, on his own, is pleasant, well behaved, kind. The only explanation is that somewhere a devil must lurk, fomenting strife. And then, just as suddenly, everything calms down, the status quo ante returns, the everyday, the ordinary—simply, provincial boredom.

IN THE SUMMER of 1990, at several points along Rustaveli Avenue, people are sitting, holding banners, posters, photographs, for any curious passerby to read and inspect. It is a form of protest, or, simply, of drawing public attention to one's problem. I remember it from Iran and Lebanon, and it is everywhere customary to refer to it in English: sit-in.

The number of people participating in any given sit-in can vary—from several to several or more thousand. There can also be one-person sit-ins, but they aren't very effective: a serious matter calls for some numerical strength. (The groups on Rustaveli Avenue number several dozen.) Sit-ins are most frequently organized on the steps of office buildings (to force the authorities to act) or on the steps of churches or mosques (because it is safest there).

Put most straightforwardly, a sit-in means that one sits, publicly demonstrating one's demands. And that's it. Nothing more. It is a remarkably peaceful and gentle form of action. No one here shouts; no one shakes his fist, curses, calls God to witness. Those who take part in a sit-in are silent. They try not to talk either among themselves or to passersby. They are focused; they are vigilant. A sit-in is a strange conjunction of protest and acceptance, mutiny and humility. The participants in a sit-in fundamentally accept reality and its most general outlines and want only to make some corrections of their own and mark their own presence in it. They accept that the world is unjust, and it is only an excess of this injustice that elicits their opposition. If someone were willing, he could readily enter into negotiations with them. That is really what they desire deep in their hearts—they need some sort of social psychiatrist, someone warmly disposed toward them and who would gaze sympathetically on their pained souls.

A sit-in is a very Eastern form of protest. In Europe demonstrators march forward in a unified mass, but such a demonstration quickly disperses and disappears. In Argentina, they walk in a circle, but this too cannot go on for long. The sit-in, however, has two principal strengths as a form of protest. First, it is long-lasting. Sitting, one can demonstrate for weeks and months. For this, of course, one needs people of the East—their stony patience, their astounding endurance and stubbornness. Second, removing sitting people is more difficult than dispersing a marching crowd.

But why would one chase off these poor souls who are sitting on the steps of the City Council building? They are not doing anybody any harm. By and large they are women, dressed in black, who want to share the tragic news: a daughter has been killed during a demonstration, a son has been killed in the Red Army. I notice that these women, holding before them photographs of their deceased children, want people to stop, to take these photographs into their hands, to gaze at the young, sometimes astoundingly beautiful faces. For us this would perhaps be difficult, but here, in Georgia, no, here mourning is celebrated openly; it is an act of public and heartrending demonstration.

OTHER SIT-IN groups spread themselves out beside the unfortunate mothers. They are independence groups who are demanding self-determination for their nation, who want the right to decide their own fate for themselves. Thus, for example, one hundred thousand Abkhazians want to separate from Georgia and form their own state. It is small wonder. Abkhazia is one of the most beautiful corners of the world, a second Riviera, a second Monaco. Well, the Abkhazians hit upon the same idea that twenty years earlier occurred to the inhabitants of that superb and eternally sunny island in the Caribbean called Antigua. The island was a British colony. In the 1970s, the inhabitants of Antigua formed a national liberation party, declared independence, and leased the island to the Hilton Hotel chain. London had to dispatch an armed expedition (four hundred policemen) in order to dissolve the party and annul the contract. So too here, in the Caucasus: the liberated Abkhazians could very well sign an agreement with some Western hotel company and finally begin to live the good life!

But will Georgia give up Abkhazia, it being such a tasty morsel? There are four million Georgians and only one hundred thousand Abkhazians. It is easy to predict the chances.

THE BUSINESS of Abkhazia (and of its ambitions for independence) best explains why matters have suddenly come to a boil in the Caucasus (and not only here), why the Caucasus is in flames. Two things have come together to create a volatile, explosive mixture. For the first time the concept of competing interests has surfaced, and for the first time the market offers easy access to arms.

In a country such as the former USSR, there existed only one interest—the interest of a totalitarian state. Everything else was ruthlessly subordinated to it; all other interests were combated and expunged in the most radical fashion. And now the state—

the monopoly—suddenly and irrevocably falls. Immediately, hundreds, thousands, of various interests, large and small, private, collective, national, rear their heads, identify themselves, define themselves, and emphatically demand the rights long denied them. In a democratic state there is of course also a multitude of various interests, but the contradictions and conflicts between them are resolved or softened by experienced, well-tried public institutions. Whereas here there are no such institutions (and there won't be any anytime soon!). So how are the natural frictions between competing interests to be resolved, since one can no longer do this through the old method of deportation and the whip.

And thus, in the place of the still-nonexistent institutions of arbitration, the simplest path emerges, the path of force. Such a resolution is abetted by the fact that weapons of all sorts have appeared on the black market, including armored trucks and tanks, owing to the disintegration of the old superpower and the loosening of discipline in the army. And so everybody and anybody is arming himself and sharpening his sword. It is easier in this country to get a pistol and a grenade than a shirt or a cap. That is why so many armies and divisions roam the roads, why it is difficult to determine who is who, what he is after, what he is fighting for. The formula of the pretender to power is being revived, typical in times of chaos and confusion. All manner of commanders, leaders, restorers, saviors, appear and disappear.

The best proof of this is to visit one of these countries repeatedly over a few months. Each time you go you will see new faces, hear new names. And what happened to those earlier ones? Who knows. Perhaps they are in hiding? Perhaps they have set up a private company? Perhaps they are announcing that they will be back at any moment? It is no coincidence that the amusement-park train ride on which one rushes up and then down at breakneck speed is called Russian Mountain. The little cars shoot along at such a pace that it is impossible to catch a glimpse of any passenger's face, all of them fly by, disappear. This is what it is like in local politics. They elect someone, then immediately eject him. It isn't long before the ejected one returns to drive out the one who took his place. In photographs, the guards of the one who has returned raise their pistols in a gesture of triumph. During this time the new exile escapes under cover of night with his guards.

"The investigator of Turkish and Mongol history in this part of the world," writes the eminent British historian Sir Olaf Caroe (*Soviet Empire*, 1967) about, among other places, the Caucasus, "is like a man standing on an upper floor, watching the unpredictable and disordered movement of a crowd gathered on some great occasion. Groups meet and coalesce, groups melt and dissolve; a sudden interest draws a mass in one direction, only to split up again; a bidder or leader may for some moments gather a knot of adherents; political or personal causes lead to rioting; a regiment goes past and there is slaughter and destruction, or even for a time a sense of purpose and direction of effort."

THE CAPITAL of Abkhazia—Sukhumi, a city of palm trees and bougainvillea. I was there in 1967. A note from that time:

> In Sukhumi Guram took me for fried fish to the restaurant called Dioskuria. It is an enchanting place. The restaurant is built on rocks plunging into the Black Sea. And the rocks against which it leans are the ruins of its namesake, a Greek colony—Dioskuria—which existed here twenty-five centuries ago. Sitting at a table, one can observe parts of the city, sunken to the bottom of the sea, transformed now into a kind of monstrous aquarium, along whose streets parade groups of fat, lazy fish.

It would be interesting to know whether Dioskuria still stands at the bottom of the sea or whether, surviving there for 2,500 years, it was finally swept away by the Georgian-Abkhasian rockets.

WITH MY HOST Giya Sartania (he is a young writer and translator), I drive out of town to make a pilgrimage to the Church of St. Nina in Santavro. Christianity is a very ancient religion in Georgia, already rooted here in the fourth century, and this little church was built at just around that time. Sometime afterward, we are in a church in Dzvaria, erected two hundred years later. And despite the difference of two centuries, the churches resemble each other, are the work of the same imagination and sensibility, which, it is evident, did not change over the centuries.

To enter these churches today is to go back in time one thousand years. Meaning this: The churches were until now either closed or transformed into museums of atheism or warehouses for fuel or wheat. And before that they had been thoroughly robbed, stripped to their severe, bare walls. In such a state they are now being handed back to the faithful. And everything is as if we had returned to the age of the catacombs. Here, amid the empty, bare walls, the first Christians gather.

> Meantime it grew completely dark, and since the moon had not yet risen, it would have been difficult for them to find the way if not for the fact that, as Hilo had predicted, the Christians themselves were indicating it. Indeed, to the right, to the left, and in the front one could see dark figures, making their way cautiously toward the sandy narrow combes. Some of these people were carrying lanterns, although covering them as much as was possible with their cloaks, others, knowing the way better, walked in the dark.

This is from Henryk Sienkiewicz's *Quo Vadis*. But with Giya I now witness a similar mysterious scene. For in this empty, freezing-cold church in Dzvaria a single object is brought in from the outside—a small metal cross standing on a bare stone altar. In front of the altar bows the priest, a hood on his head. There is silence; one hears only the sound of water trickling down the walls. And the slow footsteps of several women entering with candles. The glow of the candles illuminates the twilit church. One of the women pulls a wheat flat cake out of her bag and shares it with everyone present. There is something moving in this interior overflowing with humidity and darkness, in this silent scene with the wheat bread, in this strange behavior of the priest, who neither turns around nor looks at us.

• • •

AT DAWN by bus from Tbilisi to Baku. Almost the whole time passing through a valley between the Great and Small Caucasus. The hero of this trifling, comic odyssey is called Revaz Galidze, and he is a corpulent, even fat, man over fifty, the driver of our bus. I do not know whether being a bus driver is for him a step up or a defeat; suffice it to say that he immediately informed me that for many years he drove TIR (Transport International Routier) trailer trucks to various European countries, and so he has, but of course, worldly polish and manners. On this five-hundred-kilometer route, the bus was always full and the passengers changed frequently, yet the only people who had actually purchased tickets were two Russian women going to Kirovabad and myself. The rest would pay Revaz sums determined by him, and he would stuff the received bundles of rubles into his pockets. Revaz was the authentic king of this road, its unchallenged master and ruler.

The day was cloudy and rainy, and the area, for that part of the world, populous. Consequently we kept coming upon groups of cold, wet people standing by the roadside. Always either loaded down with bundles or leading a sheep or a goat on a rope, at the sight of the bus they would beseechingly hold out their hands. They weren't begging for kopecks or a handful of rice, but were imploring Revaz to show them a shred of mercy and take them with him. One can surmise that these people stand like this for entire days, because buses run infrequently here. The road is dangerous, battles are being fought nearby (between Azerbaijanis and Armenians), and so the courageous Revaz truly enjoys a monopoly.

And, of course, he takes advantage of the situation. Revaz conducts a cruel form of auction. That is, encountering along the route a group eager for a lift, he stops and asks how much they are paying, and for what distance. If they are paying a lot, and the distance is short, Revaz throws those who are paying less off the bus, despite the fact that they are still a hundred kilometers from home! And he throws them out having nonetheless pocketed their fare!

Revaz doesn't throw me out because, first of all, I am the only passenger who has a ticket (the Russian women have gotten off already); second, I am a foreigner; and third, I have a fever of nearly forty degrees Celsius and am dying. The closer to Baku, the greater Revaz's ruthlessness. At the start of the route there were still many of his Georgian kinsmen on the bus—and Revaz had a certain respect for them; now the whole bus is Azerbaijani peasants, flustered, shy, bewildered. The poverty of these people is depressing, and when one of them, seeing that I have a fever, takes a bottle of lemonade out of a basket and hands it to me, my throat tightens with emotion.

We are already close to Baku. A nightmarish landscape: an immense stretch of land soused with tar, smothered with crushed slag, and heaps of concrete slabs thrown helter-skelter. Everywhere heavy Baku oil flows; it runs in streams, creates stinking puddles, stagnant pools, lakes, bays. Oil on the surface of the sea, and the beaches—why, I still remember yellow sand here—are black, oily, covered in grease and soot.

To reach Baku, which lies on a bay, one must still climb along the steep and winding road into the hills surrounding the city. At one of the bends, a scene that allows me to look warmly upon Revaz. Amid this asphalt-dark, sooty, and sticky landscape stands a block of concrete, and on top of it is a live man, only a man without legs, apparently carried up by someone, his trunk inserted into a wooden fruit crate.

I am the witness of some sort of ritual, clearly established through long tradition. When we reach this place, Revaz stops the bus, greets the man, and stuffs a substantial bundle of rubles into his shirt pocket.

# Fleeing from Oneself

IN BAKU I stayed in the apartment of a Russian woman who managed to leave the city when the riots, pillaging, and arson began. I had met her in Moscow, where she came to live with her family. Giving me the key to the apartment, she said with determination: I will never go back there again. She was still frightened, terrified by the city that had fallen prey to aggressive and brutal armed bands. She told me she had reached the airport thanks only to an ambulance driver who agreed to take her there—otherwise she wouldn't have dared to show herself on the street.

IT WAS ALREADY dusk when Revaz's bus reached the station in Baku. Buses arriving from the countryside crawl amid the deafening cacophony of horns into a dense, bustling crowd, into a swarm welcoming and bidding farewell, amid sellers of tomatoes, cucumbers, and shish kebabs, groups of children asking for baksheesh, sluggish and listless policemen with clubs in their hands. The East, the real East, smelling of anise and cardamom, mutton fat and fried paprika, some sort of Eşfahān or Kirkūk, Izmir or Herāt, an exotic world, noisy, eccentric, preoccupied with itself and closed, inaccessible to anyone from the outside. Wherever its people come together, there immediately forms a colorful, agitated concourse, bazaar, souk, market; there is immediately lots of shouting, jumping at one another's throat, quarrels, but then (patience!) everything is transformed into calm, into an inexpensive little restaurant, into a chat, into a friendly nod of the head, into a small glass of mint tea, into a lump of sugar.

IN THAT STATION I quickly realize the hopelessness of my situation. How do I get from here to the house, whose exact location I do not know, carrying moreover a suitcase packed with books (a terrible mania for buying books everywhere) and suffering from a forty-degree fever? "Could you be so kind as to please tell me," I ask every person I meet, tugging at his sleeve or grasping at his lapels, "where is number 117 Pouchin Street?" But people are breaking away, pushing me away impatiently, hurrying on. I finally realize that I will learn nothing from them, for these are new arrivals from the countryside, peasants from the kolkhozes, merchants of textiles and fruit from Dagestan, from Checheno-Ingush, or even from the distant Kabardino-Balkar Republic. How are these mountain men from the Caucasus, bewildered and stunned by the big city, supposed to know where Pouchin 117 is? And so I spin around in circles, half-dead, above all from thirst. There is nothing to drink. It is already evening, and the only cistern truck selling kvass (a drink made of fermented bread) stands empty.

There are no taxis. Despairing and near collapse, I stand on the street and stretch out my hand, in which I hold a BIC ballpoint pen. I do not stand long. Children have the eyesight of hawks. One child, riding with his father in a car, spots a man who clearly wants to present him with a BIC ballpoint. At the child's request the father stops. I ask him about number 117 Pouchin Street. They let me into the car; we drive off. We drive for a long time, until we are far from the bus station. We stop in an old part of the city, near an old, dark street. (There is no snobbishness here about the old and historical, no preciousness, nothing of the splendor or priciness of the antique. Here an old house means a house untouched by any repairs, by any renovations, for seventy-three years.) I enter a dark gateway, a dark courtyard; I trip over piles of garbage. I hear a woman's voice. She asks me what I am looking for. She comes to me, takes me by the hand, and leads me to a door invisible in the darkness. "Why," she wonders, "is your hand so hot, man?"

(They say "comrade" more and more infrequently here, but they also aren't able to say "mister," for that still sounds too bourgeois, and the form "you," toward a person whom one doesn't know well, is impolite. So they address each other as "woman," "man.")

"Because I have a fever," I answer. Feeling our way in the dark, we find the doors, locked with a padlock. We enter, the woman turns on the light. I see the bed. "You know," I say to her, "there are these American postcards, on which is written 'Happiness is . . .' and then various drawings representing what happiness is. For me," I say, "now, happiness is seeing a bed."

"Yes, you really are sick," she says, and after a time brings me a pot of hot tea and a whole collection of various jams and candies on a tray.

She asks me what nationality I am.

Like peasants the world over who begin each conversation with reflections on the subject of crops, and Englishmen who start every exchange with a discussion of the weather, so in the Imperium the first step in establishing contact between people is a mutual determination of one's nationality. For much will depend on this.

In most instances, the criteria are clear and legible. Here's a Russian, here's a Kazakh, here's a Tatar, here's an Uzbek. But there is a large percentage of citizens of this state for whom self-identification presents serious difficulties, who—to put it otherwise—do not feel part of any nation. Take, for example, my friend Ruslan from Chelyabinsk. His grandfather was a Russian, his grandmother a Georgian. Their son, Ruslan's father, decided that he would be a Georgian. He married a Tatar. For love of his mother, Ruslan declared himself a Tatar. At the university in Omsk he married a friend—an Uzbek. They now have a son, Mutar. What nationality is Mutar?

Sometimes these genealogies are even more complicated, so that many do not feel associated with any nationality whatsoever. This is the *Homo sovieticus*—he is not what he is because of any particular consciousness or attitude; his sole social determinant is membership in the Soviet state. Now, after the fall of this state, such people are searching for a new identity (those, that is, who even stop to think about this at all).

THIS ETHNIC *Homo sovieticus* is a product of the history of the USSR, a significant portion of which comprises unceasing, intense, and massive migrations, displacements, transportations, and wanderings of the population. This movement begins in the nineteenth century with the deportations to and colonization of Siberia, as well as the colonial expansion into Asia, but it gathers strength only after 1917. Millions of people lose the roof over their head and spill out onto the roads. Some are returning from the fronts of World War I; others are setting off for the fronts of the great civil war. The famine of 1921 forces subsequent millions to roam in search of a piece of bread. Children whom the war and the Revolution have deprived of parents, those millions of miserable *bezprizorny*, form hunger crusades that traverse the country in all directions. And later, throngs of laborers in search of work and bread travel to the Urals and other corners of the country, where they can find employment building factories, foundries, mines, dams. For more than forty years, tens of millions of people make the martyr's journey to the camps and prisons scattered over the entire territory of the superpower. The Second World War erupts, and subsequent multitudes are displaced in all directions, depending on where the front is. At the same time, behind these front lines, Beria directs the deportation of Poles and Greeks, Germans and Kalmuks, into the depths of the Caucasus and to Siberia. As a result, entire nations find themselves in lands foreign to them, in unfamiliar surroundings, in poverty and hunger. One of the goals of these operations is to create the uprooted man, wrenched from his culture, from his environment and landscape, and therefore more defenseless and obedient vis-à-vis the dictates of the regime.

And to this picture of ceaseless and massive forced migrations of peoples let us add the dozens of more voluntary "Komsomol enlistments," the scores of migrations occurring under such slogans as "The motherland needs metal," "Plow the fallow lands," "Conquer the taiga," and so on. Let us remember too the waves of refugees that set forth with each ethnic conflict and spill across the country.

And today thousands of people are camped out still, in airports, in train stations, in barracks, in slums, in tents. The spirit and atmosphere of nomadism are still present and alive here, and an often-heard saying goes: "My address is not the number of a house, nor the name of a street, nor the name of a city, my address is the Soviet Union" (today, the Commonwealth of Independent States; I do not know what the Imperium will be called tomorrow).

And so, with these great and uninterrupted migrations, with the mixing of races that has gone on for generations, it is the similarity between or the uniformity of human types rather than their variety and distinctiveness that draws the attention of those who come into contact with the inhabitants of the Imperium for the first time.

THE FEARS of the Russian woman from 117 Pouchin Street are exaggerated fears: they do not touch Russians here. An Uzbek might fight with a Tajik, a Buryat with a Chechen, but no one will come near a Russian. Mickiewicz reflected upon this phenomenon, which seemed, at first glance, incomprehensible: A single czarist official drives an entire column of Tuvinians (a Siberian tribe) to a hard-labor camp, and not one of these unfortunate vassals will revolt. After all, they could easily kill this official and vanish into the forest. But no, they walk on obediently, meekly execute his commands, endure his verbal abuse in silence. The reason, Mickiewicz explains, is that, in the eyes of the enslaved Tuvinians, this official personifies the might of the all-powerful state, which arouses their fright, terror, dread. To raise a hand against the official is to raise a hand against the superpower, and none of them can bring himself to do that. The Tunisian writer Albert Memmi, in his book *Portrait du colonise*, accurately presents this composite of hatred and fear that characterizes the attitude of a colonized man toward his ruler, the colonizer. Fear, Memmi observes, will in the final calculation always dominate over hatred, will suppress and paralyze it.

One need only see cities over which a wave of ethnic conflict has recently rolled—even Fergane or Osh. Among the burned and devastated houses of Uzbeks, Karakalpaks, or Tajiks are visible the untouched houses of Russians. For who stands behind a poor Karachi, attacked by an infuriated Turk? At most—another Karachi. And behind a Russian? A *kalashnikov*, a tank, a nuclear bomb.

AND YET my Russian from Baku, at the first stirring in the street, at the first echoes of approaching armed bands, which—as everyone knows—are coming to bash in the heads of Armenians, and of Armenians only, packs her suitcases in haste and rushes to the airport, happy that she succeeded in getting out of hell. But where is this hell? Where is it to be found?

It is within her, within her consciousness.

I AM REMINDED of Africa, the sixties, scenes at the airports in Algiers, Léopoldville, and Usumbura; then, in the seventies, the same scenes at the airports in Luanda and Lourenço Marques. Camped out on their bundles, semiconscious from exhaustion and fear, crowds of white refugees. They are yesterday's colonizers, former rulers of these lands. Today, however, their sole desire is to get away from here, to get away immediately, leaving everything—houses awash in flowers, gardens, swimming pools, sailboats. Whence this desperate haste and determination? What is it that drives them to Europe so suddenly? What titanic force expels them so violently and ruthlessly from these comfortable, magnificent places warmed by the tropical sun? Perhaps the natives have begun the mass slaughter of their white masters? Perhaps their luxurious neighborhoods have gone up in flames? No, nothing of the sort is happening.

It is in the consciousness of the colonizer that hell has stirred, an internal hell. His unclean conscience—hitherto concealed and in a thousand ways lulled to sleep, and often simply not very clearly or fully understood—has awoken and risen to the surface. This unclean conscience need not affect every individual in the crowd of colonizers. Many of these people feel—and are—completely innocent. But they, too, are the victims of a situation that they themselves have helped to create, namely, the colonial situation, whose essence is a principle of asymmetry, the subordination of the colonized man to the colonizer. The paradox lies in the fact that even if I do not want to be a colonizer, and have even protested against colonialism, I am a colonizer by the mere fact of membership in the nation that colonizes others. Only at the price of renouncing my own country and nation, and perhaps at the price of changing my skin color (a theoretical proposition), could I rid myself of this taint, this odium. But because these are impossible choices, the scene at the airports is crowded and edgy: a dozen or so years ago at the airport in Luanda, and now, in 1990, at the airport in Baku.

But who are you fleeing from? Is it not from yourselves?

And yet a difference exists between a Portuguese or a Frenchman leaving Africa and a Russian who must depart from sunny Baku or beautiful art nouveau Riga and return to gloomy, piercingly cold Norilsk or depressingly dirty and smoky Chelyabinsk. They do not want to leave? I am not surprised! To save themselves, they set up in their former colonies various unions and parties whose slogan is "Stay put. Do not move an inch!" The Russian from 117 Pouchin Street is rather an exception, and that is because she finds herself in a position of great luxury—she has a family with an apartment, and in Moscow no less!

BAKU: I like this town. It is built for people, not against people (yes, there are cities built against people). One can walk here for days on end. Baku has beautiful boulevards, several streets of magnificent art nouveau architecture, which was transplanted here by the king of oil, Mr. Alfred Nobel. Actually, one can see every conceivable style. By the main boulevard rise several bright, luxurious, and large apartment buildings—houses that the ruler of Azerbaijan, Geidar Aliyev, constructed for his camarilla. Aliyev was first the head of the Azerbaijani KGB, later, in the seventies, the Republic's first secretary of the Communist Party. He was a pupil of Brezhnev's, who nominated him to be vice-premier of the USSR. Gorbachev removed him from this post in 1987. Aliyev was one of Brezhnev's people—a group characterized by a high degree of corruption, a taste for Oriental sumptuousness, all manner of depravity. There was not a shadow of restraint in their practice of corruption; on the contrary, it was a defiant, provocative ostentation. This colony of apartment blocks, constructed in the most important, most representative location in the city, affords a perfect example. Aliyev distributed all the apartments according to lists he himself drew up—he also personally handed the keys to the chosen. The criterion of allocation was simple—his closest family received the best apartments, after them came cousins and the higher personages of his clan. In these lands, tribal ties remain the most important, just as they were several thousand years ago.

I was in one of those apartments. Its resident, my host, worked in the local Parliament, but more important he was Aliyev's cousin. Now this man, whose official earnings amounted to a pittance, had arranged along the walls entire batteries of electronic equipment, television sets, copiers, amplifiers, speakers, lights, God knows what. But even if he were making millions of rubles, he could not buy such things in a shop, because shops do not have them. The table was set with all kinds of food, sweetmeats, dates, nuts. My host fretted and fumed the most about Sakharov. "Sakharov? What do we need Sakharov for? He has an Armenian wife!" But aside from this one problem (meaning, aside from Sakharov) all was well. He treated me to cheese from Holland, to shrimp from the Bahamas. He sat contentedly surrounded by his family. The electronic equipment twinkled at him from all directions with colorful little eyes.

• • •

THE NEXT DAY, a conversation with Professor Ayudin Mirsalinoglu Mamedov. Curious, wise, and joyful, because just now, for the first time since 1917, permission had been granted to establish a Turkic cultural society. For years the professor had been editing a periodical dedicated to Turkic. Not everyone knows that the Turkish language is the second most dominant language of the Imperium. About sixty million people speak it. An Azerbaijani can communicate not only in Ankara, but also in Tashkent and Yakutsk. His Turkish-speaking brethren live everywhere. In a certain sense, the former USSR is a Slavic-Turkish superpower. Solzhenitsyn's idea was to get rid of the Turkish element so that only a Slavic superpower would remain.

Azerbaijanis have been so called only since 1937. Before, they had "Turk" written into their identity cards. Now they regard themselves as Azerbaijanis, Turks, and Muslims.

Communism, says Mamedov, wrought the greatest destruction upon people's consciousness. People do not want to work well and live well. They want to work badly and live badly. And there's the whole truth for you.

Let us consider the universities. Four years of studying dialectical materialism, four years of cramming the history of the CPSU, four years of academically plumbing communism—and everything turned out to be a lie!

After seventy-three years of bolshevism, people do not know what freedom of thought is, and so in its place they practice freedom of action. And here freedom of action means freedom to kill. And there's perestroika for you, the new thinking.

How was communism built? Communism was built by Stalin with the help of the *bezprizorny*, the millions of orphaned, hungry, and barefoot children who wandered along Russia's roads. They stole what they could. Stalin locked them up in boarding schools. There they learned hatred, and when they grew up, they were dressed in the uniforms of the NKVD. The NKVD held the nation in the grip of a bestial fear. And there's communism for you.

What is Stalin's chessboard? He so resettled nations, so mixed them up and displaced them, that now one cannot move anyone without also moving someone else, without doing him injury. There are currently thirty-six border conflicts, and perhaps even more. And there's Stalin's chessboard for you, our greatest misfortune.

A LITTLE RESTAURANT in the center of Baku. Turkish? Iranian? Arab? Azerbaijani? In this part of the world, all these little places resemble one another. A small, detached room. Shish kebab, rice, tomatoes, and lemonade. Dinner with the leader of the Azerbaijani National Front, the writer Yusif Samedoglu. He is trying to navigate between the dictatorship of the local political bosses and the Islamic fundamentalists. But these are difficult times for liberals, for people of the center, for those who would like to reach out and hug everyone. I know what he will tell me about the situation in Baku, so I do not ask him about that; I ask him instead whether he is writing anything. He shakes his head, a resigned no. And anyway—*how* should he write? He always wrote in the Cyrillic alphabet, and now they are going to abolish Cyrillic. They will use only the Latin alphabet, as in Turkey, or will go back to the Arabic, nobody knows which. And what about the books that he wrote in Cyrillic? Translate them into other alphabets? Who is going to do this? Is it worth it? A writer in the prime of his life is left empty-handed, with work that will be illegible.

FOR THE FIRST time in my life I flew on a plane that was as crowded as a city bus at rush hour. At the airport in Baku, an enraged crowd, ready for anything, stormed into the cabin and would not even consider stepping down. The captain shouted, threatened, and cursed—it didn't help. People stood pressed together in the passageways, deaf to what was being said to them. In the end the captain waved his hand, shut the door to the cockpit, started the engines, and took off.

# Vorkuta—To Freeze in Fire

IT IS SUPPOSED to be Vorkuta at night, but we are landing in the daytime, in sunlight. So this must be some other airport.

Which?

I fidget restlessly in my seat, but right away I see that I am the only restless one, no one else's eyelids so much as twitch. I have flown maybe one hundred thousand kilometers in this country on airplanes. Two observations from those trips: The airplanes are always full—at each airport, for every destination, mobs of people are waiting, sometimes for weeks, so that finding an empty seat somewhere is quite out of the question. Second, during the entire flight there is complete silence in the cabin. The passengers sit motionless; no one speaks. If one hears a buzz somewhere, bursts of laughter, and the clink of glasses, it means that a group of Poles is on board: who knows why, but travel puts them into a state of boundless euphoria, into a near frenzy.

No, this is not Vorkuta; it is Syktyvkar.

• • •

I DID NOT KNOW where this Syktyvkar was, and I had forgotten to take a map along. We waded through snow to the airport building. Inside it was hot, stuffy, and crowded. Finding an unoccupied piece of a bench was impossible. All the benches were full of people sleeping, sleeping so profoundly and peacefully that it was as if they had long ago relinquished all hope of someday flying out of here.

I decided to stick with the passengers on my airplane, afraid that otherwise I'd miss the reboarding announcement and be left behind. We stood in the center of the large hall, for even the places against the walls were taken.

We stood and that's that.

We stood and we are standing.

I had on a sheepskin coat (I was after all flying to beyond the Arctic Circle), and in the press and swelter of the heated but unventilated hall, I started to drip with sweat. Take off the sheepskin? But what would I do with it? In my hands I had bags, and there were no hangers. We had been standing for more than an hour already, and it was becoming harder and harder to bear.

And yet the stuffiness and sweat were not the worst of it. The worst was that I did not know what next. How long am I supposed to stand like this in Syktyvkar? Another hour? Twenty-four hours? The rest of my life? And really—what am I doing here? Why didn't we fly to Vorkuta? Will we fly there at some point? When? Is there a chance of taking off the sheepskin, sitting down, and drinking some tea? Will this be possible?

I looked around at my neighbors.

They stood staring fixedly straight ahead. Just like that: staring fixedly straight ahead. One could see no impatience in their expressions. No anxiety, agitation, anger. Most important, they asked about nothing; they asked no one about anything. But perhaps they weren't asking because they already knew?

I asked one of them if he knew when we would be taking off. If you suddenly ask someone a question here, you must wait patiently. For you can see in the face of the one queried that it is only under the influence of this stimulus (the question) that he seems to awaken, comes to life, and starts the laborious journey from some other planet to earth. And this requires time. Then an expression of slight and even amused surprise crosses his face—what's the moron asking for?

The person to whom the question is addressed is absolutely right to consider his interrogator a moron. For his entire experience teaches him that no advantage accrues from asking questions, that no matter what, a man will learn—questions or not—only as much as they will tell him (or, rather, won't tell him), and that, on the contrary, the asking of questions is very dangerous and can cause a man to bring a great misfortune down upon his head.

It is true that a bit of time has elapsed since the epoch of Stalinism, but its memory is alive, and the lessons, traditions, and habits of that period remain, are fixed in consciousness, and will long influence people's behavior. How many of them (or their families, acquaintances, and so on) went to the camps because during a meeting, or even in a private conversation, they asked about this or that? How many in so doing ruined their careers? How many lost their jobs? How many lost their lives?

For years the bureaucracy and the police maintained a well-developed system of spying and informing designed to uncover only one offense: Did someone ask? What did he ask about? Give me the name of the one who asked.

A conversation between two best friends before a meeting:

> "You know, I'd like to ask about that at the meeting."
> "I beg you, please don't do that, you know they'll lock you up!"

Or the conversation of two other friends:

> "Fiedia, I want to give you some advice."
> "Yes?"
> "I've been noticing that you're asking too many questions. Do you want to hurt yourself? Be sensible, control yourself, stop asking!"

In literature (in Vasily Grossman, for example), scenes describing a return home from the camps. A man has come back after ten years of suffering in Siberia. He sits down the first evening at the family table together with his wife, his children, his parents. They eat supper, perhaps there's even a conversation, but no one asks the newcomer where he was during those years, what he did, what he experienced.

What would one ask for?

A wise sentence from Ecclesiastes: "Who gathers knowledge, gathers pain."

Developing this bitter thought, Karl Popper once wrote (I am quoting from memory) that ignorance is not a simple and passive lack of knowledge, but is an active stance; it is the refusal to accept knowledge, a reluctance to possess it; it is its rejection. (Or, in a word, antiknowledge.)

The sphere of questions—so vast and, it would seem, so indispensable to life—was not only a forbidden minefield, but an outright inimical and odious form of speech, and this was because in Soviet practice the monopoly on asking questions was reserved to interrogating police officers. Once, riding on a train from Odessa to Kishinev, I entered into a conversation with my neighbor in the compartment. He was a kolkhoz member from the Dniester region. I asked him about work, about his house, about his earnings. With each question I asked, his distrust of me increased, until finally he looked at me suspiciously and grunted: "What's this, are you a police interrogator, or what?" And he wouldn't talk anymore.

Exactly! If I were a police interrogator, then it would be all right; a police interrogator is allowed to ask questions; a police interrogator is there to ask questions. But an ordinary man? One sitting in the compartment of a train from Odessa to Kishinev?

"I'm the one who asks questions around here!" shouts the interrogating officer, Livanov, at the terrified, falsely arrested Evgeniya Ginzburg (*The Steep Wall*). Yes, only he, the interrogator, has the right to ask questions.

Yet everyone knows that the question posed by a police interrogator is not an academic, disinterested question, posed to plumb the dark mysteries of our being. No, each one of a police interrogator's questions conceals a lethal charge; the question is asked in order to destroy you, to smash you into the ground, to annihilate you. It is no accident that the expression "cross-fire questioning" is borrowed from the vocabulary of battle, the front, war, death.

Because interrogative language was appropriated by the police, by the so-called *organa*, by the dictatorship, the very inflection of a sentence expressing the desire to learn something signaled danger, perhaps foreshadowed a sinister fate. This resulted in fewer and fewer people asking questions in the Imperium and the simply fewer and fewer questions.

That is why gradually the art of formulating questions (for it is an art!) vanished, as did even the need to ask them. Increasingly everything presented itself as being what it was supposed to be. Unchallengeable and irrefutable reality was triumphing. And since that was the case, there simply were no more questions.

In their place appeared an infinite number of sayings, catchwords, and turns of phrase expressing approval of that which is, or at least indifference, lack of surprise, humble consent, resignation: Never mind! So what! Everything's possible! Well, all right! What will be will be! *Vsievo mira nie piereyebiosh!* (You cannot fuck the whole world!) You'll live—you'll see! *Nachelstvo lutshe znayet!* (The bosses know best!) Life! That's how it is! There's no need for better! A humble calf suckles two cows! You won't catch a bird in flight! Et cetera, et cetera, for it is an extremely rich language.

A civilization that does not ask questions, one that banishes from within its compass the entire world of anxiety, criticism, and exploration—the world that expresses itself precisely through questions—is a civilization standing in place, paralyzed, immobile. And that is what the people in the Kremlin were after, because it is easiest to reign over a motionless and mute world.

AFTER SEVERAL HOURS in Syktyvkar we flew off to Vorkuta (to this day I do not know what was the purpose of that stop, or of that hopeless, exhausting wait.) Flying this route in the evening is an experience of the highest artistic, painterly order. After reaching an altitude of several thousand meters, the plane suddenly enters the backstage of some grand, cosmic theater. We do not see the stage itself, which lies submerged in darkness somewhere on earth. We only see the luminous curtains hanging in the sky. They are light, pastel curtains, several hundred meters high, in shades of yellow and green.

These curtains radiate with a pulsing, vibrating light.

It is as if the plane had lost itself in these bright draperies, as if it had gone astray, lost its bearings, and began to circle restlessly amid colorful and pleated fabrics stretched in the sky. The green! The most striking was the green! "Green and blue intensify in the penumbra"—this is Leonardo da Vinci in his *Treatise on Painting*. And indeed, against the black, against the tarlike, abysmally black sky, the green lost its natural calm and equilibrium and assumed tones so intense, so imperious, that next to it other colors grew dim, receded into the background.

We were already over the airport when the spectacle of the northern lights went out, melted away in the darkness.

Temperature minus thirty-five degrees Celsius. I felt the cold immediately. Immediately the bitter bite of the frost, difficulty breathing, shivers. Everybody has scattered. The square in front of the small airport building is empty. Empty and poorly lit. What to do? I knew that I wouldn't last long in this cold. Inside the terminal was a militia post. The militiaman, hidden in an enormous sheepskin coat, said that a bus would arrive soon and that I could take it to town, to the hotel. "There is only one hotel here," he added, "you'll find it easily."

A small, old bus, crowded, packed, jammed. People tightly wrapped, enveloped, entangled in sheepskins, furs, scarves, pieces of felt—large, stiff, clumsy cocoons. When the bus stops, the cocoons abruptly tip forward; when it suddenly starts, they tip back. At each stop several cocoons vanish into the darkness, and others appear in their place (that is, I assume that they are others, for all the cocoons look more or less alike). Sometimes something kneads our feet so hard that we feel our bones are cracking—it is some little cocoon that is making its way toward the exit. A question about the hotel must be directed at the upper part of the cocoon—that is, at the spherical object directly in front of us, just as if we were talking into a microphone. One must strain one's ears to hear the reply, for it will not be aimed at us, but will float up from where a voice emerges from the cocoon. The downside of this mode of travel is that one can be riding next to a very beautiful girl and be completely unaware of it—no faces are visible. It is also impossible to see where we are—a thick hoarfrost and extremely rich, rococo bouquets of white flowers cover all the windows.

My sojourn among the cocoons doesn't last long, for, lo and behold, after a half hour we arrive somewhere in the vicinity of the hotel. When the doors open with a thud, the cocoons kindly part to both sides so that the newcomer from far away can disentangle himself from the interior of the bus, get out, and disappear into the darkness and the cold.

NO LOUVRE, no castles on the Loire, can offer so many pleasant and unforgettable sensations as the gloomy and humble interior of the Hotel Vorkuta. At work here is the immemorial law of relativity. Entering the Louvre from the sidewalks of Paris is not a passage from earth to heaven, whereas entering the lobby of the Hotel Vorkuta from the street is. The lobby saves our life, for it is warm, and warmth in this town is the most priceless thing.

I am given a key, and I run to my room. But I have barely walked in when I run out again even quicker: the window is not only wide open, but its frame is encased in a thick, massive layer of ice. Shutting it is out of the question. I rush to the chambermaid with this dismal news. She isn't the least surprised. "That's what our windows are like." She tries to calm me down; she doesn't want me to get excited. What can you do, that's life, that's what the windows are like in the Hotel Vorkuta.

An old Leninist question (or perhaps going back even as far as the times of Dobrolyubov and Chernyshevsky: What is to be done? We confer for a long time. Finally I realize that nothing will occur to her until I reach into my supplies of costly cologne made in New York. Immediately, a simple and practical idea illuminates her mind. She disappears for a time and then emerges from the darkness of the hallway carrying a hammer as triumphantly as Indian chiefs brandished their tomahawks after winning a battle against the white skins.

We set to work. It is a job worthy of a Swiss clockmaker. The point is to pry enormous hunks of ice away from the window frame without damaging the windowpanes. If we break the pane, all the work will be for naught—the chambermaid explains—because a new one cannot be installed until the summer, which is a half year away, at which point I will be long gone from here. "And until that time?" "Until that time we will suffer," she answers, shrugs her shoulders, and sighs. It takes a long time, but we chop out of the rectangular frame of ice a groove deep enough so that the window allows itself to be shut after a fashion. To cheer me up, the chambermaid also brings me a pot of hot water. The steam rising from it heats the room for a while.

I had the telephone number of a man whom I wanted to meet. I dialed. Something crackled hoarsely at the other end. "Genady Nikolayevich?" I asked. It crackled hoarsely, Yes. I was pleased; he was also pleased; he knew that I was coming; he was waiting. "Get on a bus and come," he said. I thought, But it's night, then right away realized that at this time of year it is always night here, and said: "I'm on my way."

I said, "I'm on my way," not realizing that I was on my way to my own near-death.

THE PROBLEM, the drama, and the horror of Vorkuta sprang from the conjunction of coal and bolshevism. Vorkuta lies in the Republic of Komi, beyond the Arctic Circle. Large deposits of coal were discovered here in the twenties. A coal basin rapidly came into being, built largely by the hands of convicts, victims of Stalin's terror. Dozens of camps sprang up. Before long Vorkuta, like Magadan, became a name/symbol, a name arousing fear and dread, a place of ghastly and often final deportation. Contributing to this was the nefariousness of the NKVD in the camps, the murderous labor in the coal mines, the hunger that decimated the prisoners, and the nightmarish, almost unbearable cold. Here was a cold that tormented defenseless, half-naked, chronically hungry people, exhausted to the limits of endurance, prey to the most sophisticated forms of torture.

Today Vorkuta is still a coal basin. This basin consists of thirteen mines, laid out in a large loop around the town. Next to each mine is a miners' settlement, and parts of these settlements are former camps, still inhabited. The settlements and the mines are linked by a ring road, along which two buses run in opposite directions. Because a car is still a rarity here, the bus is the sole means of transportation.

And so I took such a bus to visit Genady Nikolayevich, knowing only that I must ask for Komsomolski Posiolek, house number 6. After an hour, the driver pulled up to a place that was supposed to be the stop for Komsomolski Posiolek, opened the doors, and pointed in the direction in which I was to walk, but he pointed so indistinctly that it could have been interpreted as meaning that I was to walk in the direction of any one of the millions of stars making up the Milky Way. But the imprecision of his gesture was of no consequence anyway, for after getting off the bus I quickly lost all sense of where I was.

First, I became aware of standing in total darkness. Initially I could see nothing, but when my eyesight began to adjust to the gloom, I perceived that I was surrounded by large mountains of snow. Every few moments powerful gusts of wind struck the peaks of these mountains, lifting up toward the sky enormous clouds of white; it looked as if geysers of white lava were exploding again and again on these summits. Everywhere only mountains of snow, no lights, no people, and a cold so terrible that I was unable to take a deep breath without piercing my lungs with pain.

The instinct for self-preservation should have told me that the only way out of this situation was not to budge from the bus stop, to wait for the next bus, which would surely arrive sooner or later (although it was already after midnight). But the instinct failed me, and so, propelled by some fatal curiosity, or maybe by mere thoughtlessness, I set off in search of Komsomolski Posiolek and house number 6. The thoughtlessness lay in not realizing what it means to find myself at night beyond the Arctic Circle, in a snowy desert, in cold that gripped my face and choked me so I could not breathe.

I walked straight ahead not knowing where I was or what to do next. I would select one of the mountains as a goal, but before I managed to get close to it—floundering through deep snow, choking, and growing weaker—the mountain would vanish. It was the continuing gale, that pernicious polar purge, that moved the mountains of snow from one place to another, changed their location, their composition, changed the entire landscape. I had nothing on which to fix my eyes, nothing by which to orient myself.

At a certain point I saw before me a pit, and in the pit a wooden single-story house. I slid, partly rolled, down the ice-covered mountain slope—down into the pit. But it was a shop, locked and barred. The place seemed quiet and cozy, and I even wanted to stay here, when I remembered all the warnings of polar explorers, who said that such a warm niche, in a snowy desert, is a tomb.

So I pulled myself back up and set forth again. But where to? Which way should I walk? I could see less and less, for the snow was sticking to my face, covering my eyes. I knew only that I must keep walking, that if I were to lie down I would perish. And the fear, the animal fear of a man baited to death by some frightful force that he can neither recognize nor oppose and that—he senses—is pushing him, ever weaker and more powerless, into the white abyss.

Already at the end of my strength, but still rousing myself every now and again so as to take a few more steps, I spotted the silhouette of a woman struggling against the gale, bent, hunched over. I dragged myself up to her and gasped: "House number six." And again: "House number six"—with such hope in my voice as if my entire salvation lay concealed at this address.

"You are walking in the wrong direction, man," she said, shouting above the wind. "You are walking in the direction of the mine, and you should be walking . . . that way," and, like the bus driver, she indicated with her hand one of the millions of stars that compose the Milky Way.

"But I'm also going there," she added. "Come, I will show you where it is."

ONE ENTERS the house in which Genady Nikolayevich lives just as one enters all the other houses in this settlement. First one must spot, from a distance, the right mountain of snow; in its interior, at the bottom of it, stands the house. One must clamber up to the summit of the mountain. Below will be visible the roof of a one-story building. From the peak of the mountain to the door there are steps dug out in the wall of snow and ice. With great effort, fear, and the utmost caution one descends to the bottom. There, with the help of the residents, wrestling with the banks of snow, one forces the door open just enough to get inside.

The arrival of each new person is such an extraordinary occurrence here that all the residents of the house (there are several apartments in each) come out to greet him. Each one asks that you come visit, if only for a minute.

Genady Nikolayevich, a miner, just turned fifty and retired. Such an early retirement is one of the perks one receives for work in such dreadful, polar conditions. Although it is a rather dubious perk—only twenty percent of miners live to be fifty. A large, swollen thorax. When he talks, he is hoarse and whistles—he has advanced black lung. He arrived here to work when he was sixteen. A camp? No. There was hunger at home, in a kolkhoz near Kursk. Someone told him: If you want to eat, go to Vorkuta, there's apparently food there. And in fact he could buy bread, and sometimes even a piece of meat. Now it's worse, because the only thing one can get is reindeer meat, hard as a rock. "It's a waste of one's teeth," says Genady Nikolayevich, baring his teeth in a smile. Some are gold and some are silver. The color of teeth is important here; it indicates one's place in the social hierarchy. The higher the personage, the more gold teeth. The lower situated have silver teeth. The lowest—artificial teeth, resembling the natural ones in color and appearance. I am tempted to ask what kind of teeth Stalin had. But I know the answer: nobody knows; Stalin never smiled.

I ask him about the barracks that I saw along the way. Those are the old camps, he explains. But I saw lights in the windows! Yes, he says, because people live there. The camps were officially shut down in the sense that there are no sentences being passed out; there are no guards; there is no torture. Many of the former inmates left. But some of them stayed—they have nowhere else to go; they have no families, friends. Here at least there is a roof over their heads, and work, and buddies. Vorkuta is their only place on earth.

For Genady Nikolayevich, the border between the camp and the world beyond the camp is not very distinct. It is not the border between slavery and freedom, just a matter of degrees of captivity. It is said that he arrived in Vorkuta voluntarily. Voluntarily? He arrived because he was chased out of his home by the whip of hunger! It is also said that he could leave this place at any time. Leave? And go where? And where would he live? What would he live on? Genady Nikolayevich is rather inclined toward the opinion of Ivan Solonievich, one of the few inmates who in 1934 succeeded in escaping to the West: all of Russia is a camp.

HE KNOWS that I came here because there is a miners' strike. His mine has resumed work already, but the others are still striking. If I wish, we can go to the mine. We plunge into a sea of darkness, into snow, into a freezing gale. We hold each other so that the wind doesn't knock us off our feet or throw us in opposite directions.

In Vorkuta, for the first time, I experience cold not as a piercing, penetrating chill, but as sharp physical pain. My head feels like it is splitting from the cold. My legs and arms hurt so much I cannot touch them.

Every now and then human shadows loom in the dense and gusting blizzard, blurry silhouettes, huddled shapes bent in half.

"That's the second shift," Genady Nikolayevich, breathless, shouts in my ear. "The second shift is going home."

We are passing people who for months do not see the light of day. They walk to the mines in darkness; then, down below, in the underground, it is also dark, and when they return from work, they are surrounded by gloom. They are like the crew of a submarine—with only their watches, as well as their increasing fatigue, hunger, and drowsiness, to tell them about the passage of time.

The Komsomolskaya mine—ice-covered walls, ice-covered constructions, scanty lighting, a black, wet ooze beneath one's feet. Women distributing the carts, working some sort of levers, beams, supports. "Do you want to talk to them?" asks Genady Nikolayevich. But talk about what? Such cold, such gloom, such sadness. And the women—busy, heavy, tired, maybe something is worrying them, maybe something is hurting them? Let me show them some respect, let me offer them some relief if only by not asking anything of them, no additional effort, even one so insignificant as would be required to answer some routine question.

WE GO BACK to the house, to the room of Mikhail Mikhailovich, where he and another young miner, Yevgeny Alekseyevich, are already waiting for me. They will take me to the Vargashovska mine, where the strike continues and where a meeting is going to be held, but we still have a lot of time. Mikhail, slender, tall, dark haired, continually in motion, continually agitated, is furious that his mine (the one that I have just visited) called off the strike. The reason: the director promised that the food would be better. "This nation will never amount to anything," says the disheartened Mikhail. "Only one thing is important to these people—*pazrat'* [eat]. *Pazrat'!*" He works himself up into a fury and cries "*Pazrat'! Pazrat'! Pazrat'!*" so suggestively that one feels oneself beginning to salivate. "Hunger, that is what moves us, that is our only concern."

He clearly wants me to understand that he, Mikhail, is different, is cut from finer cloth. With pride he pulls out from a dresser drawer the thing he considers most precious—a beautiful, ornate 1900 edition of the Sergei Bible. He watches me to see if I have the capacity to be astonished and enraptured. Then he opens the enormous book at random and begins to read: "And gather yourself some wheat, barley, buckwheat beans, lentil, millet, and vetch, and put them in one dish and make yourself bread . . ."

He stops, startled and angry. Even the Bible talks about how to *pazrat'*!

"What else do you read?" I ask him later. He is reading Vauvenargues. He shows me a 1988 Leningrad edition in a green cloth cover. "There are many interesting things here," he says of the collection of aphorisms of the eighteenth-century French thinker. " 'Slavery so degrades people that they even fall in love with it.' How true that is!" He nods his head. "But in another place the Frenchman says the following: 'We do not gain much through cunning.' With this one cannot agree. Here you can attain everything through cunning."

Neighbors start to arrive; it becomes crowded in Mikhail Mikhailovich's room. Yevgeny Alekseyevich turns on the color television set on top of the dresser. The large, cherry-colored box growls as fiercely as if at any moment it were going to bristle. "Dynamo versus Spartak," Yevgeny Alekseyevich explains to me in low tones, for the others have already long known this.

I stare at the screen. There is no distinct image on it, only thousands of multicolored sparks flitting nervously across the convex glass surface. The set is broken, but if such an appliance breaks in Komsomolski Posiolek, there is no way to fix it.

I have never seen anything like it. A dozen or so people are staring intently at the screen, on which every now and then sparks explode, as they do in a fire when someone throws in some dry juniper. The spots, lines, grains of light, dance, flash, and pulsate like an ethereal and mobile Fata Morgana. What a richness of light forms this is, what an indefatigable and crazy pantomime. All these flashes seem mad and illogical, but I am wrong. A perfect order governs these wanderings of colorful particles, their ceaseless motion and rapid changes of direction. The left side of the screen suddenly starts to sparkle in red; redness vibrates there, undulates, rages, and suddenly a cry resounds in the room: "Goool! Dynamo scored!" "How do you know they've scored?" I ask Yevgeny Alekseyevich, irritated, especially since the sound on the set also isn't working. "What do you mean, how?" he replies, astonished. "Dynamo has red shirts!" After a time, at the other end of the screen there appears a great concentration of blue (Spartak's color), and the room (which is clearly rooting for the Dynamo team) groans: "They tied!" During the break the sparks calm down, and even became motionless, spread out uniformly across the whole surface of the screen, only to spring up again in new pirouettes and gambols. But it has grown late—and we have to go to the meeting.

GLIMMERING AGAINST the white, icy darkness are the lights of Vargashovska—the northernmost mine of the Vorkutaugol Company. One hundred and eighty kilometers from here is the Kara Sea (which is part of the Arctic Ocean).

I passed through the guardhouse dressed in a shabby quilted jacket and hid my face in a huge reindeer-skin hat with earmuffs. After that nobody asked me for a pass or identification card, and someone even courteously indicated where the meeting room was. It was the standard hall with a plaster Lenin, with banners proclaiming the victory of communism, and at the front a table covered with a red cloth.

The hall could seat about three hundred people. It was full. An atmosphere of curiosity, but also of a certain anxiety: experience has taught these people that provoking the authorities is no laughing matter. On the other hand, they've announced in Moscow that there is new thinking, so perhaps something will change.

From the start of the meeting—confusion, bedlam, disorder. Who is to chair the meeting? Who has the right to turn the floor over to others? Who has the right to decide that the first one to speak will be the tall one and that only later may the short one take his turn; or that the one from the back of the hall will be first, and only later this woman from the left side, who after all has been demanding to speak for a long time now? And in general—what is the goal of our meeting? We have assembled—now what? We have announced a strike—now what?

One is immediately struck by the lack of leadership. Every now and then someone tries to direct the gathering. "Kozlov! Let Kozlov preside!" Kozlov gathers his thoughts, squirms, hems and haws. He cannot decide who should speak first—this one, who is asking when they will install the windowpanes in warehouse number 5, or that one, who is shouting across the length of the hall, demanding to know when all of Lenin's volumes will be published. "Pietrov!" they call, dissatisfied with Kozlov. "Give us Pietrov!" But Pietrov also hems and haws. Pietrov also sweats; he too doesn't know what to do with the aggressive assembly.

But a solution presents itself in the end. And, of course, it is the familiar solution. Of course—the management shows up. Several directors enter the hall, on whose walls the strikers have managed to put up two slogans: "Down with the bureaucracy!" and "Down with the Partocracy!" (exactly like that—a small *b*, but a large *P*). Consternation among the strikers, but not among the directors. The directors are smiling ironically, as if to say, Exactly, down, down with us, but without us you would be unable to take a single step!

And what more is there to say—the directors are right. Nowhere can you see so clearly the division of this society into the ruling class and the ruled as you can here. This division, moreover, goes back at least to the time of Peter the Great. Only the names of the classes have changed, but the ratios of dependence, asymmetry, and bondage between them remain the same. How could it be that such an apparently simple thing as the knowledge about how to organize and conduct a meeting has already been monopolized by the ruling class. And indeed, after entering the hall, the director general stands behind the table with the same physical ease and imperious assurance with which Richard Strauss or Arturo Toscanini stood behind the conductor's lectern.

The hall grows quiet.

"Who wants to speak?" the director asks calmly. Several raise their hands. The director establishes the order in which they will do so and castigates and forces back into his seat with one glance someone who tries to jump ahead of the others. But first of all, he himself takes the floor.

"The meeting has been going on for five hours already," he says. "What have you resolved?"

Voices from the hall: "Well, nothing."

"Ah, you see," the director says, as if distressed, "you see—nothing. I, on the other hand, have taken care of the matter of the mine. Yes, I have taken care of it! I came back from Moscow yesterday." (Here, saying that one was in Moscow immediately raises one several notches in the hierarchy.)

He pauses, stares at the hall, grown suddenly still, and, after a moment, continues with pathos: "We, we alone, without any mediation from Moscow, will be exporting our coal to England and America! We, straight from Vargashovska!"

Animation in the hall, excitement, joy. What does this mean—to America? It means—dollars! And what does that mean—dollars? It means everything, literally everything!

I can see that these poor, frozen people, people who often do not see the light of day for weeks at a time, are being fooled by this man who yesterday returned from Moscow, are being fooled and hoaxed. I can see it, but there is nothing I can do about it; I cannot stand up and cry: People, don't believe him! I cannot, if only so as not to deprive them of that shred of comfort that they derive from the thought that Vargashovska will be exporting coal to England and America.

AFTER THE VOTE to end the strike, Mikhail drove me in a dilapidated but swift Moskvich to town, to the hotel. It is thirty kilometers along a road covered with thick, smooth ice. Mikhail was tearing along at one hundred kilometers per hour. We were driving and living at the mercy of that first stone that at any moment could jut out in front of us. On this road, at this speed, a stone would have meant death. Staring straight ahead, I thought: Aha, so this is what your last image of the world is like—this darkness, these headlights, and, rising before you, this shining blade of icy road, which in a moment will cut you up into pieces.

I CAME to Vorkuta to see the strike, but I also came on a pilgrimage. For Vorkuta is a place of martyrdom; it is a holy place. In the camps of Vorkuta hundreds of thousands of people died. How many exactly? This no one can measure. The first inmates were brought here in 1932, the last released in 1959. The greatest number of people died during the construction of the railroad line, along which today coal is shipped to Arkhangel'sk, Murmansk, and Petersburg. It was during its construction that one of the officers of the NKVD said: "There aren't enough railroad ties? No matter! You will serve as the railroad ties!"

And that is really how it was. It is a railroad line along which, for hundreds of kilometers, stretches a cemetery, today invisible to the naked eye. Only those who walk over the tundra that abuts the embankment (this is possible only two or three months of the year, when there is no snow) will discover in it, here and there, rotten pickets with little wooden boards nailed to them. If on a board they make out, for example, the inscription A 81, it means that in this place a thousand people are buried. This code was used by the camp bookkeepers, who kept careful accounts of the number of killed and deceased in order to reduce proportionately the number of bread rations distributed.

A man did not die here from one particular weapon, but was the victim of an entire edifice of cruelty, constructed and overseen by the NKVD.

Here, in the north, the greatest enemy of the condemned man was (besides the NKVD) the cold:

> Terrible, inhuman, penalizing labor. In the glare of blazing fires, amid the polar night, glinted hundreds, thousands of shovels, tossing the snow that was to be swept up by a bulldozer further away from the tracks. So long as one had enough good sense and strength to remain in motion the entire time, there was a chance of surviving, enduring. But each day, around the fires, a dozen or so huddled human beings gathered, wrapped in every rag they owned. They sat motionless, in a circle around the warmth flowing from the merrily crackling wood chips. They were already living corpses. Nothing could save the health or lives of these people. Warmed from one side by the heat of the fire, grilled by the biting smoke of the burning branches, they were exposed on the other side to the effects of a cold measuring tens of degrees below

> freezing. No organism could endure such a gradient of temperature occurring within it. Blood warmed in the veins of the face, hands, chest, and stomach was pumped by a weakened heart into a body reduced nearly to a state of hibernation. Something was happening inside the man which he himself could not explain, he was overwhelmed with drowsiness and nausea, overcome by an ever greater chill. He therefore moved still closer to the fire, crawled practically inside it. After several hours of sitting this way, there were only corpses by the fire, or men in final agony. Nothing could budge these people from the fire. Neither threats of force, beatings, nor attempts to stir the stiffening muscles and cooling blood—nothing helped. After they were pulled away forcibly, they fell like logs into the snow and lay motionless. Not a day passed without a dozen or so stiffened corpses being carried into the camp on stretchers. (Marian Mark Bilewicz, *I Escaped the Dark*, 1989)

I walk around dark, cold, and snow-covered Vorkuta. At the end of the main street one can see oblong, flat buildings on the horizon—those are the barracks of the old camps. And these two aged women at the bus stop? Which one of them was a camp inmate, and which one was her overseer? Age and poverty equalize them for now; soon the frozen earth will reconcile them finally and forever. I wade through snowdrifts, passing identical-looking streets and houses, no longer knowing very well where I am. The whole time I have before my eyes the vision of Nikolai Fiodorov.

Fiodorov was a philosopher, a visionary; many Russians consider him a saint. He owned nothing his whole life. Not even a coat in the cold Russian climate. He was a librarian in Moscow. He lived in a little room, slept on a hard chest, placed books for pillows under his head. He lived from 1828 until 1903. He walked everywhere. He died because there was a great frost and someone convinced him that perhaps he should after all put on a sheepskin coat and go in a sleigh. The next day he developed pneumonia and died. Fiodorov believed that fame and popularity are signs of shamelessness and published his texts under a pseudonym, but most frequently he didn't publish them at all. After the master's death, his two students collected Fiodorov's works and published them in a volume entitled *The Philosophy of the Common Cause*, in a printing of 480 copies, which they distributed free of charge.

Convinced of the eternity of life, Fiodorov believed that the most important element of Christian faith was the idea of resurrection. Excited by this thought, he devoted himself to deliberations about how to resuscitate all dead people. Everyone who ever died, in the whole world.

But what would the return of the dead of Vorkuta look like? Would there suddenly appear on the streets of the town columns of wretches driven on by guards? Starved human shadows covered with rags? A procession of skeletons? Nikolai Fiodorov dreamed of restoring them all to life. But—to what life?

On one of the streets I noticed a wooden booth. A swarthy Azerbaijani was selling the only flowers one could buy here—red carnations. "Pick out for me," I said, "the prettiest ones you have." He selected a dozen carnations and wrapped them carefully in newspaper. I wanted to place them somewhere, but I didn't know where. I thought, I'll stick them into some snowdrift, but there were people everywhere and I felt that doing so would be awkward. I walked farther, but on the next street, the same thing: many people. Meanwhile the flowers were starting to freeze and stiffen. I wanted to find an empty courtyard, but everywhere children were playing. I worried that they would find the carnations and take them. I roamed farther along the streets and alleys. I could feel between my fingers the flowers were becoming stiff and brittle like glass. So I went beyond the town limits, and there, calmly, I placed the flowers amid the snowdrifts.

# Tomorrow, the Revolt of the Bashkirs

FROM VORKUTA I returned to Moscow, to warm myself a bit, but also to find out what new winds were blowing at the summits of power.

Above all—at the summits of imperial power.

For in such a state as the former USSR (today, CIS, tomorrow . . . ?) there exists a certain class of people whose calling is to think exclusively on an imperial scale, and even more—on a global one. One cannot ask them questions like "What's happening in Vorkuta?" for they are utterly unable to answer them. They will even be surprised: And what is the significance of it? The Imperium will not fall because of anything that is happening there!

They exist for only one reason—to ensure the durability and development of the Imperium, irrespective of whatever it chooses to call itself. (And even if it should disintegrate, their task will be to set it back on its feet as soon as possible.)

In small and medium-sized countries there is no equivalent of this class of which we speak here. In such countries, the elite are busy with their own internal affairs, their local intrigues, their own closed backyard. But in the Imperium, the ruling class (and often the common people as well) are preoccupied with the imperial scale of thinking, and, even more, the global scale, the scale of large numbers, large spaces, of continents and oceans, of geographic meridians and parallels, of the atmosphere and the stratosphere, why, of the cosmos.

In Western Europe they were surprised to see on television that poor old women in Moscow abandoned the breadlines they had been standing in, gave up buying bread, to march down the street shouting the slogan "We will not give back the Kuril Islands!"

But why be surprised? The Kuril Islands are a part of the Imperium, and the Imperium was built at the cost of the feeding and clothing of these women, at the cost of their leaking shoes and cold apartments, and, what is most sad, at the cost of the blood and lives of their husbands and sons. And so they should give this back now? Never. Never ever.

Between the Russian and his Imperium a strong and vital symbiosis exists; the fortunes of the superpower truly and deeply move him. Even today.

THERE ARE two kinds of global maps printed in the world.

One type is disseminated by the National Geographic Society in America, and on it, in the middle, in the central spot, lies the American continent, surrounded by two oceans—the Atlantic and the Pacific. The former Soviet Union is cut in half and placed discreetly at both ends of the map so that it won't frighten American children with its immense bulk. The Institute of Geography in Moscow prints an entirely different map. On it, in the middle, in the central spot, lies the former Soviet Union, which is so big that it overwhelms us with its expanse; America, on the other hand, is cut in half and placed discreetly at both ends so that the Russian child will not think: My God! How large this America is!

These two maps have been shaping two different visions of the world for generations.

In the course of my wanderings over the territories of the

Imperium my attention was caught by, among other things, the fact that even in forsaken and tumbledown little towns, even in practically empty bookshops, there was for sale, as a rule, a large map of this country on which the rest of the world appeared to be almost in the background, in the margins, in shadow.

This map is for Russians a kind of visual recompense, a peculiar emotional sublimation, and also an object of unconcealed pride.

It also serves to explain and justify all shortages, mistakes, poverty, and marasmus. It is too big a country to be reformed! explain the opponents of reforms. It is too big a country to be cleaned up! janitors from Brest to Vladivostok throw up their hands. It is too big a country for goods to be delivered everywhere, grumble saleswomen in empty shops.

A great size, which explains and absolves everything. Sure, if we were a small country like Switzerland, everything here would run like clockwork, too! Look how tiny Holland is; it's no trick to achieve prosperity in a state that one can barely see on a map! Just try to give everyone here what they want—here you'll find that's impossible!

BUT BEFORE I had the time to look around in Moscow, get some information, have several important and instructive conversations, the news exploded that a large city of a million inhabitants, situated between the Volga River and the Ural Mountains—Ufa—had been poisoned. It wasn't just effluvia, combustion gases, and so forth, for these are commonplace; the city had been poisoned severely, dangerously, mortally.

"A new Chernobyl!" commented a friend who relayed the news to me.

"I'm going there," I replied. "If I can get a seat, I'm flying tomorrow."

Everyone in Moscow who was boarding the plane to Ufa was loaded with bottles, cans, canisters of water. For Ufa had been poisoned by phenol. Anyone who drinks the local water, my friend told me, will get sick or die.

Ufa is the capital of the Bashkir Republic, an autonomous

republic at the western foot of the Urals. To the south stretches Kazakhstan, to the east Siberia, and to the west Tatarstan. Nature was once beautiful here, mountains covered with forests, six hundred rivers and streams, thousands of lakes. Hordes of all kinds of quadrupeds, clouds of bustling birds, swarms of industrious bees. Until the advent of chemicals. Bashkiria was transformed into a chemical practice range, into the center of the chemical industry of the former USSR. Smoke obscured the sky; dust hung in the air; phenol flowed down the rivers. Phenol, as I read in the encyclopedia, is a brown, extremely poisonous acid necessary for the production of explosives, plastics, dyes, tannins, and a hundred other things. Because chemical plants are shoddily built here and because the proper filters and cleaners are regarded as the fabrications and whims of ecological purists, the phenol was continuously leaking into the rivers, but it was leaking quietly, so that the poisoning of people could be spread out over time, so that the pestilence would not suddenly fell the entire city.

But that is precisely what had happened now. Turning on their faucets, people saw a rust-colored, opaque substance dripping from them and smelled their apartments filling up with an atrocious odor. Phenol! Phenol! It spread from house to house, from street to street.

Still, there was no visible panic. People here accept all misfortunes, even those caused by the soullessness and stupidity of those in power, as the excesses of an omnipotent and capricious nature, on the order of floods, earthquakes, or exceptionally cold winters. The thoughtlessness or brutality of the authorities is just one of the cataclysms that nature so liberally dispenses. One must understand this; one must resign oneself to it.

IN THE STREETS, in the squares, stood kilometer-long lines. These were strange lines, for they were not fastened at one end to any one store or institution. People were waiting in expectation of the arrival of cisterns, which were supposed to bring water. From where this water was to come, when, and how much of it, no one knew.

The lines were quiet and orderly. Pregnant women stood at

the front. A certain hierarchy obtained among them—priority was given to those whose bulging stomachs were the most pronounced. The next sector consisted of women with small children. Behind them stood women who were alone. (Among them the elderly had priority.) After that the male section began—without any marked divisions or preferences.

When the cistern arrived, everyone could take as much water as he wanted. But for how long could it last? A day? Two? And the question to which no one had the answer—what next? In this country, the press, radio, and television abound in stories that begin and have no end. Battles erupt in Fergana: there are dead and wounded; the city is in flames. But the following day Fergana disappears from the field of vision—one cannot find out what is going on there. A strike in Kuzbas! Quite an event, for this is a huge coal basin. The strike erupted two years ago. What happened after that? Has it ended? Is it still going on?

ROAMING AROUND the streets of Ufa, I happened upon a museum. I knew that I was in the land of the Bashkirs, but what does this mean today—to be a Bashkir? Dr. Rim Yanguzin is showing me what he had recently found in the nearby mountains, in the ruins of old settlements, along the riverbanks. Here is a Bashkir sword, here a Bashkir necklace, and that is a clay jug for water and milk. And a boat, on which Bashkirs sailed in the seventeenth century, and an ornate harness, which their horses wore. I can also inspect a wooden plow with an iron blade, a rotting beehive, and some old snares for wild game.

All these things were made by Bashkirs, says Dr. Yanguzin, with pride resounding in his voice. Later we sit in his office, which is full of Bashkir fabrics (each tribe, and there were thirty-one of them, had its own design), Bashkir coins and rings, swords and sickles. Through the window one can see the street, the line for water, and in the background, far away, the tall chimneys of factories. And listening to Dr. Yanguzin, who is speaking with emotion about the lost paradise of Bashkiria, I can already see clearly that the reality of this city has two levels, increasingly in conflict.

On one level is chemistry, synthetic and organic, phenol and explosives. The masters of this world are Russians, and it is governed by a ministry in Moscow.

The second level is occupied by the nascent (or, more precisely, renascent) national consciousness of the Bashkirs.

A nationalistic revolution is sweeping the world today. We will sail into the twenty-first century upon its waves. But already at this moment its echoes are reaching Bashkiria and are stirring sensitive and ambitious hearts there.

There are around a million Bashkirs. What sort of place are they to occupy, what sort of posture are they to adopt in the contemporary world? Are they to acknowledge that after three hundred years of Russification, they are no longer Bashkirs? That is impossible! No amount of terror, of persecution and camps, could extirpate from the Bashkirs their Bashkirianness. Russification is itself in retreat, increasingly fewer little Bashkirs want to learn Russian. So then what, reinvigorate one's distinctness, one's nationalist sentiment? But very serious consequences will result from this! For if such a liberated, thinking Bashkir, cognizant of his national interest, takes a look around, what will he see, what will he find?

He will find first of all that only half of the territories of historic Bashkiria, which, in his opinion, stretched from the Volga to the Urals, are within the borders of the present autonomous republic. Part of the old Bashkiria belongs today to Kazakhstan, part to Tatarstan, and part to the Russian Federation (of which even the present Bashkir Republic is a part). If a cognizant Bashkir utters all this out loud, he will immediately have three enemies—Tatars, Kazakhs, and Russians. Nationalism cannot exist in a conflict-free condition; it cannot exist as a thing devoid of grudges and claims. Wherever the nationalism of one group rears its head, immediately, as if from beneath the ground, this group's enemies will spring up.

At the same time, our cognizant Bashkir, as he takes his look around, will find that his beautiful green country has been transformed into an enormous factory floor whose effluvia are poisoning the air. Reflecting upon this turn of events, he will remember that nobody asked him whether he agreed to have his country transformed into a chemical factory. Moreover—the Bashkir will realize that he derives no benefits from this gigantic and ever-so-harmful chemical production, for the Imperium pays nothing to its internal colonies. Ah, there it is—for he will quickly realize the colonial position of his Bashkiria, the fact that the Agrochima and Chimstroy so deeply entrenched here remind him a little of the Union Minière in Katanga (present-day Shaba, in Zaire) or Miferma in Mauritania.

Nevertheless, having arrived at these subversive and revolutionary conclusions, what is the Bashkir to do then? Like Gulliver, he awakens only to discover that he is so tightly entangled in a thousand threads that he cannot execute a single motion. What should he do? Demand the closing down of the factories? But nearly half of the chemical production of the entire Imperium is located here! Get on a horse and move to the mountains? And what would he do there, how would he live?

The consciousness of the cognizant Bashkir is divided, rife with contradictions. The thirst for independence is growing in him, and he doesn't see the way to quench it. He is certain that he is sitting on a sack of gold but is a pauper. Even on the large maps of the Imperium, his small, private motherland is melted into, lost in, the great expanses. The Bashkir wants to recover it again, define its borders, enclose it within a tall fence. The mood prevailing among the other smaller nations of the Imperium has also been communicated to him—the drive above all to detach oneself, to close oneself off behind another great wall of China, as if the breath of any other tribe would poison the air like phenol. For in his awakened ambitions the Bashkir is not alone. The Imperium today resembles the surface of a lake on whose bottom a volcano is coming to life. On the calm, smooth surface, bubbles suddenly appear. With time there are more and more of them. Here and there the water begins to boil. In the depths one can hear muffled rumblings.

There are today dozens of small nations and tribes like the Bashkirs in the Imperium. And they are all more and more obstinately and boldly thinking about how to partake of the feast of the gods. They reflect upon this in moments of optimism. But then comes the time of despair, the hopeless feeling of impotence and long periods of collapse.

RIM AHMEDOV. He gave me his book *A Word about Rivers, Lakes, and Grasses*, published in 1990 in Ufa. People in the former Soviet Union had resolved the problem of "the system and I" in various ways. Some supported the authorities, others were in the opposition, and many simply sought some kind of sanctuary for themselves—the further away from politics, the better (like the couple of married zoologists in the former Leningrad who chose as their subject of specialization the mimicry of monkeys).

Seemingly, but only seemingly, nature was such a subject/sanctuary. During Stalin's lifetime, the master descriptive naturalist was Mikhail Prishvin. During this time, when there was still no television or color photography, Prishvin's prose had no equal and glistened with all the colors of an autumnal forest, of pebbles at the bottom of a stream, of the crowns of mushrooms and the feathers of birds. I have always thought that these descriptions of dewdrops and of the flower of bird cherry were a kind of escape, a peaceful retreat. I said as much to the Russian poet Gala Kornilova. "But not at all!" she protested. "This was opposition writing! The Kremlin wanted to destroy our language, and Prishvin's language was rich, magnificent. They wanted everything to be without character, without distinction, gray, and in his writing Russia is so colorful, gorgeous, unique! We read Prishvin during those years so as not to forget our real language, for it was being replaced by newspeak."

And there is something similar in the prose of Rim Ahmedov. Rim does not write about the achievements of the Russian government—about the chemical industry, about plastic conductors, about faucets and tannins. Rim doesn't notice this at all. On the contrary, in opposition to the destroyers of his Bashkiria, he describes the natural beauty that still survives—the bream in the Sutoloka River, the trees on the Nurtau Mountain, the country road lined with flowers leading to the Janta-Turmush farm. He travels by boat or wanders around his country with a tent and dog.

Grasses are his favorite plant. Ahmedov is a herbalist; he collects grasses, dries them, mixes them, adds something or other to them, and makes medicines. He tells me that any single medicine meant to treat everyone is bad and cannot be efficacious. Each medicine must be prepared individually, after a conversation with the sick person. Such a conversation is necessary so that one can select just the right type of grass to awaken in that particular individual the strength to combat the disease. Without this, healing is impossible.

The creature that Ahmedov best remembers from his childhood is a small golden-green beetle—*Cryptocephalus sericeus*. Rim found it on the leaf of dead nettle—dead meaning the kind that does not sting.

And although he is now sixty years old, he has never been able to find such a beetle again.

# Russian Mystery Play

UFA—IT is the beginning of my Ural-Siberian journey.

The route: Moscow-Ufa-Sverdlovsk-Irkutsk-Yakutsk-Magadan-Norilsk-Moscow. All together (including impromptu local expeditions) around twenty thousand kilometers across a snowy desert. At this time of year (it is April), the local rivers are nothing more than wedges of ice stretching for hundreds of kilometers. And only from time to time does one find cities—like oases in the Gobi or the Sahara—closed in on themselves, living their own life, as though not bound, not connected, to anything.

The world is already accustomed to the fact that the Caucasus is burning, that bloody disorders are erupting continually in the Asiatic republics (Tajikistan, Uzbekistan, and so on), that battles are being waged on both sides of the Dniester. All these collisions, rebellions, and wars are on the distant peripheries of the former USSR; they are taking place, in a sense, outside of Russia, beyond its body.

But the awakening of the national consciousness of the Bashkirs reveals to us a new kind of conflict gathering strength in the

Imperium. All one has to do is look at the map: the Bashkir Republic, with its inhabitants standing in lines for a glass of water to drink, with Dr. Yanguzin and his collection of old swords, with Rim Ahmedov, who can cure you with a mixture of local grasses—this republic lies within the Russian Federation. And now the Bashkirs (and, together with them, other non-Russian people living within the Russian state) are beginning to raise their voice, call for rights, demand independence.

In short, following the disintegration of the USSR, we are now facing the prospect of the disintegration of the Russian Federation, or, to put it differently; after the first phase of decolonization (that of the former Soviet Union) the second phase begins—the decolonization of the Russian Federation.

Several dozen non-Russian nations and tribes live today in the territory of this federation, and they are demonstrating more and more explicitly their opposition to Moscow and stressing more and more emphatically the separateness of their interests. This movement of national emancipation is spreading with growing strength and the speed of an avalanche among the Bashkirs and Buryats, Chechen and Ingush, Chuvash and Koryak, Tatars and Mordovians, Yakuts and Tuvinians.

And it would appear irresistible, if only because these nations and tribes—for centuries persecuted, oppressed, and Russified—are at present rapidly expanding, whereas the percentage of native Russians among the inhabitants of the federation has been falling for years. Russians have a very low birthrate, and one can sense, increasingly, their resultant anxiety, uncertainty, and frustration.

IN IRKUTSK I spot a poster advertising a theatrical production entitled *A Word about Russia*.

I buy a ticket and go.

The show takes place in a church that was formerly called the Museum of Atheism.

ABOUT THE Orthodox churches:

Paradoxically, the best preserved are the ones that the Bolsheviks turned into centers for the struggle against religion—against the Orthodox rite, against Orthodox priests, against monasteries, against the churches themselves. These museums of atheism became the seats of permanent exhibits that explained that religion is the opiate of the people. Drawings and signs depicted Adam and Eve as characters from fairy tales, priests burning women at the stake, popes with lovers, and homosexuals congregating in monasteries. There were thousands of these exhibitions across the country, all organized, moreover, according to one design ratified at the highest level, and if one traveled to the Imperium in the old days, visiting a museum of atheism was an ironclad, obligatory point of the program.

After visiting such a museum, foreigners sometimes expressed shock and indignation that a place consecrated to the worship of God had been transformed into the headquarters of the struggle against God. But they were wrong to feel that way! Let us assume that a certain church was assigned a role in the struggle against God, that is, that it was turned into a museum of atheism. The wives of local dignitaries would then be employed there, and so they would see to it for the sake of their warmth that there were panes of glass in the windows, the doors shut properly, the little stove was lit. It would also be relatively clean inside—the walls would be whitewashed from time to time, the floor occasionally swept. The fate of churches that were not ordered to struggle against God was entirely different. They were transformed into stables, cow barns, into fuel storerooms, into warehouses. A motorcycle-repair shop was set up in the beautiful Franciscan church in Niesterov, near Lvov. Neither it nor the thousands of churches in which for years oil and artificial fertilizers were kept can be saved. Nor can those churches be saved that fifty, sixty, years ago were robbed, devastated, closed, exposed to the destructive effects of the cold, rain, and wind, abandoned to rats and birds. Perhaps the synagogue in Drohobych can be saved—it has a strong roof and serves as a furniture warehouse, so no chemicals are ruining it. The majority of salvageable churches today are precisely yesterday's museums of atheism (in recent years frequently renamed "museums of icons").

About icons:

That same wild and primal, and later premeditated and methodical, barbarism that ruined and demolished the churches also destroyed the icon.

How many icons fell victim to it?

From October 1917 until this decade, twenty, thirty, million icons were destroyed in Russia!

This figure is cited by the Russian art historian A. Kuzniecov in the monthly *Moskva* (January 1990). Kuzniecov lists the destructive uses icons were put to:

In the army—for target practice
In the mines—as pavement for tunnels flooded with water
In the marketplace—as raw material for building potato crates
In kitchens—as boards for chopping meat and vegetables
In apartments—as fuel for stoves in winter

The author adds that massive piles of icons were also simply set afire or driven out to country and city garbage dumps.

The church in Irkutsk (the one that was saved, the one that was not destroyed so that a Party-committee building could be built on its foundations) has high, whitewashed walls against which icons glow, their aged varnish shining. From these dark paintings, framed in silver friezes and frames, gaze at us the faces of saints, evangelists, apostles, and mystics, who in a moment, when the light dims, will draw back into their secretive and enigmatic darkness.

Benches have been arranged in the nave. There are about two hundred spectators sitting on them—all the places are occupied. People are bundled in their coats, they are cold; this is Irkutsk, eastern Siberia.

Onto the stage, which was set up in the chancel, enter seven tall young men. They are dressed in old-Russian linen shirts, girdled with a ribbon, and ballooning linen pants stuffed into high leather boots. They wear their hair in the old Slavic fashion, with bangs, in a pageboy, and have long beards. Three of them are holding clarions like those of the trumpeters of Prince Vladimir's brigade, and every now and then one of them beats a drumroll. At the head of this battle-ready troupe stands the Commander, the Standard Bearer, the Ideologue. He delivers a sort of hymn to Russia, which in places turns into a bold and lofty historical lecture and elsewhere into a fervid anthem interrupted by a long litany to Russia. It is loudly seconded by his fellow old-Russian warriors and ends with the roar of clarions and an explosion of drumbeats.

"Russia!" cry the warriors, "you were always great and holy! Glory unto you, Russia!" (Clarions, drum, the warriors make the sign of the cross, bow to the ground.)

"Yes," says the Standard Bearer, "Russia was powerful, and the Russian nation led the world!"

"The whole world!" cry the warriors (clarions, drum, the sign of the cross, bowing). "Kings from Europe and from all the continents came to genuflect before our czars, brought them gifts of gold, silver, and precious stones!" (Bowing, drum.)

"But Russia's greatness awakened the hatred of its enemies. Russia's enemies had long been lying in wait for her ruin, desiring her extermination!"

The Standard Bearer falls silent and looks around the audience. We are all sitting motionless, staring and raptly listening. And suddenly, in this churchlike, profound silence, rising up on his toes, as if to take off in flight, and stretching his body, he shouts: "The October Revolution!"

He shouts in such a way that I feel a cold shiver run down my spine.

"The October Revolution was an international conspiracy against the Russian nation!" And after a moment: "The October Revolution was supposed to wipe Russia off the face of the earth!"

"Russia, they wanted to put you to death!" the warriors chime in (clarions, drum, bowing).

"Everyone colluded," says the Ideologue, "everyone took part in the plot, Latvians, Jews, Poles, Germans, Ukrainians, the English, the Spanish, everyone wanted the ruin of the Russian nation! Three forces," he rounds out the thought, "stood at the head of this conspiracy—imperialism, bolshevism, and Zionism. These were devils which brewed up seventy-three years of hell for us!"

"Begone, begone, Satans, save yourself, Russia, save yourself!" cry the warriors, crossing themselves, blowing on the clarions, and banging on the drum.

Jews enrage the Ideologue the most.

"The Jews," he calls out in a tone of the greatest contempt and outrage, "want to appropriate the Holocaust. But after all, the true holocaust was perpetrated against the Russian nation!"

He waits until the warriors finish singing a song about the strength and immortality of the Russian land, then presents the following argument.

"In 1914," he says, "there were 150 million Russians in the world. As our scholars have calculated, if these Russians had lived and multiplied normally, there would be more than three hundred million of them today. But how many of us are there in reality?" he asks, addressing the auditorium, and immediately answers: "There are only one hundred and fifty million of us. So I ask, where are the other one hundred and fifty million Russians, one hundred and fifty million of our brothers and sisters? They died, were murdered, shot, tortured to death, or were never even born, because their young parents got a bullet in the head before they could see their offspring.

"I want to say something more. I ask you, if they want to destroy a nation, who do they always strike at first? They strike at the best, at the most talented, at the wisest. So it was in Russia. The best half of our nation perished. That is the real holocaust. The imperialists, Bolsheviks, and Zionists, that internationale of torturers and Satans, could not bear the fact that the Russians were the greatest white nation in the world! The greatest!"

The clarions blare and the drum thunders.

I look around at the people. They sit engrossed, listening, but their faces express nothing, no emotions, no feelings. They say nothing, burrowed in their coats, wrapped in shawls and scarves; they do not move. Around us, on the white walls, the icons glow darkly, hung in rows, as seven young Russians in the chancel sing a song about the ruin of their nation.

When the singing comes to an end, the Standard Bearer resumes: "The world should humble itself and ask Russia for forgiveness for having dealt her such a terrible blow, for having stabbed her with the October Revolution as with a poisoned sword."

"Let the nations ask Russia for forgiveness!" the warriors cry out.

"The world must cleanse itself of this guilt, of this sin it has committed against Russia!"

My God, I think, you have befuddled his mind.

I am freezing, but I don't want to leave, I am waiting to see what will happen next.

"The Russian people immediately came out against the Bolsheviks," says the Ideologue. "Uprisings and mutinies were breaking out everywhere, in each county, in each province. Let me read to you what one soldier who was fighting against Russian peasants in the Tambov province wrote: 'I have taken part in many battles against Germans,' this soldier writes, 'but I never saw anything like this. The machine gun is mowing people down in rows, and they keep coming, as if they didn't see anything, they are walking over corpses, they are walking over the wounded, they are unstoppable, terrifying eyes, mothers are holding children in front of themselves, they are calling, Holy Mother, Intercessor, save us, have pity on us, we are all dying in your defense. There was no longer any fear in them.' "

The Standard Bearer puts away the card with the quote. There is still silence everywhere.

"The Bolshevik army," he says in a calm voice, "murdered during communism's martial years more than ten million Russian peasants. Another ten million then died of hunger. Today they are trying to blame everything on Stalin. But Stalin wasn't yet in power. In point of fact it was Mr. Bronstein and Mr. Dzierzynski who were ruling. Neither of them was a Russian.

"The conspiracy continues!" the Standard Bearer cries out, and points at the enormous doors of the church, as if at any moment the international conspirators were going to burst in and throw us in jail.

"The conspiracy continues," he repeats, "and the nation perishes."

A long, mournful beating of the drum.

Silence, total silence in the audience.

Again the Ideologue speaks, this time recounting in a matter-of-fact tone how Russians in the Imperium have the worst life of anyone. "If the average life expectancy in Lithuania is seventy-two and a half years, in Russia it is sixty-eight. The Lithuanian! The Lithuanian lives five years longer than the Russian!" He does not care merely that someone is living longer than someone else. The point is that an insignificant Lithuanian is living longer than a great Russian!

He is mainly concerned that Russia, native Russia, is becoming depopulated. In the five most Russian districts of the Imperium (Pskov, Tula, Kalinin, Tambov, Ivanovo), the population is progressively diminishing. The old Russia is emptying out. Most deserted is the countryside. Recently, the population of the countryside has been decreasing by ten percent annually. There are many abandoned villages. Drive in the summer; you may see in one place only some old women sunning themselves on an earthen bench outside a cottage. There are no men, not even old ones. You don't see a horse; you don't see a hen; you don't see any livestock at all. And in the winter, you won't even see those old women. In the winter, it's as if a plague has passed through.

"What's the solution?" he asks, staring so intently at the auditorium that one might assume he had driven the several thousand kilometers from Moscow to Irkutsk in the hope that here precisely he would find the answer to the questions tormenting him. But we sit in silence. Several men shift slightly in their seats, as if they feel obligated to speak up and give some salutary advice, but after a moment they too grow still.

"Russia is wise and eternal," the Standard Bearer responds to our perplexed and ineffectual silence. "Russia will find a solution, Russia will be saved."

He has a program for, as he puts it, the "reanimation of

Russia." It essentially comes down to transplanting Russians to Russia. So that they might return, as he puts it, to "the deserted cradle of Russia." This is difficult, not only because Russians are trying to leave Russia, not return to it, but also on account of the dimensions and expense of such an operation: twenty-four million Russians live outside the borders of the Russian Federation.

"Return, return to the womb of Mother Russia!" the warriors cry out, crossing themselves and bowing down to the ground. But the nave does not react in any positive way.

During the course of this great campaign of returning the Russians to Russia, one will have to be careful that some Uzbeks, Turkomans, or Georgians do not use the occasion to move here themselves.

"Russia for Russians!" cries out the Standard Bearer (clarions, drum, the cross).

It is an important but problematic declaration. The problem is that the consciousness of the contemporary Russian is torn by an irreconcilable contradiction. It is the contradiction between the criterion of blood and the criterion of land. What should one strive for? According to the criterion of blood, the point is to maintain the ethnic purity of the Russian nation. But such an ethnically pure Russia is only part of today's Imperium. And what about the rest? According to the criterion of land, the point is to maintain the full extent of the Imperium. But then there can be no hope of maintaining the ethnic purity of the Russians.

Contradictions, contradictions.

The Standard Bearer understands this, and having let fly the slogan "Russia for Russians," he immediately backs down from it.

"Russia," he calls, "must remain a great world power! They want us to become like the Indians on an American reservation. They are trying to make us drunk, they are trying to poison us. But we will not become Indians. We will not be a banana republic!" (Clarions, much drum beating.)

He threatens us with his fist. "Do not dance to the music of the West! Do not hang bottles of Coca-Cola around your necks!" (The drum alone.)

"Our objective is the salvation of the nation and the state," he says emphatically, resolutely, forcefully. "Our objective is: one state, one territory, one spirit, one Russia!" (Many clarion calls, much drum beating.)

"Very soon," he adds with hope, but also with conviction in his voice, "the nation will have had enough of this pluralistic chaos, of this whole messy masquerade, and will come to understand that only the czar can bring salvation!"

Yet another litany to Russia begins.

"Russia, forgive us our sins," says the Standard Bearer, "the sin of faithlessness, the sin of weakness, the sin of losing sight of the goal. We vow to restore your strength, we vow fidelity. Let your sun, Russia, shine over the world in the name of the Father, the Son, and the Holy Ghost!" (Long clarion calls, loud drumming, crosses and more crosses, bowing and more bowing.)

I WALKED OUTSIDE. It was a cold, starry night, beautiful, windless. I was returning to the hotel, which lay in the same direction as Lake Baikal. Yesterday, with Oleg Voronin, a splendid, brave young scholar from the local university, I took the bus to the lake, to a place called Listvyanka. A heavy rain mixed with snow was falling, obscuring everything.

The lake was frozen, rusty carcasses of barges jutted out through the ice. One could not see the other shore; one could not even see all of Listvganka well. There were two stores and a bar in the settlement—everything was closed. There was nowhere to go, nothing to do. Waiting for the bus, we walked for several hours along the empty road. Although I understand that it is very beautiful everywhere around here, mountains, forest, water, one must come in the summer, when there is sun.

We returned half-dead to the city, and strictly speaking I had not seen Baikal. But I bought a book in Irkutsk, from which I can learn much about it. The author—G. I. Gagazy—writes that Baikal is a very deep lake, with a great deal of water. He asks: If humanity's only remaining source of water were Baikal, how much longer could it survive? And he replies: Forty years.

# Jumping over Puddles

"WHAT'S YOUR NAME?"

"Tanya."

"And how old are you?"

"In two months I'll be ten."

"What are you doing?"

"Now? At this moment? I'm playing."

"What are you playing?"

"I'm jumping over a puddle."

"And you're not afraid that you'll get hit by a car?"

"No car is going to be able to drive through here!"

Tanya is right. The temperature went up yesterday, at noon it is even two degrees above freezing, and the entire city is sinking into mud. The city of Yakutsk, a veritable Siberian Kuwait, the capital of an extremely rich republic reposing on gold and diamonds. Half of all those diamond marvels with which rich ladies around the world adorn themselves, or that one can observe in the windows of jewelry shops in New York, Paris, and Amsterdam (to say nothing of the diamonds used for geological drilling and metal cutting), come from Yakutsk.

Tanya has a pale little face. It is always dark here in winter, and even when the sun does appear, it doesn't feel warm; it shines brightly, hurts the eyes, but is distant and cool. The girl is dressed in a coat that is too short, made out of fabric with large green-and-brown checks. Too bad about its being short, but then after all one cannot have a new coat every year. Where would Mother get the money for that? And even if she had that much money—Tanya smiles dreamily—who is going to stand in lines and wait until they deliver to Yakutsk a shipment of coats perfectly sized for ten-year-old girls? And in addition ones so thin and tall?

Tanya analyzes and judges all this in a very adult fashion.

She applies the same reasoning to jumping over puddles. One must jump so precisely and accurately as not to get one's shoes wet, because where would one get another pair to change into?

"Of course," I agree, "and furthermore you could catch cold and get the flu."

"Catch cold?" The girl is amazed. "Now, when the ice is already melting and it's getting warm? You probably don't know what real cold is."

And the little Siberian looks with unmistakable although discreet superiority at the man who is plainly older yet seems to have no idea what great cold is.

ONE CAN RECOGNIZE a great cold, she explains to me, by the bright, shining mist that hangs in the air. When a person walks, a corridor forms in this mist. The corridor has the shape of that person's silhouette. The person passes, but the corridor remains, immobile in the mist. A large man makes a huge corridor, and a small child—a small corridor. Tanya makes a narrow corridor, because she is slender, but, for her age, it is a high one—which is understandable; she is after all the tallest in her class. Walking out in the morning, Tanya can tell from these corridors whether her girlfriends have already gone to school—they all know what the corridors of their closest neighbors and friends look like.

Here is a wide, low corridor with a distinct, resolute line—

the sign that Claudia Matveyevna, the school principal, has already gone.

If in the morning there are no corridors that correspond to the stature of students from the elementary school, it means that the cold is so great that classes have been canceled and the children are staying home.

Sometimes one sees a corridor that is very crooked and then abruptly stops. It means—Tanya lowers her voice—that some drunk was walking, tripped, and fell. In a great cold, drunks frequently freeze to death. Then such a corridor looks like a dead-end street.

I DO NOT at all regret coming to Yakutsk, since I was able to meet here such a splendid, wise girl, and to meet her accidentally, while I was walking the streets of the neighborhood that is called Zalozhnaya. Tanya was simply the only living creature that I saw in the vacant landscape of this neighborhood (it was noon; people are at work at that hour), and, since I had lost my way, I wanted to ask for directions to Krupska Street, where I had an appointment.

"I will take you there," Tanya volunteered cheerfully, "because you might not find it yourself." In practice this meant that I had to join in her game, because one could reach Krupska Street in only one way—by jumping over puddles.

This is the Zalozhnaya neighborhood: wide streets at right angles to one another, no asphalt, not even cobblestones. Each street is a long, flat archipelago of puddles, mud holes, swampy pools. There are no sidewalks; there aren't even any footbridges made of planks, which we had at home in Pinsk. Along the streets stand wooden, single-story little houses. They are old; their wood is blackened, wet, rotting. Tiny windows, the panes thick, in frames lined with cotton wool, felt, rags. Because of these panes one has the impression that these houses are looking at one through the kind of thick glasses worn by old women who can barely see.

In Zalozhnaya, the cold is salvation.

The cold maintains the surroundings, the environment, the soil, in a rigorous discipline, in an ironclad order, in a strong and stable balance. Embedded in the frozen earth, which is hard as concrete, the houses stand straight and sure; one can walk and drive over the streets; the wheels don't sink into slimy quagmires; shoes don't stay behind in gooey sludge.

Yet all it takes is a day like the one on which I met Tanya, meaning: all it takes is for warmth to arrive.

Released from the grip of the cold, the houses become limp and slide deep into the earth. For many years they have been standing considerably below street level; that is because they were built on permafrost and the warmth they have radiated over time has hollowed out niches for them in the icy soil, and with each year they sink into these more and more. Each little house stands in a separate and increasingly deep hole.

Now the wave of April warmth hits Zalozhnaya, and its lopsided, poor little houses twist, grow misshapen, sprawl, and squat ever closer to the earth. The entire neighborhood shrinks, diminishes, sinks in such a way that in some places only the roofs are visible—as if a great fleet of submarines were gradually submerging into the sea.

"And do you see that?" Tanya asks.

I looked in the direction she is indicating with her hand and see the following: the thawing, loosened muck is starting to flow, snaking its way in little streams, channels, chinks, straight down into the houses. Nature in Siberia is extreme, everything here is violent and radical, and therefore if the mud in Yakutsk is threatening houses, it is not a dripping, trickling, watery dark-gray goo, but a loosened avalanche that suddenly and irresistibly takes off in the direction of porches and doors, fills passageways and yards. It is as if the streets were overflowing their banks and pouring themselves into the houses of Zalozhnaya.

Inside the house one walks in mud; mud covers the floors; it is everywhere. "It smells a little unpleasant," Tanya adds, "for Zalozhnaya has no sewage system, so in all of this there are various things. . . ." She wrinkles her forehead, searches for the appropriate words, finally capitulates and repeats—"simply various things."

I am supposed to pay attention to one other thing, to the signs thrust here and there into the ground, warning that one cannot dig anywhere. Why? Well, because the electrical wiring runs just underfoot, simply placed into the ground, and so if someone drives in a shovel and hits a wire, the current will kill him. In Zalozhnaya, therefore, one can not only get soaked up to one's waist, soiled, and smeared in mud, but also fall into a sewage drain and—even—electrocute oneself. That is why it is safer in the winter; in the winter it wouldn't occur to anyone to dig in the ground.

Nearing Krupska Street, we encounter an old woman outside a little house who is trying with the energetic strokes of a broom to halt the muddy deluge crawling onto the porch.

"Hard work," I say, to start a conversation.

"Ah," she replies, shrugging her shoulders, "spring is always terrible. Everything flows."

Silence falls.

"How's life?" I ask the most banal and idiotic question, just to keep the conversation going somehow.

The granny straightens up, leans her hands on the broom handle, looks at me, smiles even. "*Kak zyviom?*" she repeats thoughtfully, and then in a voice full of pride and determination and suffering and joy she offers in reply what is the crux of the Russian philosophy of life—"*Dyshym!*" (We breathe!)

LIKE THE SLUM neighborhoods in Latin America (*favelas* in Rio de Janeiro, *callapas* in Santiago in Chile, and so on), Zalozhnaya in Yakutsk is a closed structure. Poverty, dirt, and mud create here a homogeneous, coherent, consistent landscape in which all the elements are linked to one another, are correlative. As far as the eye can see, there are no contrasts here, no symbols of prosperity rising above the panorama of penury. The essence of such a closed structure is that one cannot improve one individual thing—the other links in the chain will immediately stand in the way. One cannot, for example, bring about that people have clean shoes: the ubiquitous muck will not allow it.

One can only demolish Zalozhnaya and move its residents into new housing. But the newer buildings are not much better. It is even possible that they are worse. Barely finished, the apartment blocks, constructed out of large slabs, are already crooked, cracked, and the plaster has fallen off the walls in sheets. Hot and cold water, as well as the entire sewage output, are conducted through pipes that run on the exteriors of houses and cut across yards, squares, streets, in all directions. One can see these pipes everywhere, wrapped in flocks and rags, in various metal sheets and tapes, and tied up with wire and ropes.

The pipes often burst. If it is winter (as it is nine months out of the year), huge mountains of ice that no one ever removes form in the cracks. One can see these mountains here and there—massive, heavy, glittering in the sun. This tangle of pipes, wires, joints, faucets, through which run the streets, makes the new neighborhoods of Yakutsk look like enormous factory workrooms over which there hasn't yet been the time to put a roof.

In one of these workroom/neighborhoods stands a long, patient line. I come closer, up to the stand at which two saleswomen dressed in white aprons are working. I want to see what they are selling, what this crowd of people is waiting for. Cakes for sale. One kind of cake, one type only, with one pattern of pink icing identically inscribed on all. You can pick up the cake just like that—with your hands. It won't fall apart—it is frozen solid.

SO INSTEAD of diamonds, gold, and Kuwait I found Zalozhnaya and an entire city of poverty. Yakutsk never sees or touches the diamonds. They are shipped straight from the mines to Moscow, where they are used to pay for the production of tanks and rockets, and for the international politics of the Imperium.

I return to Oktiabrska Street, to my hotel. I'm in room number 506. To open the door, one must try turning the key a number of times. It takes from eight to sixteen attempts. Expecting results at attempt number 8 is optimistic, but expecting them at number 16 is also in a certain sense optimistic, for by the sixteenth time the door will open for sure. The worst thing is that it cannot be locked from the inside, and it is hung in such a way that, unlocked, it opens of its own accord onto the corridor. I had no choice but to ask the tenant from the adjoining room (a Buryat, technician) to lock my door for me. (We developed a certain ritual: I would knock at his door, my neighbor would come out, together we would open my door, my neighbor would lock it.)

In the little bathroom, there is both cold and hot water from the faucet above the washbasin, but in the shower there is only hot. Not knowing this, I turn on the shower. Seething, boiling water gushes forth with a roar. Because it is cold in the bathroom and in the room itself, thick clouds of steam form instantly. I cannot see. I throw myself at the shower, but it won't turn off. I make a dash for the window, to let out the steam, but the window does not open; it is sealed up with adhesive plaster—and, anyway, the handle for opening it has been removed. If I open the door of the room, the steam will burst out into the corridor; I will create confusion and scandal. But why scandal? How am I at fault here? I'm already thinking about how to explain and defend myself. Everything in this country is somehow thought out, arranged in such a way that the man on the street—no matter what he is doing, in what situation he finds himself, in what straits and difficulties—will always have a feeling of guilt. Because (as I said) it is cold in my room, the steam immediately condenses on the walls, on the windowpanes, or the glass of a little picture frame, and on the sliver of a mirror. I make a final, heroic effort and, soaked through, half-suffocated, and scalded, I finally manage to turn off the shower, swearing to myself to touch nothing else. It is damp, water is everywhere, but for a moment it is also a bit warmer.

I walked out onto the corridor to check whether anyone had noticed the cataclysm that had just shaken my room. But it was empty, dead. A television set was on in the common room, but no one was watching. The writer Vladimir Solouhin was saying: "Because of Lenin a river of blood flowed in the Soviet Union, an ocean of blood was spilled." He said that sixty-six million people died, not counting the victims of the Second World War. "All this," said Solouhin, "was done in the name of creating paradise on earth." And he concluded: "Paradise! Ha, ha! And today we are walking around without pants."

After him a laborer came on, who, despite the fact that Lenin no longer counts, announced with pride that he had just read fifty-five volumes of Vladimir Ilyich in just several evenings. "It's very simple," he said, clearly pleased with himself. "I read each volume for no longer than one hour. I simply knew that Lenin wrote the most important things in his texts in italics. So I quickly flipped through the pages and read only the parts in italics. I recommend it to everyone!" he encouraged the empty room at the Hotel Yakutsk.

At the end of the program, Yuri Lubimov, the director of the Moscow theater Taganka, said in a critical but also despairing tone: "We have lost our minds, we have lost our conscience, we have lost our honor. I look around and I see barbarity!" Lubimov's powerful, theatrical voice filled the common room, spilled out into the corridor and lobby.

At the newsstand in the lobby, the only foreign newspaper on sale was the French *L'Humanité*. I bought it for the sake of one photograph, to which normally I wouldn't have paid the least attention. But now I sat in my room and stared at this picture on the last page. It showed an elegant and clean highway, L'Autoroute A6, along which stretched unending lines of elegant and clean cars. All this suddenly fascinated me: the white stripes on the road and the large, distinct road signs, and the bright light of the lanterns. Everything was washed; everything was clean; everything went with everything else.

"*Le grand week-end pascal*," said the caption, "*est commencé*."

People have had enough of Paris; they want to rest.

This is so far away, I thought, looking at the photograph. As if on Venus.

And I started to mop up the bathroom full of water.

IN THE MORNING hotel guests can buy breakfast in the bar. At that time of day, they are most often dressed in sweat suits. They stand in line. There is absolute silence. If someone wants to address his neighbor, he speaks in a whisper. This silence can at times be deceptive, treacherous. For suddenly, without reason, cries break out, yelling, a brawl! Two things characterize such situations. First, the cause is usually completely irrational. What was the reason? What happened? Why? It is impossible to ascertain; no one knows; everyone shrugs his shoulders. The atmosphere is charged with conflict, like a cloud packed with thunderbolts, and the slightest trifle can unleash the destructive energies. Second, the explosion occurs instantaneously; there are no intermediate degrees, no jeers, pouts, sulks, grimaces, only a straight shot from silence into screams—like a leap over a precipice! It is as if this war could take place on only one frequency, not one hertz lower or higher. This terrible, enraged, senseless shrieking and swearing lasts a short while and just as suddenly as it started—it dies out. Again, silence descends. Again, if someone wants to address his neighbor, he speaks in a whisper.

And now comes our turn to step up to the barmaid. The scene consists of a minimum of words and has a very businesslike character. The barmaid looks at the guest and remains silent—this means that she is waiting for the order. There is no "Good morning" here or "How are you"—the guest gets straight to the point. He says: A glass of cream, an egg, farmer cheese, cucumber, bread.

He does not say thank you; he does not say anything at all superfluous. The barmaid hands him the food, takes the money. Also without a word. She closes the cash register and looks at the next guest.

People here eat quickly, urgently, they swallow everything in seconds. Although several times I was the first in the bar, I was invariably the last to leave. Those who had arrived after me left long before I did. I do not know to what degree the specter of continually recurring famines, so deeply encoded in the collective memory, plays a role here—the subconscious fear that perhaps tomorrow there will be nothing to eat.

AN EVENING at Vladimir Fiodorov's. Fiodorov, an ethnic Russian, is an eminent figure in the local cultural world. He is the editor in chief of the local bimonthly *Zwiezda Vostoka*, in which I read a report about a village in the Yakut countryside, Syktiach (in the summer, six days by ship on the Lena River to the north). Tuberculosis is raging in the village, whoever can is escaping; to get a loaf of bread one must ride two hundred kilometers over roadless wilderness, over snow, over the taiga—to the town of Kiusiur.

Fiodorov's little apartment (for his wife, himself, two daughters) is very well cared for, tasteful, cozy, measures thirty square meters. But his family is away, and so we are spending the evening alone. Fiodorov was born in Yakutia, on the banks of the Lena; he knows the entire republic, has traversed it lengthwise and widthwise. He has experienced, and carries in his imagination, a world that to me is unknown and inaccessible. The taiga, rivers, lakes—I have never been there, I do not know what a man feels after he has killed a bear, or when he is walking around hungry and suddenly catches a large fish.

I continually have on the tip of my tongue a question about the Yakuts, but I somehow feel awkward about posing it. In Yakutia, the Yakuts are a minority—there are four hundred thousand of them. What are their relations with the Russians? The Russians have been here only since the seventeenth century. Does Fiodorov believe that something like a colonial situation exists? Colonial dependence and exploitation?

"How so!" Fiodorov would answer. Yakutia (in the fall of 1991, the Republic of Yakutia changed its name to Sacha) is his country; he was born and raised here; he lives and works here. It is the argument of Afrikaners in South Africa: they were born there, they have no other country! Besides, Russians and Yakuts are equally exploited here, a great state is exploiting them—the Imperium. It is the Imperium that takes away their diamonds and orders them to live in Zalozhnaya.

Yakutia is full of pain. There were many gulags here, mainly near the gold mines. If a prisoner turned in gold over and above the quota, he received for each gram of extra gold a gram of alcohol or a gram of tobacco or bread. Cheating proliferated, becoming epidemic among the overseers. But one of them, Pavlov, once gave out three hundred grams of alcohol for three hundred grams of gold, and the prisoners discovered that the alcohol was not diluted with water, was honestly high proof. News of Pavlov's deed spread through the camps, he himself passed into legend, and this extraordinary episode is, as one can see, recounted to this day in the Republic.

Fiodorov speaks about terrible things. When criminals escaped, they would persuade one of the political prisoners—naive and unsavvy—to go with them. This they did as insurance against death from hunger, which was always a threat. At a certain point they would kill the victim and divide up his flesh.

When an escape took place, the NKVD would inform the local population, who understood the bounty system. It was enough to deliver to the authorities the escaped prisoner's right hand; identity was confirmed by comparing fingerprints. For each prisoner "returned," the reward was a sack of flour. Many died accidentally this way, many hunters, travelers, geologists.

Stalin ordered a road built between Yakutsk and Magadan. Two thousand kilometers across the taiga and the permafrost. They started building it simultaneously from both ends. Summer came, thaws, the permafrost melted, water underran the soil, turned the road into a quagmire, it drowned. Together with the road drowned the prisoners who worked on it. Stalin ordered the work to start anew. But it ended up the same way. Once again, he commanded. The two ends of the road never met, but their builders perhaps met in heaven.

# Kolyma, Fog and More Fog

I WAITED FOUR DAYS at the airport in Yakutsk for my airplane to Magadan to take off. Snowstorms raged over Kolyma; everything was covered over, buried under, and for that reason scheduled flights were suspended.

This is what traveling around Siberia is like.

The majority of airports are poorly lit; the craft that fly through them are old and break down frequently; sometimes one also has to wait somewhere for fuel to be delivered to the airplanes from another part of the continent. The entire time he is traveling, a person lives in tension, with nerves, in fear that these unexpected stops and delays will cause him to miss a connecting flight, lose a reservation, and then—drama, disaster, catastrophe. For here one cannot be capricious, change tickets, select other times and routes. One can get stuck for weeks on end at an unknown and always crowded airport, with no chance of getting out quickly. (All tickets are sold out months in advance.) What then would one do with oneself, where would one live, what would one live on?

I now find myself in just such a situation in Yakutsk. I also cannot return to town, for what if the storm in Kolyma suddenly abates? If it does, the plane will take off immediately, so we have to hold on with all our might, because if it gets away—if it flies off—we are lost.

So the only thing to do is sit and wait.

OF COURSE, it is a dreadful sort of idleness, an unbearable tedium, to sit motionless like this, in a state of mental numbness, not really doing anything. But on the other hand, don't millions and millions of people the world over pass the time in just such a passive way? And haven't they done so for years, for centuries? Regardless of religion, of culture and race? In South America, we need only go up into the Andes or drive through the dusty streets of Piura or sail down the Orinoco River—we will encounter everywhere poor mud villages, settlements, and towns; and we will see how many people are sitting on earthen benches in front of houses, on rocks and stools, sitting motionless, not really doing anything. Let us travel from South America to Africa, let us visit the lonely oases on the Sahara and the villages of black fishermen stretching along the Gulf of Guinea, let us visit the mysterious Pygmies in the Congo jungle, the tiny one-horse town of Mvenzo in Zambia, the handsome Dinka tribe in the Sudan—everywhere we will see people simply sitting. Sometimes they will utter a word or two, in the evening they will warm themselves by the fire, but really they are not doing anything, only sitting idly and without motion; and moreover they exist (or so we can suppose) in a state of mental lethargy. And is it different in Asia? Driving along the road from Karachi to Lahore or from Bombay to Madras or from Djakarta to Malang—will we not be struck by the fact that thousands, why, millions of Pakistanis, Hindus, Indonesians, and other Asians are sitting idly, without motion, and are looking at who knows what? Let us fly to the Philippines and to Samoa, let us visit the immeasurable territories of the Yukon and tropical Jamaica—everywhere, everywhere that same sight—people sitting motionless, for hours on end, on old chairs, on bits of plank, on plastic crates, in the shade of poplars and mango trees, leaning against the walls of slums, against fences and window frames, irrespective of the time of day or of the season, of whether the sun is shining or the rain is falling, phlegmatic and expressionless people, as if in a state of chronic drowsiness, not really doing anything, living with neither desires nor goals, and also (one can assume) submerged into mental torpor.

And here around me, at the airport in Yakutsk? Is it not the same? A crowd of people sitting wordless, motionless, an inert crowd which will not so much as twitch, which, it seems to me, isn't even breathing. So let us stop getting excited and thrashing about, let us stop tormenting the stewardesses with questions for which they have no answers, and, following the example of our brothers and sisters from the sleepy village of San Juan near Valdivia, from the settlements on the Gobi desert crushed by the heat, and from the littered outskirts of Shiraz, let us sit motionless, staring off into space, and every hour sinking deeper and deeper into a state of mental numbness.

AFTER FOUR DAYS the storm in Kolyma passes, the buxom stewardess runs around the terminal, wakes the sleeping as she calls out loudly: "Magadan! Who for Magadan?" Hurriedly, nervously, we collect our bags, sacks, packages, suitcases. Wrapping ourselves in scarves, buttoning sheepskins, and pulling big hats with earmuffs down on our heads, we dash chaotically to the airplane, which immediately wheels toward the runway. We're flying. A woman is sitting beside me—she is going to visit her son, who is serving in the army in Kolyma. She is worried by his letters; it is clear from them that he is not tolerating *diedovshchyna* very well.

Have I heard about *diedovshchyna*? Yes, I have. It is a system of sadistic treatment of recruits by NCOs and older soldiers. One of the malignant tumors eating away at the Red Army. Soviet society scaled down to the size of a platoon or company and dressed up in uniform. The essence of this society: the cruelty of the strong toward the weak. The recruit is weak, so those above him by virtue of rank or length of army service make him their slave, pariah, shoeblack, spittoon. The recruit must buy his way into this brutal community, must lose his personality and dignity. Toward this end they mistreat the recruit, harass him, break him, destroy him. They beat and torture him. Sometimes he cannot stand the baiting, the cruelty and the terror; he tries to escape or commits suicide. The recruit who endures the hardships and the ruthless prison house of the *diedovshchyna* will live with only one thought in mind—to recoup, to get revenge, to retaliate for his humiliation, for the fact that they dragged him through the mud and the filth, that he had to smell the foot rags of the corporals, that they kicked him in the face with their boots. But who can yesterday's recruit retaliate upon? Whose packages from home can he steal, whose kidneys can he injure? Naturally, only someone weaker than he, and, therefore, the new recruit.

Adding fresh fodder to this traditional, ordinary sadism, ethnic and religious conflicts have flared in today's army: the Uzbek is killing the Tajik, a platoon of the Orthodox (Russians) clashes with a platoon of Muslims (Tatars), the shamanist (Mordovian) sticks a knife into the back of the atheist (German).

Alarmed and appalled mothers have started organizing into various unions and associations to force the authorities to combat *diedovshchyna*. One can meet them at various demonstrations and marches as they walk holding two photographs before them: in one, a young boy, a picture given to his mother as a keepsake when he was leaving for the army; in the other, the same face, the same head—already in a coffin. If the mother is relatively wealthy, these photographs are framed, behind glass. But one can also see poor women, who carry shabby, frayed photographs. The rain and snow wash away and smudge the features of the young face. If you stop for a moment as you are walking past, the woman will thank you for the gesture.

My neighbor on the plane tells me about the torments of her son, the recruit. She whispers, into my ear, for she is after all betraying the secrets of the great army. I do not know if she has read Mikhaylovsky's study of Dostoyevsky. An old, large text written in 1882. Mikhaylovsky was a Russian essayist, thinker. He rejected Dostoyevsky, called him a "cruel talent," but at the same time marveled at his perspicacity, his genius. Mikhaylovsky writes that Dostoyevsky discovered a horrifying attribute in man—unnecessary cruelty. A tendency in man to inflict suffering on others—without cause and without purpose. One man tortures another for no reason, except that torturing gives him a pleasure to which he will never admit out loud. This trait (unnecessary cruelty), combined with power and pride, gave rise to the world's most ruthless tyrannies. It was Dostoyevsky who made this discovery, Mikhaylovsky emphasizes; in the story "The Village of Stiepanchykovo and Her Inhabitants" he describes a small, provincial creature named Foma Opiskin—tormentor, monster, tyrant. "Give Foma Opiskin the power of Ivan the Terrible or Nero," writes Mikhaylovsky, "and he will not be outdone by them in anything and will astound the world with his crimes." More than half a century before Stalin solidified his position in the Kremlin and before Hitler came to power, Dostoyevsky conceived in the figure of Foma Opiskin the progenitor of both these tyrants.

Preying upon his victims, Foma is satisfying the need to act sadistically, to torment, to cause pain. Foma is not a practical man ("he needs that which is unnecessary"); by inflicting suffering on others he does not achieve anything—therefore one cannot understand him in terms of any rational, pragmatic categories. He does not think about the fact that behaving sadistically toward others has no purpose and does not lead to anything—what is important to him is the process of sadistic activity itself, the tyrannizing itself, the cruelty for cruelty's sake. Foma "beats a completely innocent man without reason." This gives him pleasure and a feeling of absolute power. This pure, immaculate disinterestedness in the act of inflicting suffering, defined as "unnecessary cruelty," is what Mikhaylovsky sees as Dostoyevsky's great psychological discovery.

But why, Mikhaylovsky wonders, did people of Foma Opiskin's type find such fertile ground in Russia? Because, he answers, "the main characteristic of the Russian, encoded in the Russian nation—is the incessant pursuit of suffering." Yes, it had to be a Russian who described the personage of Foma, who discovered his dark soul, filled with "indomitable, self-generated anger," who showed us his ghastly, inconceivable Underground.

BENEATH THE WINGS of the aircraft, a white, still plain unrolls, here and there darkly stained by forests, a monotonous and empty space, gentle hills in the shape of flat, squat mounds—nothing that would catch the eye, nothing that would hold the attention. That is Kolyma.

In Magadan it is more than fifty kilometers from the airport to town, but luckily I found a taxi, a dented, rusty Volga. I was riding with my heart in my mouth, for I didn't have a pass to enter the city. I was afraid of being turned back, after having thought for so long about coming here, to see this most terrible—next to Auschwitz—place on earth. We were driving along a snow-covered highway, between hills, occasionally passing thin young pine forests. From one of these young woods two young men suddenly emerged, in dark glasses and in elegant Western coats with raised collars. Like characters from a crime film. They stopped us and wanted to know if we would give them a ride to town. The driver looked at me, but I was of the opinion that there was no question that we should take them. It turned out that a good angel had sent them, for ten kilometers farther on there was a checkpoint and we had to stop. Seeing the militiamen from a distance, I removed and hid my glasses. Here people wear spectacles with yellow or brown plastic frames, and my frames are metal, light, they immediately attract attention for being different, not from here; and whenever I wish to disappear, I hide the glasses. In my cheap wool quilted jacket and reindeer-skin hat I looked like someone from Omsk or Tomsk. The militiamen at once became interested in our young men's dark glasses, a quarrel started, a row, a struggle, and they were dragged out of the car. In short, the militiamen stopped the young men and ordered us to keep going.

"Caucasian mafia" was how the taxi driver characterized those detained. The word "mafia" is enjoying a tremendous popularity these days. It is increasingly replacing the word "nation."

Here where one hundred nations once lived "in harmony and brotherhood," one hundred mafias have now appeared. The nations have vanished, have ceased to exist. Three large mafias have taken their place—the Russian mafia, the Caucasian mafia, and the Asiatic mafia. These large mafias are divided into an infinite number of smaller ones. There are Chechen and Georgian mafias, Tatar and Uzbek, Chelyabinsk and Odessian. The smaller mafias are divided into even smaller ones, and these in turn into utterly small ones. Small, but dangerous, armed with pistols and knives. Thus there are mafias operating on a national scale, on the scale of the republic, on the scale of the city, the neighborhood, a single street—even a single courtyard. The geography of the mafias is most complicated, but as to who belongs to what mafia, this the other mafiosi know precisely, for it is after all on this kind of discernment that their life depends. All the mafias have two characteristics: (a) their members do not work but live well, and (b) they are continually squaring accounts. Stealing, smuggling, or squaring accounts—that is what the everyday life of a mafia member looks like.

This obsession with the mafia—the annoying habit of thinking about everything in terms of the mafia—didn't arise totally out of thin air, but has deep, tragic roots. The great cataclysm that occurred in the first three decades of this century—the world war, October 1917, then civil war and mass starvation—deprived millions of children in Russia of their parents and their homes. These millions of orphans, millions of *bezprizorny*, wandered the roads of the country, through villages and cities, searching for food and a roof over their heads. (There is indeed a difference between being hungry and homeless in Africa and being so in Russia; in Russia, without a warm corner somewhere, one freezes to death.) Many of these *bezprizorny* lived by theft and robbery.

The grandfathers of many of today's Russian mafiosi are these homeless and frequently nameless *bezprizorny*. Breaking with one's past was not easy, and at times downright impossible. Whoever once came into conflict with the authorities handed down his embattled status to his son and grandson. In today's post-Soviet society there exist not only individual criminals, not only criminal elements, but an entire criminal class possessing a genealogy and tradition different from the rest of society. Each successive crisis—the Second World War, the postwar purges, the corruption of the Brezhnev era, the disintegration of the USSR—reinforced and augmented the ranks of this class.

The maniacal, obstinate view of the world as a great, all-encompassing network of mafias (who is trying to secede from Georgia? The Abhazian mafia. Who is attacking Armenians? The Azerbaijani mafia, and so on) has additional sources. The first is the conspiratorial theory of history, for years promulgated by Stalin: behind everything that is bad stand conspiracies, organizations, mafias. And the second is the tradition, practice, and climate of mysteriousness that is characteristic of the political and social life in this state. (Who was in power? Gorbachev's mafia. Who will be ruling in the Kremlin in a few years? Some other mafia!)

IN TOWN, nobody asks me anything. Despite the fact that the receptionist in the Magadan Hotel is severe and looks at me (I do not know why) reprovingly, she gives me a bright and warm room, number 256. From the window I can see the snow-covered street and the bus stop and, farther on, a wall behind which stands an old prison.

One can come to Magadan like the three Japanese from a textile firm in Sapporo, whom I met in the hotel.

They do not know where they are.

They are conducting business and bowing—courteous, clean, efficient. They want to sell their textiles; that is what brings them here. But while they arrive here laden with elegant fabrics, one can also come with an utterly different type of baggage, that is, the baggage of knowledge—about the place in which I now find myself talking with the Japanese. The fact is that we are standing on top of human bones. And even if, as a result of this awareness, one were to spring back a step or even run several hundred meters, it would not matter: everywhere it's just cemeteries and more cemeteries.

Magadan is the capital of the northeastern territory of Siberia called Kolyma, after the river that flows here. A land of great cold, permafrost, darkness. An empty, barren, almost uninhabited terrain, visited only by small nomadic tribes—Chukots, Evenkis, Yakuts. Kolyma aroused Moscow's interest only in our century, when news spread that there was gold here. In the fall of 1929, on the Bay of Nogayev (the Sea of Okhotsk, constituting part of the Pacific), the first base was built. This settlement was the beginning of Magadan. At that time one could reach this place only by sea, sailing north from Vladivostok or Nahodka, for eight to ten days.

On November 11, 1931, the Central Committee of the Greater Russian Communist Party (the Bolsheviks) adopts a resolution to create in Kolyma a trust to excavate gold, silver, and other metals—it is called Dal'stroy. Three months later the ship *Sachalin* sails into the Bay of Nogayev, carrying the first director of Dal'stroy—a Latvian Communist, the general of the GPU, Edvard Berzin. Berzin is thirty-eight years old at the time. He will live five more years. Berzin's arrival marks the creation of the Gehenna, which, under the name Kolyma, will pass, together with Auschwitz, Treblinka, Hiroshima, and Vorkuta, into the history of the greatest nightmares of the twentieth century. In colloquial Russian, Kolyma was transformed, bizarrely, into a word denoting the consolation of relativism. That is, when things are truly bad, awful, frightful, one Russian consoles another: "Don't despair, it was worse in Kolyma!"

In the frozen desert of Kolyma, people are needed to work. That is why, simultaneously with Dal'stroy, Moscow calls into being here a directorate of the Northeastern Camps of Correctional Labor (USVITLag). USVITLag fulfilled the same role vis-à-vis Dal'stroy as the concentration camp Auschwitz/Birkenau did vis-à-vis IG Farben—it supplied the slaves.

THE BEGINNINGS of Magadan coincide with the onset of the great terrors of the Stalin era. Millions of people are imprisoned. In the Ukraine, ten million peasants die of hunger. But they are not all dead yet. One can still deport countless throngs of "kulaks" and other "enemies of the people" to Kolyma, limited only by the transportation bottleneck. For only one railroad line goes to Vladivostok, and only a few ships ply the waters from there to the port in Magadan. It is along this very route that for twenty-five years, nonstop, living human skeletons are transported from across the entire Imperium to Magadan.

Live ones, but also the already dead. Varlam Shalamov, who spent twenty years in the camps, tells about the ship *Kim*, which was carrying three thousand prisoners in its holds. When they mutinied, their escort flooded the hold with water. It was forty degrees below zero. They arrived in Magadan as frozen blocks. Another ship, carrying thousands of deportees, became stuck in the Arctic ice. It reached the port after a year—none of the prisoners survived.

The ship *Dzurma*, carrying condemned women, had reached Magadan. Many of these women were already dying from cold and exhaustion. Such people, in a state of slow agony, are called *dohodiags*, "coming to the end," in the language of the camps.

> The *dohodiags* were carried out one by one on stretchers. They were carried out and arranged in rows on the shore, clearly for the purpose of facilitating accounting, to avoid confusion during the making out of death certificates. We were lying on the rocks and looking around for our group, which was dragging itself to town for the torture of communal sauna and disinfection. (Evgeniya Ginzburg, *The Steep Wall*)

The people who boarded the transports were already exhausted by months of imprisonment, interrogation, hunger, and beatings. Now they faced weeks of torment in crowded cattle cars, in filth, the delirium of thirst (for they weren't given anything to drink). They did not know where they were going or what awaited them at the end of the journey. Those who survived this Gehenna were driven in Magadan to the enormous staging camp. Here a slave market operated. The commanders of the camps set up near the mines would come and select for themselves the most physically able prisoners. The higher the commander stood in the hierarchy of power, the stronger the convicts he was able to choose for himself.

There were 160 camps—or, as they are also called, Arctic death camps—in Manadan and Kolyma. The convicts changed over the years, but at any given moment there were around half a million residents. Of these, one-third died in the camps, and the rest, after serving years of hard labor, left as physical cripples or with permanent psychic injuries. Whoever survived Magadan and Kolyma was never again the person he or she once was.

The camp was a sadistically and precisely thought-out structure, having as its goal the destruction of the individual in such a way that before death he would experience the greatest humiliations, sufferings, and torments. It was a barbed net of destruction from which a man, once having fallen into it, could not extricate himself. It consisted of the following elements:

| | |
|---|---|
| (cold) | clothed in wretched and thin rags, the convict continuously suffered from the cold, froze |
| (hunger) | he experienced this cold all the more keenly because he was always bestially, obsessively hungry, having for nourishment only a piece of bread and water |
| (hard labor) | hungry and frozen, he had to work hard, punishingly, past the point of endurance, digging the earth and carting it off in a wheelbarrow, crushing rocks, chopping down the forest |
| (lack of sleep) | frozen, hungry, exhausted by work, and most often sick, he was purposefully deprived of sleep. He could sleep for only a short time, in an icy barracks, on hard boards, clothed in the rags in which he worked |
| (filth) | he was not allowed to wash himself, and be- |

| | |
|---|---|
| | sides there wasn't the time or the place for it, so he was covered in a crust of sticky dirt and sweat, he smelled, stunk unbearably |
| (vermin) | he was consumed the whole time by vermin. Lice nested in his rags, bedbugs caked the plank beds in the barracks, in the summer swarms of mosquitoes tormented him, and terrible Siberian flies, attacking in swarms |
| (NKVD sadism) | the escorts and guards—the NKVD overseers—incessantly inflicted their rage upon him. They shouted, beat him about the face with their fists, kicked him, baited him with dogs, and for trivial reasons—shot him |
| (terror of the criminals) | political prisoners were terrorized, robbed, and tormented by the criminal ones. To them belonged the effective control of the lower rungs of power |
| (the feeling of injustice) | it was psychological torture to endure the feeling of having been done the gravest injustice. All these political prisoners were utterly innocent, they had done nothing wrong |
| (homesickness and fear) | all were tormented by the longing for their dearest, for home (sentences ran to twenty-five years), by being completely cut off from the world, by an unknown, increasingly horrifying tomorrow, by fear that death would arrive any day |

"It is a terrible thing to see a camp," wrote Varlam Shalamov of Kolyma. "No one on earth should know camps. In the camp experience everything is negative—every single minute of it. A human being can only become the worse for it. And it cannot be any other way. There is a great deal in the camps about which a man should not know. But seeing the very bottom of life is not the most dreadful part of it. What is most dreadful is when a man appropriates this bottom as his own, when the measure of his morality is borrowed from the camp experience, when the morality of criminals finds application in life. When man's intellect attempts not only to justify those camp sentiments, but also to serve them."

And later: "The camp was a great test of character for a man, a test of ordinary human morality, and 99 percent did not pass this test. Together with those who did not pass it, died those who did manage to, by trying to be better than the rest, harder on themselves . . ." (*Kolyma Tales*).

ON DECEMBER 1, 1937, Berzin is recalled to Moscow. Stalin has decided that this executioner has acted too gently and orders him arrested and shot. That same December 1, the ship *Nicolai Yezov* reaches Magadan, bringing, as Berzin's replacements, the two new rulers of Kolyma—the director of Dal'stroy, Col. Karp Pavlov (he will shoot himself in 1956), and his deputy, the chief of Kolyma's death camps, Col. Stiepan Garanin. Garanin is thirty-nine years old. He will live one more year.

Garanin is Kolyma's dark legend.

"Ivan Kuzmich, do you remember Garanin?"

> Do I remember? You must be kidding. I saw him from close up, after all, just like I'm seeing you now. He was reviewing a column of prisoners. And he wasn't alone, but with an entourage. Before he appeared, they were relaying messages over the telephone: he might pull up here, so as to personally conduct an inspection of the camp. He was still in Magadan when we were already standing at attention. Everything cleaned, painted, the ground strewn with yellow sand. The command frets and fumes; it cannot control its nerves. Suddenly, whispers: They're coming, they're coming. The gate of the camp

opens wide. And he drives through it with his escort—several passenger cars, several trucks carrying his personal guards. He steps out of the first car, and his entourage arranges itself quick as lightning on both sides. All of them with Mausers [a type of gun], in short sheepskin jackets. He himself in a coat of bear fur. A fierce expression on his face. Drunken eyes, heavy as lead. The commander of our camp, a major, runs up to him and reports in a trembling voice: "Comrade commander of USVITL-NKVD. The independent subcamp of the camp system ready for inspection." "Are there prisoners here who shirk their work?" "There are," the major answers fearfully. And around twelve people step forward from the ranks. "So, you don't want to work, sons of bitches?" And he already has a pistol in his hand. Bang! Bang! Bang! He gets them all. Any that still move are finished off by the entourage. "And are there record setters here, those that exceed the quota? Super-quota workers?" "There are, comrade chief of USVITL-NKVD." A joyful, cheerful line of super-quota workers steps forward. They don't have anything to fear. Garanin walks up to them with his entourage, still holding the Mauser with the empty magazine. Without turning around, he hands it backward to his people. He gets from them a new loaded pistol, which he puts into a wooden holster, but he doesn't take his hand off the butt. "So, super-quota workers? You exceed the quota?" "Yes," they answer. And he asks them again: "Enemies of the people who exceed the quotas? Hmm . . . you, cursed enemies of the people! One must liquidate the likes of you. . . ." And again: Bang! Bang! Bang! And again around ten people are lying in a pool of blood. Then he appears cheered up, his eyes have grown calmer. He has sated himself with blood. The camp commander leads his dear, honorable guests to the mess hall for a prepared feast. And he is happy that he has himself dodged the bullet. When Garanin felt like it, he shot at the commanders of the camps as well. It was a terrible lawlessness, when Garanin was chief. People fell like flies. (Anatoly Zygulin, *Black Stones*)

Garanin shot several, a dozen, or sometimes several dozen people a day. Murdering, he laughed or sang cheerful ditties. Beria ordered him shot suddenly and for obscure reasons, ostensibly for being a Japanese spy. But it is after all quite likely that this burly, muscle-bound hulk, son of a Belorussian peasant, a blacksmith by profession, semiliterate, did not even know that such a country as Japan exists.

ARRIVING IN MAGADAN, I had three telephone numbers with me. I dialed the first—a young male voice answered and informed me that the woman I was calling was no longer alive. The second—endless ringing, no one picked up. I dialed the third number: 23343. A deep, good-humored voice answered. I introduced myself and heard such a friendly, even joyful, response as if the one on the other end of the line (I did not know him personally) had been waiting years for my visit. We arranged to meet. He would try to borrow a four-wheel-drive car somewhere, so that we could go around a bit, see something.

IN THE MORNING a green GAZ van pulled up. The driver was a woman who said that she was forty-seven years old. It's strange, but I do not remember her name (perhaps she didn't give it), only her age. "Forty-seven Years" was a massive, robust woman in whom everything was pushed forward, bulging, popping, most of all her eyes and breasts. She had powerful, strong shoulders, and I couldn't imagine the dimensions of the man next to whom she might have felt a shy, weak, small thing. Nothing (and, I also think, no one) could possibly resist her.

Next to the driver sat the man I had spoken to yesterday, Albert Miltahutdinov, a writer, who had spent his entire adult life—more than thirty years—in Kolyma, writing and also studying the geography of this part of Siberia. (Because formerly one could reach Kolyma only by sea, it became customary to speak of it as an island, which further underscored its isolation from the rest of the world. Anyone leaving Kolyma said: "I'm going to the continent.")

"*Pojechali!* (Let's go!)," said Forty-seven Years in a tone that was at once a question and an order. We had barely set off when she started to go into ecstasies over Romanians. "*Molodcy Rumyni!* (Brave young Romanians!)," she exclaimed. "They cut off Ceauşescu's head!" Although this happened already some time ago, it had clearly made an impression on her. "When will we cut off the heads of those in the Kremlin?"

I thought: I am in Kolyma. I was terrified not so much by her words as by the fact that, while holding the steering wheel with one hand, she was demonstrating with the other how heads should be properly cut off; and we were driving along a street with such terrible ditches, potholes, and chasms that I felt like an astronaut in a vacuum chamber—I was riding not knowing where my head was, where my legs were. The vehicle would at one moment rear up vertically, as though to take off for the sky, and in the next, plunge as though into a bottomless abyss.

But Forty-seven Years took no notice of the road—she had a more important problem. "Oh, what fools they made of us!" she would say with rage. "What fools they made of us!"

Her energy, her fury, all the guns of her hatred, were aimed at the Kremlin. There resided those who for forty-seven years had made an idiot out of her, promulgating preposterous things, which they ordered her to believe.

"But we will get them!" She was getting drunk on her blinding, angry vision.

WE REACHED the Bay of Nogayev and stopped at the water's edge, near some abandoned, rusting cutters. This is a place-symbol, a place-document, with a symbolic weight similar to that of the gate to Auschwitz or the railway ramp in Treblinka. This bay, the gate, and the ramp are three different stage designs for the same scene: the descent into hell.

Of the millions of people who were disgorged upon this rocky shore covered with gravel, on which we are now standing, three million never came back. The bay looks like a large lake with a calm, gray-brown surface. The entrance to it, from the Sea of Okhotsk, which separates it from Japan, is so narrow that even in stormy weather there are no large waves here. In all directions one can see dark gray, almost black hills with gentle slopes, bare, without a trace of greenery, like so many heaps of coal or slag long ago abandoned. A dreary, monotonous, lifeless world. Without trees, without birds. One can see no movement; one can hear no sounds. Low clouds, crawling along the ground, always seemed to be drawing in our direction, straight at us.

This environment provokes extreme behavior, one can fall into a delirium here, into madness, or succumb to the most crushing depression; the most difficult thing is to preserve a sense of normalcy and the faith that nature can be friendly, that it does not want to rid itself of us. In a place like Kolyma, nature pals it up with the executioner, helps him in the destruction of the defenseless and innocent victim, serves the criminals, grovels before them, always slipping them new instruments of torture—biting cold, icy winds, banks of snow a story high, enormous, impassable cold deserts.

To this bay came the ships carrying in their hatches prisoners jammed together, half-dead from hunger and suffocation. Those who were still moving walked down the gangplanks to the shore. It was then that they saw the bay for the first time. The first impression, noted in dozens of memoirs: From here I will not return. They were ordered into columns. Then the counting of the prisoners began. Many of the guards were illiterates, and counting large numbers caused them great difficulties. The roll call lasted for hours. The half-naked deportees stood motionless in a blizzard, lashed by the gales. Finally, the escorts delivered their routine admonition: A step to the left or a step to the right is considered an escape attempt—we shoot without warning! This identical formula was uniformly applied throughout the entire territory of the USSR. The whole nation, two hundred million strong, had to march in tight formation in a dictated direction. Any deviation to the left or to the right meant death.

From the bay they were now marched along the main street

of Magadan, on which today stands my hotel. It was the first street in the town. Berzin built it and gave it his name—the chiefs of the NKVD gave their names to cities, squares, factories, schools, until a veritable NKVD-land had come into being. In 1935 Berzin opened in Magadan a park of culture, giving it the name of his superior, the chief of the NKVD, Yagoda. Three years later Berzin and Yagoda were shot. Berzin Street was renamed Stalin Street, and Yagoda Park was renamed after the new chief of the NKVD, Yezov. A year later they shot Yezov, and the park received the name of Stalin. In 1956 Stalin Street was changed into Marx Street, and Stalin Park was renamed Lenin Park. For how long—no one knows. Eventually, the town council hit on a good idea, and is now giving streets apolitical names. So there is Gazetnaya, Pochtovoya, Garaznaya, Nabierzhaya. After all, newspapers, post offices, garages, and shorelines will always be around.

After passing through the street of Berzin-Stalin, the exhausted columns vanished inside the gates of transit camps, of which there were several in the town and its immediate environs. Until recently Magadan had barely a couple of brick buildings, and the whole town, comprising numerous small wooden houses above which rose the watchtowers, looked like one large camp scattered over the hills, covered by snow in the winter, drowning in mud in the summer.

After several days the prison columns set forth once again, pushed along by the shouts of their escorts, by rifle butts, by the baying of dogs. The most important thing was to reach one's final destination, for whoever weakened and fell was finished. The columns shuffled deep into Kolyma, to their designated camps and to primitive gold, platinum, silver, lead, and uranium mines, hollowed out with pickaxes. For decades they marched from Magadan sometimes daily, sometimes weekly, one after the other, hundreds upon hundreds, thousands upon thousands, walking toward their appointed places along the town's only road—the northern one—and one after another vanishing into the eternal, thick, and cold fog.

• • •

"ALBERT," I asked, "can we see the old camps?" We proceeded to drive up from the bay, along the trail of the prisoners, to town.

Forty-seven Years was cursing the local bureaucracy. It turned out that Magadan and the state of Alaska had made an arrangement. A group of American children was invited here for two weeks. Each child was to live with a Russian family. War broke out in town because everyone wanted to have such a child at their home. What was at stake, naturally, wasn't just a young American, although, being extremely generous, the people here were more than glad to have them. The point was that whoever was assigned such an overseas guest would see an immediate overhaul of their entire apartment building: walls would be painted, lightbulbs replaced in the stairwells, panes inserted into windows, the courtyard swept, the sewage pipes repaired, the faucets fixed, the sinks and bathtubs exchanged, locks and hinges on doors oiled. It just so happened that someone in the apartment block where Forty-seven Years lived was trying for such a little Yankee, but, as she told us amid shouts, laughter, and curses, he offered too small a bribe. So the stairwell is still dark and there is no hot water.

In general life is hard.

A resident of Magadan, K. I. Ivankienko, complains in a letter to his newspaper:

> Several days ago, in the periodical *Krestianka*, I read my horoscope, from which I deduced that a likelihood existed that I would succeed in buying something expensive, but useful. Consequently I lined up in front of the doors of the Melodia shop, before it even opened, in the hope that I could buy a television set. Unfortunately, I didn't succeed. But right next door, after all, is a shoe store, so I rushed in to buy shoes. Unfortunately, here too I didn't succeed. I went to three vegetable shops in a row—there were no potatoes anywhere. I started walking from shop to shop trying to buy something, anything at all, no longer necessarily expensive or necessarily useful, but I couldn't

> get anything anywhere. Finally I found myself in shop number 13, commonly known as Three Pigs. They were selling beer. But it was no matter, since it turned out that they would sell you beer only if you had brought a tankard from home. (*Magadanskaya Pravda*, April 27, 1990)

WE DIDN'T HAVE far to drive. The old camps have remained in the old neighborhoods, near snow-covered streets without sidewalks or streetlights. Some of them were turned into warehouses or depots. The rest are decaying and falling apart. The watchtowers are still standing, visible here and there, crooked, leaning, rotting. In the snow and the mud lie shattered gates, fences, and posts without wire—the wire was stolen. The majority of the barracks were torn down for firewood; several are still standing, but they are empty, without doors and windows.

Everywhere, in Vorkuta, in Norilsk, in Magadan, one is struck by the squalor of the camp world, by its extreme, shabby poverty, its clumsy, careless provisionality, slovenliness, and primitivism. It is a world stitched together from patches and rags, nailed together with rusted nails driven in with an ordinary ax, tied together with a burlap rope, secured with a piece of old wire.

If one wanted to erase the evidence of the crime, nothing here would need to be broken apart, dismantled, blown up. Half of the gulag archipelago has already sunk into the mire. Half of the camps in Siberia have been overgrown by forests, and the roads to them washed away by spring floods. In the cities, new neighborhoods, factories, sports stadiums, already stand on the sites of many of the camps.

In the summer, if one drives across Kolyma on the northern road—toward Karamken, Strelka, Bol'shevik—and one knows where the old camps lie, concealed by forests and hills, one will find there piles of rotting poles, a piece of iron rail, the clay remains of a kitchen. It is doubtful that one would find any object of use: there will be no spoon or bowl, no pickax or shovel, no brick or plank—all that was taken by the prisoners or their guards or later scavenged by the local population, for each of these things has its price here, its value.

In a few more years every last trace of the world of the camps will be erased from existence.

ALBERT, I asked again, is nothing left in Magadan of those years? No physical evidence?

He grew thoughtful. "Virtually nothing," he said after a while. "The headquarters of Dal'stroy was torn down. The barracks of the NKVD—torn down. The prison where interrogations took place—torn down. There are already new houses everywhere and new streets.

"But there is still one building. It has survived because it's a little out of the way, hidden between the apartment buildings of a residential neighborhood. It's the old House of Political Instruction of the NKVD cadre of the Kolyma camps."

We went there, scaling enormous snowbanks. It is a single-storied old building that appears small today. In the main hall a dozen or so schoolgirls, pale and serious, were practicing their ballet steps.

In was in this very hall that the briefings of murderers took place. It was here that they determined the frequency and size of executions. Here came Garanin and Pavlov, Nikishov and Yegorov. And hundreds of others whose gun barrels were still warm.

Before their eyes, with their help, and sometimes by their very hands—three million people died.

We walked around the empty building. "And here?" I asked Albert, pointing at a door.

Behind it was the bathroom of the executioners. It was the size of an average room. No toilet bowls. Only six oval holes in an unevenly laid, concrete floor. Gray walls covered with brown water stains. A broken faucet.

"Is this everything that's left, Albert?"

"That's everything," he replied.

I HAVE TWO books with me: Varlam Shalamov's *Kolyma Tales* and Alex Weissberg-Cybulski's *The Great Purge*. The juxtaposition of these authors, of their outlooks and stances, is fascinating. The comparison enables one to penetrate, if only slightly, into

Russian thought, into its riddle and its nature. Both books are documents of the same experience—that of a victim of Bolshevik repression—but how different are the minds of the two authors!

Both were members of the same generation (Weissberg was born in 1901; Shalamov, in 1907). Both were arrested in 1937: Shalamov in Moscow (for him it was the second time); Weissberg in Char'kov, where he was working as a contract engineer. Both tormented, tortured, harassed, humiliated by the NKVD. Completely innocent, pure, honest men.

But here the differences begin.

The question is as follows: Which will prevail within us, determine our relation to life, to reality? The civilization, the tradition in which we grew up, or the faith, the ideology that we possess and profess?

The Austrian Weissberg is a man of the West, reared in the spirit of Cartesian rationalism, of penetrating and critical thought.

Shalamov is a Russian through and through; he never traveled outside Russia; he encountered Western ideas only sporadically; everything about him is Russian from start to finish.

At the same time, the man of the West, Weissberg, is an ardent and committed Communist, while the man of Russia, Shalamov, is a profound anti-Communist.

What attitude will each one of them now have toward his situation as a victim of barbaric repressions and "unnecessary cruelty," toward the whole nightmarish surrounding world of Stalinist purges, prisons, gulags, and executions?

Weissberg is convinced that he has found his way into an insane asylum, that the investigating officers of the NKVD are demented people, that the Soviet Union of Stalin's epoch is a world of lunacy, paranoia, of the absurd. That which takes place here, he writes, "is completely senseless, these are the escapades of a debauched *aparat*, defying all rational interpretation." Or: "I grabbed my head. Was I in a madhouse?" Or: "Everything is after all the sheerest folly. I simply lack the words to characterize this." Et cetera, et cetera. And all the while, not for a moment does he abandon his beliefs: "I am a German Communist," he flings at the interrogating officer, "and I arrived in this country to take part in the building of socialism. I am a patriot of the Soviet Union."

Convinced that he is in an insane asylum, that he is in a ghastly land of madness and surreal paranoia, Weissberg does not break down; under the most horrifying conditions, in crowded, dirty prisons dripping with blood, his mind, the mind of a Western rationalist, works intensively—it searches for a rational, reasonable explanation for that which is happening around him. In each cell they throw him into, Weissberg strives to discuss, to question, to exchange opinions.

But it is precisely Weissberg whom his Russian fellow comrades in adversity look upon as a madman! What are you thrashing around for? they say. What are you trying to accomplish here? Sit quietly and suffer!

Between these two attitudes there is no communication, no common language. That is why I do not know whether Weissberg and Shalamov could have understood each other.

Shalamov believes that everything that surrounds him is part of the natural world. The camps belong to the natural order of things, and not to the human order. Can a man rebel against the fact of a great frost or a terrible flood? If a flood comes and someone starts to shake his fist at the river, people will say that he is mad, that he escaped from an insane asylum. If a flood comes, one must climb the highest tree and wait patiently until the water recedes. That is rationality, that is the only reasonable response. If a man finds himself in a camp, he shouldn't revolt, because they will shoot him for that; he should just live in such a way that ensures he will survive. Maybe, sometime, the water in the river will recede; maybe, sometime, they will release him from the camp. Nothing more can or even need be done.

In *Kolyma Tales*, the world beyond the wires of the camp does not really exist. News about the end of World War II reaches here after a lag in time and does not make an impression. The real and only world is the camp. The camp is a complete and logical structure. Why did Weissberg find all this absurd? If the camp were absurd, it would have collapsed instantly. The camp does have a logic, and that is the logic of murder—a kind of rationality different from the one that the Austrian engineer-Communist was searching for.

It is Shalamov's mind that is rational and logical and Weissberg's mind that is astray, lost in abstractions.

"Each intervention in that which fate was bringing, in the will of the gods, was something unbecoming and contradictory to the code of camp conduct," Shalamov recalls. And between the lines: whoever thinks that he can behave differently has never touched the true bottom of life; he has never had to breathe his last in "a world without heroes."

This difference between Shalamov's and Weissberg's stance vis-à-vis the world of repression, the "other world" (Herling-Grudzinski) into which they were cast, is explained by perhaps the greatest Russian philosopher, Vladimir Soloviev: "The opposition between the two cultures—the eastern and the western—was already sharply delineated at the dawn of human history. If the East built the foundations of its culture on the ruthless subordination of man to a higher power, the supernatural, then in the West it was the opposite, man was left to his own invention, which allowed for a broad, self-generated creativity."

ONE WALKS ALONG the streets of Magadan through high-walled corridors dug out in the snow. They are narrow, and when another person is passing one must stop to let him by. Sometimes at such a moment I find myself standing face-to-face with some elderly man. Always, one question comes to my mind: And who were you? The executioner or the victim?

And why am I moved to wander? Why am I unable to look at this man in an ordinary way, without that perverse and intrusive curiosity? For if I could summon up my courage and ask him this question, and if he responded sincerely, I might hear the answer: "You see, you have before you both the executioner and the victim."

This too was a characteristic of Stalinism—that in many instances it was impossible to distinguish these two roles. First someone, as an interrogating officer, would beat a prisoner, then he himself would be thrown into prison and beaten; after serving his sentence he would get out and take revenge, and so on. It was the world as a closed circle, from which there was only one exit—death. It was a nightmarish game in which everyone lost.

I VENTURED FAR, right up to the bay. In this place one could no longer hear the city. Above all, one could not hear Kolyma. Somewhere beyond the hill descending toward the bay, in silence and darkness, its dead lay. In one memoir I read that Kolyma's permafrost so preserves corpses that the faces of those buried maintain even their expressions. The faces of people who saw that which, as Shalamov warns, man should not see.

I thought about the terrible uselessness of suffering. Love leaves behind its creation—the next generation coming into the world, the continuation of humanity. But suffering? Such a great part of human experience, the most difficult and painful, passes leaving no trace. If one were to collect the energy of suffering emitted by the millions of people here and transform it into the power of creation, one could turn our planet into a flowering garden.

But what has remained?

Rusty carcasses of ships, rotting watchtowers, deep holes from which some kind of ore was once extracted. A dismal, lifeless emptiness. Not a soul anywhere, for the exhausted columns have already passed and vanished in the cold eternal fog.

# The Kremlin: The Magic Mountain

I AM RETURNING to Moscow from Magadan by way of Norilsk. From Kolyma to Norilsk it is more than three hours by plane over northern Siberia. It is a clear, sunny noon; the air so transparent and bright that it creates the effect of a great close-up—as if one were looking at the earth through a magnifying glass.

Below, as far as the eye can see, white and more white, a smooth, taut flatness polished by winds to the utmost, absolute luster. Over this blinding and lifeless smoothness, a small, solitary dark blue creature laboriously wends its way—the shadow of our airplane, a mobile sign that it is flying, that we are alive.

White, like every color, is in and of itself indescribable. It exists, but it begins to individuate and submit to definition only in juxtaposition with other colors. And here there are no other hues. There is only the boundless white cosmos and, sunk into it, like an insect trapped in a lump of amber, the microscopic shadow of our IL-62.

But at a certain moment, we observe that on the bright, clean surface below us, a line appears. For a time it runs solitarily. But then we see a second line. Now the two run parallel to each other, straight, until the place where they are intersected by a more distinct, stronger line. For some time nothing happens, just three lines stretched across a flat, vast background. Suddenly the white boundlessness begins to be covered with ever new lines, now there are more and more of them, laid out closer and closer together. The hitherto homogeneous, monotonously uniform plane breaks into squares, rectangles, rhombuses, and triangles, into an intricate geometric structure, forms piling up here, dissipating in all directions there: it is Norilsk, the mining and metallurgical basin of Siberia—like the Polish Śląsk, the German Ruhr, the American Pittsburgh, only beyond the Arctic Circle.

BETWEEN NORILSK and Moscow lie the Ural Mountains. During the flight over them a change of season takes place. Until now it has been winter and more winter, and now, after passing the summits of the Urals, one flies straight into spring. The earth regains its gray-brown hue—natural in this region—the riverbeds fill up with running silver, and here and there stretch spots of pale green. Along the way there will still be some cities, there will be the Volga, there will be forests, and beyond the forests—Moscow.

IN MOSCOW I immediately fall into a whirl of discussions, the capital's gossip, polemics, and quarrels. Everywhere encounters, meetings, conferences, and symposia. Every day all kinds of people stand around the statue of Pushkin, from morning to night, trying to outshout one another, sticking their fingers into one another's eyes, shoving handfuls of leaflets under one another's noses. These times are a paradise for debaters, for the silver-tongued, for polemicists and prattlers, preachers and orators, swordsmen of the word and seekers of the truth. There are dozens, hundreds, of such street-debating clubs in this country. You will see rabid debaters in the squares of Lvov and Omsk, Arkhangel'sk and Karaganda . . . everywhere. It all looks like a scene from the old photographs of the February Revolution of 1917.

Although there are plenty of interesting and even extraordinary things in these verbal geysers, one day I decide to escape from the polemicists and the debaters and go to the Kremlin.

I HAD LONG thought about going to the Kremlin. That intention was revived whenever, traveling to the city center from Leninski Prospekt (where I was staying), I passed the Kremlin's lofty walls, buildings, and towers rising up on the right. I was always struck then by the immense stone wasteland surrounding the Kremlin complex on all sides—large, unending squares, wide bridges, concrete embankments, vast, desolate areas covered in asphalt and concrete slabs, stretching for kilometers.

On these squares that spread out in all directions, packs of cars, scattered, some here, some there, take off every few minutes, dash wildly along, taking every possible shortcut, and hurriedly disappear into the throats of streets that begin somewhere far from here. The infrequently stationed militiamen wisely stand out of their way. But besides them one cannot meet a living soul here, despite the fact that we are in the center of a city of ten million. One feels this desolateness especially on Sunday or during bad weather. The wind rips across the wasteland, driving rain or snow along with it. I sometimes ventured into these unpeopled spaces. Below, the river Moscow rolled its gray waters. To one side was the leaden massif of the apartment building for the elite—the only residential structure in the area. I was suspended in the vacuum that separates the inaccessible government (the Kremlin) from the living tissue of the city. There was no movement or buzz of the street here—rather, the silence and boundlessness of the steppe.

THE KREMLIN is a large complex of medieval and modern edifices standing on a hill and enclosed by a brick-and-stone wall. This mighty wall is crowned by twenty towers of various sizes, the largest being Spasskaya, Nikolskaya, Naroznaya, Troitskaya, and Borovitskaya. Inside are various government buildings as well as former Orthodox churches and cathedrals, turned into museums. Above all, the Kremlin is the workplace, and often also the residence, of the most important person in the Imperium. In short, since 1918, when Lenin moved the capital from Petersburg to Moscow (safety considerations decided the matter: Petersburg was too close to the sea, too close to Europe), the Imperium has been ruled from the heights of the Kremlin.

The shortest route to the walls of the Kremlin is from Red Square. Here is where, if the day is sunny and warm, one can encounter the greatest number of people. On one side of the square stands a long, long line to Lenin's mausoleum. On the other side is the Spasskaya Tower. Black government ZILs (Soviet-made limousines) fly out every now and then through this gate at great speed. They are all identical (except that the most important ones don't have registration plates), but as for who is riding in them, one cannot tell, for the windows are veiled with curtains. These vehicles drive out so frequently that one could easily be led to believe that there is a car factory in the Kremlin and that new models are leaving the assembly line one after the other.

To walk into the Kremlin just like that, simply to walk in, without a reason or a goal, is impossible. One can gain access for only three reasons: (a) to visit the museum as part of a group excursion from one's place of work (it is a form of distinction and reward), (b) to attend one of a variety of important congresses that from time to time take place here (delegates and accredited journalists can enter then), (c) at the summons of one of the dignitaries who officiate here. In each of these cases, one is required, after having passed the gate, to move by the shortest route possible to the preordained destination—there and back.

I TRIED entering from the west side, from the Troicka gate, because I know that it is the entrance for people who come here on foot, for the commoners. Two officers of the militia stopped me: "A pass!"

I showed them my press credentials.

"That's not enough! The pass to the Kremlin! Where are you going?"

"To the congress of the small nations of Siberia."

As a matter of fact there was such a congress in progress. They sent me back for a pass. It was four o'clock in the afternoon.

Office workers, secretaries, janitors, were leaving the Kremlin through the same gate. All of them were carrying bags stuffed with items from the Kremlin shops, nets full of veritable treasures—cold cuts, cheeses, oranges. Loaded down, they swayed in the direction of the distant bus stops and metro stations.

The next day at the same time I appeared at the Troicka gate with a pass. They inspected it, compared the photograph with the original, and made certain that I knew where the congress was taking place, in which building. In reality I didn't know, for I also had no intention of listening to the debates of the Siberians. I wanted to see the Kremlin.

But this would not be easy, as I quickly realized. Having exited from the twilight of the deep and massive gate, I saw before me inside the walls a great stone-paved emptiness. In front of me stretched the flat expanse of the old Senate Square. On the right I had the modern marble mass of the Palace of Congresses, and on the left the rectangular arsenal building, painted yellow. It was empty everywhere and clean everywhere. The sidewalks quite obviously freshly swept, the shrubs trimmed evenly, in a uniform shape, the curbs whitened with lime. When the wind blew, dry leaves appeared on the square and the sidewalks, but they too seemed clean to me. This aseptic and severe cleanliness deepened in a strange way the bareness and desolation of the place. I had the impression that I was here alone, that I was of no concern to anyone. But that was an illusion.

FACING ME, slightly to the left, stood the building that interested me the most—it was an eighteenth-century structure that had served as the Palace of the Senate and later the seat of the government of the USSR. Erected on a triangular plan, it stood inside the Kremlin itself. Lenin, Stalin, and Brezhnev had each ruled from here. They were shielded from the rest of the city and from the country by, as it were, a double guard: first, they were isolated by the enormous emptiness of the broad squares and open, bare spaces surrounding the rise upon which the Kremlin stands, and second—within the fortress—were sheltered by the powerful Kremlin brick wall and the other buildings standing nearby.

That was not enough!

In 1920, H. G. Wells, while visiting Lenin in the Kremlin, noticed a third barrier sheltering the leaders:

> The Kremlin as I rememebered it in 1914 was a very open place, open much as Windsor Castle is, with a thin trickle of pilgrims and tourists in groups and couples flowing through it. But now it is closed up and difficult of access. There was a great pother with passes and permits before we could get through even the outer gates. And we filtered and inspected through five or six rooms of clerks and sentinels before we got into the presence. (*Russia in the Shadows*)

But even that was not enough!

Neither the depopulated squares around the Kremlin, nor the walls and gates of the fortress, nor the empty spaces inside the fortress, nor the checkpoints in the buildings and rooms, gave the leaders a feeling of adequate security. So they went below the surface; they burrowed underground:

> Before the Second World War, between the Kremlin and the Central Committee building on Nogin Square, as well as certain other buildings in the center of the city, long underground passages were built, so that the members of the government and the higher military commanders could pass from one area in the Kremlin to another without going out into the street. . . . Admiral Isakov remembers: "We are walking with Stalin along long Kremlin corridors, at their intersections stand sentries and, in accordance with the regulations of the internal security service, with their gaze they meet and follow each passerby, until, in their mind's eye, they have delivered him into the care of the next sentry. I'd barely had the time to think about this when Stalin said, in a tone of hatred seasoned with bitterness: 'They protect . . . But at any

> moment they will shoot you in the back.' " (Roy Medvedev, *Under the Judgment of History*)

Well, all right—the surface of the globe is secured, inside the Kremlin walls everything is also under control, and no one can dig through underground; but isn't there still a menace from the air? Yes, they thought of that too. The sky above the Kremlin is tightly controlled. Only in the muddle of perestroika did oversights occur, and when a young German, Rust, suddenly landed, Gorbachev had to punish several generals for the gaps in the aerial security of the Kremlin.

This sheltering of the leadership, despite the fact that in 1920 the entire security system was still childishly lax and makeshift, led Wells to a thought that troubled him:

> It is very possible that all this is indispensable for ensuring Lenin's personal safety, but it also after all renders difficult the maintaining of direct contact between Russia and him, and—what seems even more important, insofar as the effectiveness of governmental action is concerned—contact between him and Russia. For if what reaches Lenin is passed through a filter of some kind, then similarly everything that comes from him must be filtered, and in the course of such machinations serious distortions can occur.

It is possible that the observation about what fatal consequences the overly tight isolation of the Soviet leaders might have for their thinking occurred to Wells when this distinguished Englishman of impeccable manners, who always took morning walks and afternoon tea with milk, was attacked by Lenin with a series of questions:

> Our talk was threaded throughout and held together by two—what shall I call them?—*motifs*. One was from me to him: "What do you think you are making of Russia? What is the state you are trying to create?" The other was

> from him to me: 'Why does not the social revolution begin in England? Why do you not work for the social revolution? Why are you not destroying Capitalism and establishing the Communist State?" These *motifs* interwove, reacted on each other, illuminated each other. The second brought back the first: "But what are you making of the social revolution? Are you making a success of it?" And from that we got back to two again with : "To make it a success the Western world must join in. Why doesn't it?"

I WALKED in the direction of the Palace of the Senate. At first no one stopped me, and, in fact, I saw no one around. In the silence I could hear the echo of my own footsteps, and so I tried to walk without making any noise. Yes, it was precisely in this building, now standing before me, that Stalin's apartment was located. It was here that his wife, Nadiezdha Alliluyeva, committed suicide:

> Nadiezdha Alliluyeva's life with Stalin was becoming increasingly difficult. On November 8, 1932, a number of families of bolshevik leaders who were friendly with one another gathered in the Kremlin to celebrate the fifteenth anniversary of the October Revolution. Nadiezdha Alliluyeva was also present, but Stalin was late. When at last he arrived, Nadiezdha took the liberty of making an ironic comment about him. Stalin exploded with rage and answered her with an impertinence. Sometimes he smoked cigarettes instead of a pipe. Wanting to vent his anger on his wife, he suddenly threw the burning cigarette in her face, and it landed in the décolletage of her dress. Nadiezdha pulled out the cigarette and jumped to her feet, but Stalin quickly turned around and walked out. Nadiezdha walked out practically upon his heels. As it turned out, Stalin went to his dacha, and Nadiezdha to their Kremlin apartment. The festivities were ruined, and several hours later something even worse happened. . . . In the morning

> Svetlana's [Stalin's daughter] nanny, and Stalin's housekeeper, Caroline Tiel, was the first to see Nadiezdha Alliluyeva lying beside her bed in a pool of blood with a tiny pistol in her hand. (Roy Medvedev, *Under the Judgment of History*)

From that time on Stalin lived alone, and his entourage consisted almost entirely of men. But after all, one had to have some fun, especially when the long winter nights arrived and snowstorms raged and the wind wailed over the Kremlin's deserted expanses.

> Stalin finished a late dinner by raising a toast in Lenin's honor:
>
> "Let us drink to Vladimir Ilyich, our leader, our teacher—our everything!"
>
> We rose and solemnly drank in silence, then promptly drunkenly forgot about Lenin. Stalin, however, continued to wear a serious, solemn, and even sullen expression on his face. We left the table, but before we had started to disperse, Stalin walked up to a large, automatic gramophone. He even tried to dance some of his native dances. And he wasn't devoid of a sense of rhythm. Nevertheless he soon stopped, offering an explanation full of resignation:
>
> "Age has caught up with me and I am already an old man."
>
> But his friends, or, rather, courtiers, began to reassure him:
>
> "No, no, nonsense. You look terrific. You are holding up amazingly well. That's right, for your age. . . ."
>
> Later Stalin put on a record, on which the coloratura chirrup of the singer was accompanied by the howling and barking of dogs. He laughed with an exaggerated, excessive amusement. . . . (Milovan Djilas, *Conversations with Stalin*)

> Stalin put on dance music and we began to dance. The only good dancer among us was Anastas Ivanovich Mikoyan. Mikoyan danced, then Voroshilov danced. Everyone danced. I never move my feet, I dance like a cow on ice, but I too danced. Kaganovich danced. He too is a dancer of a class no better than mine. Same with Malenkov. Bulganin used to dance, probably in his youth; he tapped something Russian with his foot to the beat of the music. Stalin also danced—he shuffled his feet and spread his arms. . . . We sang. We sang, meaning we accompanied the records that Stalin put on. Later, Svetlanka appeared. . . . Stalin immediately ordered that she dance. After a time she grew tired, I could see that she was just barely moving . . . Stalin himself was already staggering, but he said: "Well, Svetlanka, dance!" And she: "But I've already danced, daddy, I'm tired." But Stalin grabbed her like this, by the hair, a whole fistful, I mean by her forelock, as it were, and pulled, you understand, very hard . . . pulled, jerked and jerked. (Nikita Khrushchev, *Memoirs*)

I WAS WALKING in the direction of the Palace of the Senate when suddenly two men appeared in front of me. Young, well built, in gray suits. I do not know where they came from; it was instantaneous. Instantaneous, resolute, imperious. One of them raised his hand, giving the signal—stop. Nothing more, but it all looked very serious and final. They didn't ask a single question—it was a scene without words. I stood for a moment, deliberating what I should do, then turned around and started to walk in the direction of the Arsenal.

I walked, and the setting sun shone in my eyes. Maybe that is why I saw the two men in front of me so late. Young, well built, in gray suits. The same as their predecessors, even identical, but of course different. One of them raised his hand in the practiced gesture—stop. I stopped, again seconds of hesitation, but then I turned to one side. They vanished at once.

I did not know where to go, what to do with myself—I knew the Kremlin only from photographs. But I spotted the rectangular silhouette of the Palace of Congresses, familiar to me from pictures. I set off in that direction. The Congress of the Siberians, however, must have been located in another building, for as soon as I walked up closer, two young men materialized before me. Well-built, in gray suits. The interior of the palace, moreover, was dark, all entrance doors closed. I decided to go south, for I saw in that direction the glittering cupolas of the Orthodox churches and cathedrals. I was hoping that there, perhaps, they would let me go in somewhere and see something.

At this stage of my wandering I theorized that I could succeed in my expedition if I walked everywhere with a determined step and even with a certain haste, moving in a straight line from point *A* to a previously selected point *B*.

But even this method did not save me from encounters with ever new pairs of well-built men in gray suits. It was as if, walking, I were inadvertently pressing down on some secret stone and releasing an invisible spring, which continually flung in my direction pairs of men who resembled each other as closely as twins. I retreated or turned to one side, and they—as quickly as they appeared—vanished.

IT WAS STILL empty everywhere.

An early evening wind had arisen, and in the silence that prevailed here I heard only its sporadic murmurs and laments. I was walking across Cathedral Square, having passed along the way the enormous Uspienski Cathedral and the towering belfry of Ivan the Great. Everywhere here man feels small, crushed by the immensity of these temples, stunned by the uniqueness of their architecture.

Finally I reached the Borovitskaya Tower, closely guarded because the top leadership drives into the Kremlin through its gate. I wanted to see this place, for I was just reading a book about Beria, and on June 26, 1953, Beria entered the Kremlin this way for the last time. Stalin had already been dead for four months. His place had been taken by Khrushchev. Khrushchev was afraid that Beria would shoot him and seize power himself; therefore he wanted to forestall the blow and had Beria arrested.

In the book I mentioned (*Beria: The End of the Career*), the then commander of the Moscow district, Marshal K. G. Moskalenko, recalls: "On June 25 at nine o'clock in the morning Khrushchev called me. He said that I should take some trusted people and come to the Kremlin, to the office of Premier Malenkov, in which Stalin once officiated. He added that I should bring maps, and also some cigars. I told him that I don't smoke, that I had given up smoking during the war. Khrushchev started to laugh and said that there would be a need for cigars, but not the kind I'm thinking of. Only then did I understand that I was supposed to bring weapons."

Khrushchev was speaking about cigars, and not about pistols, because everyone was eavesdropping on everyone else and the whole plot might have come to light.

At eleven Moskalenko and his people arrived at the Kremlin in the limousine of Marshal Bulganin (then the minister of defense). They waited.

> After several minutes Khrushchev, Bulganin, Malenkov, and Molotov came out to meet us. They started to tell us how lately Beria had been behaving insolently toward the other members of the Political Bureau, spying on them, eavesdropping on telephone conversations, snooping, watching to determine who went to see whom, whom the members of the Bureau were meeting with, treating them in a boorish manner, etc. They told us that the Political Bureau was about to convene and that at a given signal we were to enter and arrest Beria.

Marshal G. K. Zhukov relates further:

> Together with Moskalenko, his aide-de-camp, and the generals Niedielin and Batick I was sitting in a room and waiting for the two rings that were the agreed upon signal. I was forewarned that Beria was physically strong and knows jujitsu.
>
> "That's nothing," I answered, "I am strong too."

> An hour passed, and no ringing. I started to worry whether by chance Beria hadn't outsmarted everyone. But then the rings. I got up, we went to the hall of the Bureau meetings. Beria was sitting at the table, in the center. My generals encircled the table. They approached Beria from the rear and ordered:
>
> "Get up! You are under arrest!"
>
> Beria hadn't yet had time to get up when I twisted his arms to the rear and pulled them up, so that he wouldn't be able to tear them away. I looked at him, and he was pale, very pale. And stunned.
>
> We led him into the waiting room, then into another room. Here we searched him thoroughly. Oh, I forgot. In the moment when I twisted Beria's arms, I quickly reached for his belt, to check whether by chance he wasn't armed.
>
> We held Beria in the locked room until ten in the evening, and then under cover of darkness we drove him out of the Kremlin, wrapped in a carpet and thrown upon the car floor. The point was for the Kremlin guard not to notice him and not to inform his people.

Then they tried Beria—not for his crimes, but for wanting to seize power. And they immediately shot him.

Moskalenko drove Beria out of the Kremlin through the gate in the Nikolskaya Tower, situated closest to the city.

I now walk out through that same gate onto Tverskaya Street (formerly Gorky Street). Some young people are demonstrating, and I come up closer to hear what they are chanting. They are marching, holding hands, and shouting: "Coca-Cola hurrah!!!"

Moving in the same direction, up Tverskaya Street, are the tired and hungry people who today stood in line for several hours to get into the mausoleum and see Lenin. They are now getting in a second line—the one for McDonald's, for hamburgers with ketchup and fries.

# The Trap

THESE EVENTS TOOK place in the summer of 1990. I could not recount them earlier, for doing so would have endangered the people who had helped me.

THE DAY BEFORE leaving for Yerevan I met with Galina Starovoytova in Moscow. (Galina Vasilievna Starovoytova, professor at the University in Petersburg. At the time a deputy to the Supreme Soviet of the USSR, from Armenia. Subsequently an adviser to Boris Yeltsin on affairs of nationalities.) I was seeing her then for the first time. She was a portly woman, with an engaging manner and a warm, friendly smile. I knew that she was flying to Yerevan the next day. "We will meet there," she said. And added: "Maybe we will be able to help you, but I don't know, we will see."

The skepticism in her voice was understandable to me. I was asking to get into Nagorno-Karabakh, which was a practically hopeless matter. Access via an overland route did not exist: the entire district of Nagorno-Karabakh—which is an Armenian enclave in the territory of Azerbaijan—was encircled by divisions of the Red Army and of the Azerbaijani militia. They guarded all passages, highways, tracks, and paths, guarded the rocky clefts and faults, the passes, precipices, and peaks. There was absolutely no question of forcing one's way through this vigilant, tightly woven net. Even those who knew these parts well did not make such attempts. Therefore only the air route remained—namely, a small Aeroflot plane that flew from time to time (most irregularly) from Yerevan to Stepanakert, the capital of Nagorno-Karabakh. But with this too I had no chance. It wasn't merely a matter of getting a seat on the plane—difficult enough since people camp out for weeks at the airport in Yerevan (and I had neither the time nor the money to do this). The greater problem was that buying a ticket required a Soviet passport with proof of residence in Nagorno-Karabakh, or a permit from the General Staff of the army in Moscow. In my case, neither one of these documents could possibly be obtained.

I ARRIVED in Yerevan during the night. The entire next day I spent in the hotel, waiting for a telephone call. I had some ancient Armenian chronicles with me. Beautiful, thousand-year-old texts, but one cannot read much of them, for they contain so much despair, so much pain, and so many tears. The fate of Armenians: centuries of persecutions, centuries of exile, diaspora, homeless wandering, pogroms. All that is recorded in the chronicles. On each page someone is praying for endurance, someone is begging for his life. On each page there is terror, in each verse trembling and fear.

THE NEXT MORNING the telephone rang. I heard the voice of Galina Starovoytova. "Since yesterday," she said, "we have been thinking about you. We are deliberating, we are searching for a way. Wait patiently until a young man comes to you."

The young man was called Guren. He was well built, stocky, with energetic, vigorous movements. When he saw me, he immediately became worried. "What's wrong?" I asked. He opened his briefcase, in which he had several Soviet passports. They were the passports of Armenians, but of teenage Armenians; the oldest was twenty-four years old. All of them were no longer alive.

"This one was burned to death in Sumgait," said Guren, "and this one was choked to death in Nagorno-Karabakh."

"And this one?"

"I don't know how this one died." From the photographs, eyes equally black, serious, and concentrated stared out at us. Finally Guren picked a passport in which the photograph was somewhat blurred (water? sweat?) and told me to take that one.

Next, he put me into a completely dilapidated Moskvich in which nothing but the motor and (I hoped!) the brakes were working, and we set off across town. Immediately I felt that I was in the Third World, as if I had suddenly found myself on a street in Tehran, in Calcutta, or in Lagos, where no one observes any regulations, any lights or signs, and yet all the deranged, chaotic, frenzied traffic follows some sort of internal logic (invisible to the eye of a European), which ensures that although everyone drives exactly as he pleases, in a manner chosen purely at will—across, backward, in a zigzag, in a circle—in the end everyone (in any case, the majority) reaches his goal. We too—a particle of this rickety, wildly honking mass reeking of exhaust fumes—were heading toward our goal. What that was, I had no idea. But experience has taught that whenever people are taking me on a hazardous, uncertain, improbable expedition, it is inappropriate to ask questions. If you ask, it means you don't trust them; you are uncertain; you are afraid. But you had said that you wanted to do this. Make up your mind—are you ready for anything or not? Besides—there is no time! It is too late for indecision, for hesitation, for alternatives.

An old apartment building in the center of town. Guren leads me to the second floor. A typical Soviet apartment—cluttered, crowded. A daily, murderous struggle to maintain even a touch of cleanliness and order. A struggle without allies—without soap, without detergents, often without water. Actually, most frequently without water, because the city is drying up; there is water only rarely, sometimes here and sometimes there. One must search for it; one must wait for it. In the apartment in which I now find myself, the balcony has been converted into a veranda whose glass walls give onto a courtyard planted with trees; on this veranda a table stands and several people are sitting. I know only one of them—Galina Starovoytova. The others are mainly young men with beards. The presence of the bearded men indicates that there is a battle front somewhere in the vicinity, one front or another—for liberty, for power. In Armenia there are two fronts—the one in the war against the Imperium, and the other against Azerbaijan. The city is full of fedayeen—they stand on the streets, ride in trucks, armed with whatever they can manage to obtain, dressed in any old way, but all of them with beards. The fedayeen sitting at the table greet me very warmly, but after the initial effusiveness they all grow still, silence descends.

"Ryszard"—I hear someone's voice—"you will fly today to Stepanakert. On the same plane as Deputy Starovoytova. But you will fly as a pilot. And you and Galina Vasilievna do not have to know each other. You understand?"

"Of course," I said, "I understand." It sounded almost as though I had sworn a grand, solemn oath.

I wasn't in this apartment for long before Guren said it was time to drive to the airport.

SHALL I DESCRIBE the airport in Yerevan (which I also know from various other occasions)? Shall I describe morning at this airport? How a crowd of hundreds, of thousands of people awakens, people who have slept on benches, on the marbled concrete floor, on the stone steps? How these people begin to rise amid profanities, curses, the crying of infants? How long have they been sleeping here? Well, some not so long; this is only their first night. And those over there, the crumpled up, unshaven, unkempt ones? Those—a week. And those others one cannot even get closer to because they stink so terribly? Those—a month. So all of them, like one man, awake, look around, scratch themselves, yawn. A man gets up and attempts to stuff his shirt back inside his pants. A woman tries to stick her hair under a kerchief. Black, shining hair, magnificent, like Scheherazade's. It is the time when everyone would like to relieve himself. The glancing around begins, an increasingly anxious glancing around—where is there to go, where is there to hide, where is there to squat down? There are four toilets at the airport. Even if one were to assume, optimistically, that they are working, it would take several hours for everyone to visit them. Unfortunately, they are out of order, or, more accurately, one cannot avail oneself of them. This is what happened. Once, long, long ago, the toilet bowls became clogged. Because they were clogged and a towering mountain grew in them, people started to fill up the space around the toilet bowls. With an extraordinary, astounding punctiliousness, they filled up every square centimeter of the floor. Because they could no longer find any field of activity for themselves in the area around the toilets, they started to advance farther, to spread out, with an understandably natural determination to conquer new territories, ever wider and wider.

Well, all right, let us assume that the adult seekers of a secluded place, at the sight of these foul constructions that have stiffened at the doors of the four toilets, will suppress their need for several hours. But the children? After all, young children . . . have to. This two-year-old girl has to, and even this five-year-old boy, although he's already so big, has to. So is there any sense in the commander of the airport, who walks around and fumes at the children for relieving themselves, without any great shame, in the corners?

Some of the people are running here and there trying to find out about a flight. Will there be one? When will there be one? And so on. As to whether or not there are seats available they do not ask, for everyone knows that there never are any seats available. Those who run around like crazy trying to find out something are novices, naive and inexperienced; they have probably spent only one, perhaps two, nights here thus far. The veterans do not go anywhere. They know that there is no point to it and prefer to guard their places on the benches. They sit on them motionless, as though autistic, without any connection to their surroundings, like people in institutions for the mentally ill.

• • •

SHALL I DESCRIBE the scenes in the small, crowded room in which complaints are heard? The Armenian who is on duty here, judging by his appearance, must have been some kind of boxer, a circus strongman, a wrestler. But only such a gladiator could physically restrain the pushing, cursing, threatening crowd, whose raised fists are ever rolling toward him, like a torrent of lethal stones. How many misfortunes, how many dramas, in this crowd. This woman must make it to the Urals today, for the funeral of her son, who died in the army. I will not attempt to describe her shouts, her face, her fingers clutching her hair. This man has suddenly lost his eyesight. He must fly to Kiev, for an operation. It is his only chance to avoid becoming blind forever. Along the wall of the room stands a quiet line of women, who also should, somehow, fly out. They stand calmly; they cannot become tense. Their stomachs are bulging, labor could start at any moment.

Guren and I forced our way through the human thicket—through the crowd obstinately, rabidly pushing at something (at someone?)—and reached the pilots' room. At the sight of us one of them rose in greeting. He was thin, slightly taller than me. His name was Suren. He told me to follow him and led me to the parking lot, to his car. In the trunk he had a uniform—a jacket and pants. "I was ironing all night," he said with pride. "We still have to get you epaulets and a cap," he added. I changed in the car and we stuffed my own clothes into a plastic bag. We returned to the building. Suren found a stewardess, I could see him telling her something. She disappcared, and we waited for her, talking about the weather. Finally she returned and nodded her head to indicate that I should follow her. She had the key to the pilots' locker room. There she picked out for me the appropriate epaulets and cap. I was to fly as the captain of the plane. She led me out into the corridor and said: "I will stay in the locker room—you go by yourself back to Suren." She didn't want us to be seen together.

I went, but was immediately confronted by an unexpected situation. For I had barely shown myself in the hall of the airport when people, spotting a pilot, threw themselves upon me with questions—where are we flying to, would we take them and when?

I would have somehow handled this, but now, jostling aside the passengers, two men—or, as it quickly became apparent, two competitors—forced their way over to me and in an imperious tone almost simultaneously announced to me: "All tickets for the plane through me only!" (In short, possessing an officially purchased ticket was barely a preliminary or even a prepreliminary step on the thorny road of securing a piece of paper that would have the actual value of a valid ticket. Whether someone would take off or not depended on a bribe given to one of the mafias, whose leaders I now had before me. Here is precisely the kind of situation in which many Westerners lose themselves, inclined as they are to treat all reality just as it usually presents itself to them: limpid, legible, and logical. With such a philosophy, the man of the West thrown into the Soviet world has the rug pulled out from beneath his feet at every moment, until someone explains to him that the reality that he knows is not the only one and—most certainly—not the most important one, and that a plurality of the most diverse realities exists here, interlaced into a monstrous knot that cannot be untied and whose essence is multilogicality: a bizarre confusion of the most contradictory logical systems, now and then erroneously called illogicality or alogicality by those who assume that there exists only one system of logic.)

Conscious of the fact that the slightest misstep might now, in my situation, have disastrous consequences, I was forced into decisive action. I pushed everyone aside vigorously and walked to the pilots' room. Suren introduced me to the second pilot with whom we were to fly. He was called Averik. We immediately liked each other. Averik knew that this entire operation entailed a great risk, but something about it all fascinated him, and from the very first moment he was prepared for everything. He knew that if they caught me, he too would go to prison. But at the time I met him he was cheerful and full of energy. The complete opposite of Suren—who was always composed, closed, taciturn.

• • •

THE AIRPLANE that Suren and Averik were piloting was a small jet, JAK-40, intended for twenty-six passengers. In Yerevan, during takeoff, there were no problems. A bus drove us together with the passengers to the plane, which stood far from the terminal. Among the passengers I saw Starovoytova and Guren (he was flying as her assistant). The rest were exhausted Armenians, already so worn out that they weren't even able to look joyful about the prospect of finally going home. Suren, Averik, and I entered the cockpit and shut the door. Suren started to activate the engines. The atmosphere in the cockpit was good, for the whole plan of my expedition rested upon rather solid foundations. An eminent Soviet personage, a very well-known and popular deputy to the Supreme Soviet, is visiting her electoral district. She is bringing gifts for the schools and wants to meet with those who voted for her. It is therefore only natural that she will be received with joy and respect, and I, in this atmosphere of general hospitality and cordiality, will be appearing as—perhaps—her personal pilot. (If this part proves for some reason unsuccessful, I am to pretend that I do not know Starovoytova.)

Our small jet covers the distance from Yerevan to Stepanakert in three-quarters of an hour. One flies between two mountain ranges of Nagorno-Karabakh (also called Upper Karabakh, for there is also a Lower Karabakh). Upper and Lower Karabakh form the eastern spur of the Caucasus, which, in ever gentler declivities, as if gradually losing its vigor and impetus, metamorphoses into the valley of the Kura River. Another two, three, hundred kilometers farther west and the clear waters of this river will flow into the dark, oil-polluted Caspian Sea.

Suren and Averik at the controls. We sit in the cockpit as if in a theater box suspended in air, from which one watches an extraordinary pantomime—dancing mountains. This dance is slow, somnambulistic, almost motionless, and yet these silent, petrified shapes are moving, are changing their position, are turning around, are leaning low to the ground or straightening up high—to the clouds. Couples, groups, processions, ever new ones.

All around—Switzerland. Here herds of grazing sheep, there rushing streams, over there green forests and clearings.

THE VOICE of the air-traffic controller from the Stepanakert airport tears me from this contemplation—we are starting our descent. One can already see the small valley, a barely visible line of habitation, and then, after a moment, Suren points out the thread of the landing strip. This runway will turn out to be uneven and very short; no larger plane could land here. As a matter of fact, we ourselves come to a stop at the very end of it, and just ahead is a pile of rubble. Slowly we taxi toward the barracks—that is the airport terminal. As we draw nearer, Suren and Averik's expressions stiffen: the place is surrounded by troops. The militia is everywhere. There is a state of war in Nagorno-Karabakh, and the district is governed by the military commissioner. The troops are units of the KGB brought here from deep inside Russia.

"There were never this many," Suren mutters.

He has barely cut the engines when I see armed commandos encircling the plane and officers approaching. Suren says something to Averik and points at me. Averik nods his head knowingly.

"Walk ahead of me," he says. We walk out of the cockpit. The only door in the plane is located in its tail. Averik opens it, the steps drop to the ground. I feel the blast of tropical air and see the soldiers gathering at the foot of the steps.

"Get out, get out and immediately walk straight ahead." I hear Averik's voice.

I know I cannot now hesitate for even a second or make an uncertain gesture, an unnecessary motion. I run down the steps, I pass the officers already crowding at the bottom, I pass the commandos and militiamen, I march straight ahead. Averik is walking beside me, and he (I am counting on this) knows what to do next. The most important thing is that no one is calling after us, no one is ordering us to stop. We walk straight into a line of armored trucks and soldiers sitting in the shade of these trucks. And here too no one stops us—we are wearing pilots' uniforms, after all, everyone saw that a moment ago we brought in a plane.

We walk the length of the trucks for about a hundred meters, until we reach a gate near which stands a small wooden building. Inside is a sort of bar, which offers one thing only—warm lemonade. Averik buys me a glass (in the confusion I forgot to bring money) and says to me: "Sit here and wait," and, without a good-bye, he vanishes. After a period of time a young man with a beard appears whom I have never before seen and who, walking past me, mutters through his teeth, "Sit here and don't move, from now on you are under my protection," and vanishes.

The waiting starts to stretch out, longer and longer. I sit as if on burning coals. There are several tables in the bar, but they are empty; I am the only one sitting here. But there is nevertheless a lot of activity; people are continually coming in for lemonade. The greatest threat is the military patrols. Just imagine: a small, makeshift airport deep in the countryside, high up in the mountains. Sometimes a small airplane arrives, which, moreover, takes off again almost at once. The sole attraction is the bar, which sells lemonade. It is hot, everyone is thirsty. The military patrols are the most thirsty of all, for they are walking around in helmets, in bulletproof vests, and on top of that they are loaded down with hardware. What do these patrols have to do? Nothing, really—to walk and snoop, to walk and search, observe, question. And then, amid this deadly tedium and do-nothingism, they are presented with this tasty morsel: in the bar (the only one!), in the empty bar, sits an Aeroflot pilot. And what if one were to simply walk up and ask him a question. Let's say—where are you from? Or let's say—where are you going to? After all one can ask, especially if one is part of a military patrol on duty, in wartime conditions, in such a trouble spot as Nagorno-Karabakh. People come here very rarely. It is difficult to come here. They don't just let anybody in.

If a Russian patrol accosts me—that won't be so bad: I will pretend to be an Armenian; I will speak Russian, but with an Armenian accent. If an Armenian patrol accosts me—that won't be so bad either: I can speak Russian with the kind of accent a Lithuanian or a Latvian might have. It is the mixed patrols,

Russian-Armenian, that fill me with the greatest fear. That I won't be able to weasel out of.

The second problem lies in the fact that I don't have any documents. Yes, the edge of a Soviet passport protrudes from the pocket of my shirt. But it is the passport of a young Armenian murdered in Sumgait.

After an hour the bearded man reappears.

"Listen," I say, "I cannot sit here, they are going to catch me here." I see that his nerves are on edge.

"Sit," he replies, "there is no way out. Sit." And he vanishes.

Despite the heat, I pull the cap down over my eyes and pretend that I am dozing. It is a large cap, imposing, covered with all kinds of trimmings, stripes, and oak leaves. I treat it now as a sort of shield, a screen behind which I can hide. I also try to assume a pose that will discourage all contacts. The pose of some kind of a misfit, a grump, a Neanderthal, one that will signal to everyone: Better not come close!

Two hours after first sitting down in this bar I hear the roar of the departing plane. I feel even more lonely and trapped. Fortunately, now the bearded man appears again and says: "Follow me." I walk out of the bar feeling as though I were leaving behind the walls of a hard prison. We go along the road leading from the airport to town, but no farther than a hundred meters, to a place where, beside the road but slightly below it, is a parking lot. At its entrance, in the shade of a roadside tree, sits an old Armenian. He and my young bearded man exchange knowing nods of the head, whereupon my guide leads me to a canary-yellow Lada. He says, "Sit here and don't move," and . . . vanishes. On the one hand I feel more at ease here than in the bar, where I had been a sitting duck, but on the other hand, the car, which had stood all day in the sun, is like a furnace inside. I want to get out and take a walk around the parking lot when the old man squatting in the shade of the tree hisses: "Don't get out, they are right nearby!" Indeed, maybe fifty meters farther is a roadblock and next to it a military guard post. There would be nothing simpler than, upon seeing an Aeroflot pilot suffering in the sun, to invite him into the tent for a sip of refreshing tea and then, if only to keep the conversation going, to ask him who, what, how, where. After all, one has to talk, it's natural, it's human to talk, especially now, when there is glasnost, now one can chat even with a stranger.

The worst thing is that I still do not know what is going on. Clearly, our optimistic plan, prepared in Yerevan, has failed. Starovoytova was to have been greeted at the airport by local notables. This ceremony would have lasted a quarter of an hour, well, maybe a half hour. Next, we were to have gone in cars to town, eaten dinner, given presents to the schoolchildren, toured the park, met with the inhabitants of Stepanakert. It was supposed to have been warm, hospitable, idyllic. Whereas in fact no notables were waiting for us at the plane, only KGB commandos. There is no atmosphere of welcome at all; we have fallen straight into an ambush.

I ask the old man (he sits the entire time under the tree staring in the direction of the airport and doesn't move his head even when he exchanges a few words with me) if Starovoytova has already gone to town, but he answers no in a worried tone of voice. That means, I reason, that either they are holding her at the airport or they have ordered her to return in our airplane to Yerevan. But the Armenian does not know.

THAT OLD ARMENIAN in the shade of a roadside tree. All the conspiracies of the East depend on such people. They dwell motionless as boulders in the rocky landscape of this country. They sit leaning against canes in the clay back alleys of Oriental cities. They see everything; they know everything. Nothing can throw them off balance. No one can cheat them. No one can defeat them. Now, too, thanks to the presence of this man under the tree, I felt better.

I AM DEVISING a story in the event that they catch me.

Where did you get the uniform? the interrogating officer will ask me.

Where? I bought it in Warsaw. You can buy any uniform you

want there from the Russians. A captain's, a colonel's, even a general's. You can also buy arms, but, as you can see—I'm not carrying any.

If what you are saying is true, why did you buy the uniform of an Aeroflot pilot?

Because for a long time now I have wanted to get into Nagorno-Karabakh, and I knew that there was no other way to get myself here. I wanted to be in this place at all cost, because I have always been moved by the fate of people condemned to extermination, and the inhabitants of Nagorno-Karabakh are condemned to extermination.

You think so? the interrogating officer will ask.

Alas. I fear that yes. This is a small island of Christianity, which in a few years will be flooded by the ocean of Islamic fundamentalism. The waves of this ocean are already rising. Don't you see them?

Where did you get the passport of that man from Sumgait?

That passport was lying on a windowsill at the Yerevan airport. No one was paying any attention to it.

Who let you onto the plane?

No one did, I walked on myself. I got on the bus together with the passengers, and we went on board together. It would have been strange if the passengers were to ask a pilot why he is flying on a plane.

Guard! The interrogating officer calls the militiamen. Take this prisoner to his cell!

I had a lot of time on my hands, and so I composed various other alternative depositions in which I had one aim only—not to implicate anyone, not to burden anyone.

FOUR HOURS had passed since our landing when, from the direction of the town, a black limousine pulled up and stopped at a certain distance from the guard post. It was the kind of car in which only higher officials of the Imperium ride, so I thought, Aha, they sent the car, so they'll probably let Starovoytova into town. A moment later the bearded man appeared (the whole time very tense, conspiratorial) and said: "Walk in a decisive way!"

He didn't have to say that—I knew that in such situations walking decisively is half the battle.

We got in, slamming the door energetically behind us, and the car took off at once. We were driving in the direction of the town, several kilometers along an asphalt road lined intermittently with armored cars and small tanks; the entire area resembled a large army camp. Suddenly, tall, massive concrete blocks appeared before us on the highway, forming a labyrinth. Cars had to slow down and maneuver cautiously between them before stopping to be inspected by the soldiers stationed here. At the sight of this obstacle, the bearded man said: "Lie down and pretend to be dead drunk." He couldn't think of anything else. I immediately collapsed on the rear seat and covered my face with the cap. I heard the bearded man saying to the soldier who stuck his head into the car: "Drunk. Drunk and tired."

Once again we were speeding toward town, on our right a hill, on our left a deep ravine with the thread of a dead railroad line visible at its bottom. "You can sit up now," the bearded man said, "but if they stop us again pretend again to be drunk." But all the sentry posts we subsequently passed just waved us on. Little streets soon appeared, planted with many trees, shady, at right angles to one another. Then the car entered a courtyard surrounded by apartment buildings, and the bearded man said: "Get out." I jumped out, and the car pulled away at once. I didn't even have a chance to take a look around before an elderly woman ran up to me, pulled me by the arm, and shoved me into a stairwell, saying only, "Third floor," before disappearing. I walked up to the third floor, where a door was already open, and I found myself in an apartment encircled by a crowd of women and children. Everyone was shouting with joy, hugging me, embracing me, calling something out to me. I saw flushed, triumphant faces. "Rogues! Knaves! Occupiers!" The women were getting carried away. "How much longer still are they going to torment us this way, hold us captive!" And as they uttered their unceasing and ever more inventive curses and threats against the regime, they heated up for me a dinner that had long gone cold.

Several men came in, and they too embraced me. With their

arrival, the whole brouhaha momentarily died down; the children disappeared somewhere into the corners; the women stopped lamenting and execrating. I could go change. They gave me some civilian clothes.

THE EVENING PASSES in conversation. That is why I have come here. I have come in order to meet the people from the Karabakh Committee, who are not permitted to leave this place, who are condemned to silence, to a mute resistance, whereas what they want is for the world to know about the fate of the local Armenians, their adversity, their drama. That desire—for one's voice to be heard somewhere—is characteristic of enslaved peoples, who cling to their belief in the possibility of justice in the world the way a drowning man clings to a plank, who are convinced that being heard is being understood and that by that means alone they can prove their argument and win the case.

Darkness is starting to fall. We are sitting in a large room, at a long, heavy table. It is a typical Armenian apartment: the table is the most important piece of furniture, the central point of the house and home. The table should always be set with whatever one has, with whatever is at hand, just so that it is not bare, for a table's nakedness alienates people, freezes conversation. The more things a table is set with, the greater the goodwill and respect being shown.

"Our question," says one of those present, "is, How do we survive? It has been weighing on Armenians for hundreds of years. For centuries already we have had our own culture, our own language and alphabet. For seventeen centuries the Christian religion has been the national religion of Armenians. But our culture has a passive character, it is the culture of the ghetto, of a defensive fortification. We have never imposed our customs, our way of life, upon others. A sense of mission or a desire to rule are foreign to us. But we find ourselves surrounded by people who, brandishing the banner of the prophet, have always wanted to conquer this part of the world. In their eyes, we are a poisoned thorn in the healthy body of Islam. They are thinking about how to remove this thorn, meaning, how to efface us from the surface of the earth."

"Nagorno-Karabakh is in the worst predicament," someone else speaks up. "We were once an inseparable part of the territory of Armenia, but in 1920 the Turkish army came in here and cut down to a man the Armenian population that lived between the border of today's Armenian republic and Nagorno-Karabakh. Our forefathers saved themselves by hiding in the mountains of Karabakh. The depopulated belt of land between Armenia and Karabakh was settled by Caucasian Turks, meaning Azerbaijanis. This belt is barely thirteen kilometers wide, but it is closed off by them and one cannot drive or walk through there. In this way we have become a Christian island in the heart of the Islamic Republic of Azerbaijan. And on top of that the Azerbaijanis are Shiites, their inspiration is Khomeini; they will not rest until they have disposed of us."

"Stalin," a man sitting next to me adds, "Stalin knew the Caucasus well. He was himself from the Caucasus, after all. He knew that a hundred nations live in these mountains, nations that have always waged wars against one another. It is a back alley of the world, quadruple locked: cut off by two seas, the Black and the Caspian, barricaded behind two towering mountain ranges. Who will come here? Who will have the courage to venture deep inland? Stalin knew how to add fuel to the fire. He knew that Nagorno-Karabakh will always be a bone of contention between Turks and Armenians. That is why he did not unite Nagorno-Karabakh with Armenia, but left our district in the middle of Azerbaijan, under the control of Baku. In this way Moscow assumed the position of the highest arbiter."

"Despite the fact that we live so far from Paris and Rome," says an older man from the end of the table, "we are part of Christian Europe, or—strictly speaking—its tail end. Let us look at the map. The western part of Europe ends with a distinct line of coasts—beyond that is the Atlantic. But in the East? Where should one draw the borders? In the East this isn't at all clear. Here Europe melts away, thins out, dissipates. We have to adopt some kind of criterion. In my opinion, the criterion should not be geographical, but cultural. Europe extends to the easternmost place inhabited by people faithful to the ideals of Christianity. We, Armenians, are such a nation, the most southeasterly."

"There are two lines of confrontation between Islam and the rest of the world," someone from the same end of the table adds. "One runs along the Mediterranean Sea, and the second along the crests of the Caucasus. If one considers that more and more Turks and Algerians are coming to live in Europe, one can assume that our children will live to see the day when Stepanakert will be one of the few Christian cities in the world."

"If we last that long," several voices speak up simultaneously. To demonstrate the uncertainty of the proposition, my host leads me to the window. It is already dark. Rows of lights are suspended high in the sky. "Up there on the mountain," he says, "lies the Azerbaijani town of Shusha. They have us in the palm of their hand, they can shoot at us at any moment."

Uncertainty, fear, hatred. That is what one breathes here.

"Armenians," says someone, "have never reconciled themselves to the loss of Nagorno-Karabakh. Every few years riots and insurrections have erupted in Armenia over this matter. Despite Stalin's cruelties, despite Brezhnev's repressions. In June of 1988, the Supreme Council of Armenia complied with the request of the Supreme Council of the District of Nagorno-Karabakh for joining us to Armenia. Baku said no. Moscow will always take the side of the stronger, and Azerbaijan is much stronger than we are. Nagorno-Karabakh occupies barely five percent of the surface area of Azerbaijan, and barely three percent of the population of the Republic lives here. Moscow took advantage of the fact that Baku threatened to occupy Nagorno-Karabakh, declared a state of war, and installed its own troops here. We are in a trap. We are under occupation by Moscow, but if Moscow departs from here, we will fall under occupation by Baku."

AS THIS DISCUSSION was taking place, we heard a sudden commotion in the stairwell, the door opened, and Starovoytova entered with a small entourage. She appeared tired and tense, but attempted to remain calm and to create a cheerful, cloudless atmosphere. She told us her story. She had barely left the plane when she was arrested by several officers—envoys of the military commander in chief of Nagorno-Karabakh. They declared that she had no right to fly into Stepanakert and tried to persuade her to return to Yerevan. But Starovoytova refused and announced that she would not return unless they carried her back onto the plane. The officers realized that this would be a problem. First, because Starovoytova is a woman of a certain physical stature, and, second, because an international scandal would break out. Endless consultations and deliberations began—what to do? As it turned out, the catalyst of the whole affair had been the first secretary of the Central Committee of the Communist Party—Ayaz Mutalibov (until 1992 the president of Azerbaijan), who telephoned Gorbachev from Baku and vowed an offensive against Stepanakert if Starovoytova was not expelled. For its part Moscow wanted to maintain good relations with Mutalibov, with Islam, with Turkey, with the Near East, and so on; who cares about Starovoytova and Nagorno-Karabakh! Starovoytova was playing for time, for she wanted at all costs to remain here and meet with the people. She wanted them to feel that someone remembered them. She had one strong argument: the pilots, seeing what was happening and taking advantage of the confusion, had flown off. They knew that the airport in Stepanakert was not illuminated and that it was already too dark for them to be forced to attempt another landing that same day.

STAROVOYTOVA had opponents in Baku, because Azerbaijanis, like Armenians, divide mankind into two opposing camps.

For Armenians, an ally is one who believes that Nagorno-Karabakh is a problem. The rest are enemies.

For Azerbaijanis, an ally is one who believes that Nagorno-Karabakh is not a problem. The rest are enemies.

The extremism and finality of these positions is remarkable. It isn't merely that among Armenians one cannot say, "I believe that the Azerbaijanis are right," or that among Azerbaijanis one cannot maintain, "I believe that the Armenians are right." No such stance even enters the realm of possibility—either group would instantly hate you and then kill you! In the wrong place or among the wrong people even to say, "There is a problem" (or, "There is no problem") is enough to put oneself at risk of being strangled, hanged, stoned, burned.

It is also unimaginable to make the following speech in either Baku or Yerevan: Listen. Decades ago (who living among us can even remember those times?), some Turkish pasha and the savage Stalin threw into our Caucasian nest this terrible cuckoo's egg, and from that time on, for the entire century, we have been tormenting and killing one another, while they, in their musty graves, are cackling so loudly one can hear them. And we are living in so much poverty, after all, there is so much backwardness and dirt all around, that we should really reconcile our differences and finally set about doing some work!

This person would never make it to the end of his speech, for the moment either side realized what he was driving at, the unfortunate moralist and negotiator would be deprived of his life.

Three plagues, three contagions, threaten the world.

The first is the plague of nationalism.

The second is the plague of racism.

The third is the plague of religious fundamentalism.

All three share one trait, a common denominator—an aggressive, all-powerful, total irrationality. Anyone stricken with one of these plagues is beyond reason. In his head burns a sacred pyre that awaits only its sacrificial victims. Every attempt at calm conversation will fail. He doesn't want a conversation, but a declaration that you agree with him, admit that he is right, join the cause. Otherwise you have no significance in his eyes, you do not exist, for you count only if you are a tool, an instrument, a weapon. There are no people—there is only the cause.

A mind touched by such a contagion is a closed mind, one-dimensional, monothematic, spinning round one subject only—its enemy. Thinking about our enemy sustains us, allows us to exist. That is why the enemy is always present, is always with us. When near Yerevan a local guide shows me one of the old Armenian basilicas, he finishes his commentary with a contemptuous rhetorical question: "Could those Azerbaijanis build such a basilica?" When later, in Baku, a local guide draws my attention to a row of ornamental, art nouveau houses, he concludes his explanations with this scornful remark: "Could Armenians construct such apartment buildings?"

ON THE OTHER HAND, there is something one can envy both the Armenians and the Azerbaijanis. They are not beset by worries about the complexity of the world or about the fact that human destiny is uncertain and fragile. The anxiety that usually accompanies such questions as: What is truth? What is the good? What is justice? is alien to them. They do not know the burden that weighs on those who ask themselves, But am I right?

Their world is small—several valleys and mountains. Their world is simple—on one side we, the good people, on the other they, our enemies. Their world is governed by an unambiguous law of exclusivity—us or them.

And if another world exists nevertheless, what might they want of it? Only that it leave them in peace. They need to be left in peace so as to thrash each other all the more thoroughly.

THE SUN AWOKE me in the morning. I jumped out of bed, walked to the window, and stopped, speechless. I was in one of the most beautiful corners of the world! It was like somewhere in the Alps, in the Pyrenees, in Rhodope, like Andorra, San Marino, or Cortina d'Ampezzo. Yesterday, because of the tension, I hadn't noticed the panoramas surrounding me. Only now did I see what was unfolding all around. Sun, sun everywhere. Warm, but at the same time brisk, as in the mountains. Azure everywhere, intense, profound, limpid, cobaltlike. The air clean, crystalline, bright. Far away, up high—mountains crowned with white snow. And closer, also mountains, but green, a strong green, all awash in dwarf mountain pines, in wild grasses, in meadows, in mossy trails.

In this enchanting, luscious landscape are set the shabby, dilapidated concrete apartment blocks of Stepanakert's neighborhoods, heavy, large slabs clumsily and sloppily assembled, slovenly, mean. In the place where I had spent the night the buildings form a closed quadrangle. Between them, between balconies, residents had stretched steel wires. Little pulleys move along the wires, with drying laundry attached to them. Manipulating the pulleys, one can keep one's laundry in the direct line of sunlight all day—it will dry more quickly that way. Because there isn't a great deal of room, some sort of timetable must be enforced, some sort of agreed-upon schedule delineating who can hang out how much of his laundry when. Judging by the laundry's kind, composition, and appearance, one can discover a great deal about the intimate life of one's neighbors. One can also obtain important shopping information. Where did the neighbor from across the way get such fine stockings? This network of wires stretched above the courtyard, above the trees growing here, is so inventive and intricate that probably only the local women know how to direct, skillfully and smoothly, this entire parade of shirts and slacks, underwear and stockings, that every now and then comes to life as it moves now forward, now to the side or back.

STAROVOYTOVA is returning to Yerevan, and, in the apartment where I am being hidden, the Armenians have been conferring since morning—what is to be done with me? How can I be gotten out of here? The reports brought back from the airport by various messengers sound dire. The military commander of Nagorno-Karabakh (a general whose last name I do not remember), wanting to allay the anger of Secretary Mutalibov and his allies in Moscow, has decided on a show of force: he will do everything to ensure that Starovoytova will never again want to set foot here, that she will depart in an atmosphere of intimidation and hostility. All cars along the road to the airport are being searched; the airport itself is swarming with soldiers; commandos have even been positioned along the runway.

I can see that my Armenians are nervous and are starting to quarrel. I do not understand the precise content of these disputes, but it is certain that they are about me, because every now and then they interrupt the discussions and let fly in my direction: "Get dressed in the uniform!" (I get dressed.) After a while: "No! Put on the civilian clothes!" (I put these on.) After another round of quarrels: "No! Get back in the uniform!" I obediently execute these contradictory orders because I discern that the situation is truly serious: I am in a trap. I will not be able to make my way to the plane through such a densely laid net.

THE MATTER IS further complicated by the fact that news of the arrival of Starovoytova (who is immensely popular here) has spread all over town, and a crowd is gathering in front of our building. If there is a crowd, then troops will soon appear; if troops arrive, they will start to inquire about why the crowd is gathering, et cetera; and thus they will follow the thread until they reach the spool—our hiding place. The Armenians are growing increasingly nervous; the temperature of their quarrels rises violently.

Finally one of the messengers arrives (it is that splendid bearded man who yesterday got me out of the airport) and tells the Armenians something. They fall silent at once and look out the window. After a time, one of them says to me: "You see that militia car with the rotating beacon?" On the roof of the car standing in front of our building a sky-blue beacon was slowly spinning round. "You will go downstairs," says the Armenian, "you will push your way through the crowd, and you will get into the backseat of that car, behind the driver. You must make it look like you know exactly what you are doing."

NOW, in the uniform of an Aeroflot pilot, I walk down to the courtyard. I see the faces in the crowd; I push my way through and walk straight to the militia car. Only the driver is inside, an Armenian sergeant. I sit down in the back and wait. Starovoytova appears and the crowd encircles her. Just then an army patrol pulls up—blonds, therefore Russians: the situation is becoming dangerous. Starovoytova cuts short the meeting and gets into the Volga standing to the side. Two militiamen, Armenians, get into the car I am sitting in, and a militia captain—also Armenian—takes the place next to the driver.

We pull out first, the Volga behind us. Patrols along the road—disoriented, because they are supposed to be checking every car, but this, after all, is a militia car, its siren blaring. We somehow manage to drive through the labyrinth of concrete blocks, and then through the raised barrier. The soldiers in these patrols are all young, tall blonds—Slavs. Blue-eyed, Russian-speaking.

Sun, heat. It is nearing noon.

The captain sitting next to the driver is very tense. He knows how much he is risking at this moment. I am thinking that the rest of us know it too. Although we are driving quite quickly, the road becomes a psychological Golgotha, elongating into infinity.

Finally—the airport. I see the parked JAK-40. The airplane is here! But what a long way we still have to go to get to it! We must still surmount the most difficult obstacle—the gate leading to the runway. Near the gate, a throng: commandos, officers. We stop some distance before it; the car carrying Starovoytova pulls up behind us. One of the militiamen gets out of my car, and she takes his place. We reach the gate and are immediately surrounded by soldiers. The captain takes out his identity card and says: "Captain Serovian from headquarters. I have orders from the military commander to drive Deputy Starovoytova to the airplane!" And he starts to repeat this over and over to the soldiers crowding at our windows. "Captain Serovian from headquarters. I have orders . . ." et cetera, et cetera.

Slowly, the soldiers step aside and raise the barrier. We are driving in the direction of the airplane when Starovoytova stops the car and says: "I will go say good-bye to the commander of the airport, and you meanwhile install Ryszard on the plane."

Suren and Averik are standing by the steps leading to the aircraft. "Get into the cockpit," says Suren (he says this softly, for the troops are everywhere), "sit down at the controls, and put on the headphones." I board the plane and find a soldier inside, checking the walls and floor with a metal detector—he is searching to see that weapons haven't been smuggled in.

After a time the passengers are let on. Then Starovoytova boards. Suren and Averik are already there.

The pilots start the engines and we taxi slowly to the runway. "Can we still be turned back?" I ask Suren. "We can," he says.

On both sides of the runway stand evenly spaced commandos, their helmets camouflaged with twigs of rosemary.

We take off toward the east, into the sun, toward the mountains, toward the snow, and then we turn and fly west, toward Yerevan and Ararat. Perhaps a half hour goes by, then a hoarse voice resounds in the headphones. Suren turns on his microphone. They talk for a moment. Suren takes off his headphones and says to me: "They won't turn us back now. You are free."

He looks at me, smiles, and hands me his handkerchief.

Only then do I feel that from under my large cap sweat is pouring down my face.

# Central Asia— the Destruction of the Sea

THE AIRPLANE DELIMITS a wide circle, and when its wing dips, one can see sand dunes stretching down below, wrinkled by the wind. It is the new desert of Aral Kum—or, more precisely, the bottom of a sea that is disappearing from the face of the earth.

IF WE LOOK at the map of the world from west to east, we will see in the southern part of the Eurasian continent a chain of four seas: first the Mediterranean, which changes into the Black; then, beyond the Caucasus mountains, the Caspian; and, finally, the easternmost, the Aral Sea.

THE ARAL SEA draws its water from two rivers: the Syr Darya and the Amu Darya. These are long rivers—the Syr Darya measures 2,212 kilometers, and the Amu Darya, 1,450—cutting across all of Central Asia.

CENTRAL ASIA is deserts and more deserts, fields of brown weathered stones, the heat from the sun above, sandstorms.

• • •

BUT THE WORLD of the Syr Darya and the Amu Darya is different. Arable fields stretch along both rivers, abundant orchards; everywhere profusions of nut trees, apples trees, fig trees, palms, and pomegranates.

IT WAS A GREAT pleasure to sit down in the shade of one's own garden, under the roof of a breezy veranda, and delight in the calm of a cool evening.

THE WATERS OF the Syr Darya and the Amu Darya, as well as of their tributaries, allowed famous cities to arise and to flourish—Bukhara and Khiva, Kokand and Samarkand. This way, too, passed the loaded-down caravans of the Silk Road, thanks to which the markets of Venice and Florence, Nice and Seville, acquired their importance and color.

IN THE SECOND HALF of the nineteenth century, the lands through which both rivers flow were conquered by czarist armies commanded by Gen. Mikhail Chernaev and became part of the Russian Imperium—or, rather, its southern colony, called Turkestan because the local population (with the exception of the Tajiks) speaks Turkic languages. The faith prevailing here is, without exception, Islam—the religion of hot climates and deserts.

IN 1917 the anticzarist revolt in Turkestan is kindled not by Uzbeks or Kirghiz but by the local colonials—Russians—who, now being Bolsheviks, thereby hold on to power. In 1924 Turkestan is divided into five republics—Turkmenistan, Tajikistan, Uzbekistan, Kyrgystan, and (in several stages) Kazakhstan.

DURING THE YEARS of Stalin's rule, large numbers of peasants, the Muslim clergy, and almost the entire intelligentsia (which did include many) fell victim to repression. The latter group was replaced by Russians as well as by assimilated local activists and bureaucrats—Uzbeks, Tajiks, Turkmen, and so on.

• • •

ABANDONING MASS repressions, Khrushchev, and later Brezhnev, introduced a new politics of domination in their colonies. A Russified local stood at the head of every institution, but his deputy was always a Russian who received his instructions directly from Moscow. The second principle of the new politics was based on the renascence of old local tribal structures and the handing of power to trusted clans whose allegiance had been bought. Later, during the years of perestroika, astonishing communiqués were issued by the office of the attorney general of the former USSR about the battle against the terrible corruption prevalent in the Imperium's Asiatic republics: entire local Central Committees and Councils of Ministers were going to jail. What? Was everyone stealing? Yes, everyone, for it was under the name of the Central Committee or of some other governing institution that the elders of the ruling clan covertly operated, connected and linked by major interests. If rival clans existed and an understanding between them could not be reached, a local civil war erupted, like the one in 1922 in Tajikstan. At the head of each republic stood a vizier—the first secretary of the Central Committee of the local Party. In accordance with Eastern tradition, his rule was for life. Dinmukhamed Kunayev was the first secretary of Kazakhstan for twenty-six years, until finally Gorbachev had to depose him. Shafar Rashidov was the first secretary of Uzbekistan for twenty-four years, until his death in 1983. Geidar Aliyev was the chief of the KGB, and later the first secretary of Azerbaijan for twenty-three years. Whenever one of them passed through town, it was an event long remembered, long reminisced about. The system of indirect rule once invented by the British in Asia and in Africa and adopted by Moscow allowed those in power complete license.

THIS DIGRESSION about the system of rule will enable us better to understand the extraordinary history of the destruction of the sea, its background and circumstances.

WATER IS the prerequisite for life, especially valuable in the tropics, in the desert, because there is so little of it. If I have sufficient water for only one field, I cannot cultivate two fields; if I have water for one tree, I cannot plant two trees. Every cup of water is drunk at the expense of a plant—the plant will dry out because I drank the water it needed to live. An unceasing battle for survival takes place here between people, plants, and animals, a battle for a drop of water, without which there is no existence.

A BATTLE, but also cooperation, for everything here depends upon a fragile and shaky equilibrium, the upsetting of which means death. If the camels drink too much water, there will not be enough of it for the oxen; the oxen will die of thirst. If the oxen die, the sheep will perish, for who will pull the treadmill that carries water to the meadows? If the sheep perish, what meat will man eat and what will he cover himself with? If man is weak and naked, who will plant the fields? If no one farms the fields, the desert will encroach upon them. The sands will cover everything; life will disappear.

THEY GREW cotton here for years. Cotton fabric is light and strong, and also healthy, for it cools the body. For centuries there was a good price for it because it was never overcultivated—the constraint always was (and still is) the tropics' chronic shortage of water. To cultivate a new field of cotton one would have to take water from the gardens, cut down forests, kill off the cattle. But then how would one live, from what, and what would one eat? Everyone in India, in China, in America, in Africa, has known this dilemma for thousands of years. And in Moscow? In Moscow they also know it!

THE CATASTROPHE begins in the sixties. Two more decades were then needed to turn half of the fertile oases of Uzbekistan into desert. First, bulldozers were brought in from all over the Imperium. The hot metal cockroaches crawled over the sandy plains. Starting from the banks of the Syr Darya and the Amu Darya, the steel rams began to carve deep ditches and fissures in the sand, into which the water from the rivers was then channeled. They had to dig an endless number of these ditches (and they are still digging them now), considering that the combined length of the Syr Darya and the Amu Darya is 3,662 kilometers! Then along these canals, the kolkhoz workers had to plant cotton. At first they planted upon desert barrens, but because there was still not enough of the white fibers, the authorities ordered that arable fields, gardens, and orchards be given over to cotton. It is easy to imagine the despair and terror of peasants from whom one takes the only thing they have—the currant bush, the apricot tree, the scrap of shade. In villages, cotton was now planted right up against the cottage windows, in former flower beds, in courtyards, near fences. It was planted instead of tomatoes and onions, instead of olives and watermelons. Over these villages drowning in cotton, planes and helicopters flew, dumping on them avalanches of artificial fertilizers, clouds of poisonous pesticides. People choked, they had nothing to breathe, went blind.

KHRUSHCHEV wanted to have his fallow lands under plow in Kazakhstan, Brezhnev his land of cotton in Uzbekistan. Both were very much attached to their ideas, and no one dared question what the cost would be in either case.

THE PICTURE of the land changed rapidly. The fields of rice and wheat, the green meadows, the stands of kale and paprika, the plantations of peaches and lemons, all vanished. Everywhere, as far as the eye could see, cotton grew. Its fields, its white downy sea, stretched for tens, hundreds, of kilometers.

Cotton grows for several months. Then comes the harvest.

> During the period of the cotton harvest in Central Asia, everything dies down. For two to three months, schools, institutes, and offices are closed. Businesses and factories work at half-time: everyone goes to pick the cotton, to work beneath the burning sun. Schoolchildren, students, nursing mothers, old people, doctors, teachers. No one, on any account or under any circumstances, will be relieved of this obligation. We have a saying here: if you do

> not plant cotton, they will plant you [in prison], if you do not collect cotton, they will come and collect you. During harvest time everyone talks about cotton, everyone follows the news bulletins about the accomplishment of the plan. Newspapers, radio, television, everything serves one goddess—cotton. Around 20 million people live in the countryside in Central Asia. Two-thirds work with cotton and really with nothing else besides. Farmers, gardeners, orchard keepers have all had to change profession—they are now employed as laborers on cotton plantations. Coercion and fear compel them to work with cotton. Coercion and fear, for it surely isn't money. One earns pennies harvesting cotton. And the work is tiring and monotonous. To fulfill his daily quota, a man must bend down ten to twelve thousand times. An atrocious, forty-degree heat [Celsius], air that stinks of virulent chemicals, aridity, and constant thirst destroy the human being, especially women and children. But, after all, the more cotton the happier and richer our country! And in reality? In reality people pay with their health and their life for the personal well-being and power of a handful of demoralized careerists. (Grigory Reznichenko, *The Aral Catastrophe*, 1989)

THE ALLUSION to demoralized careerists: it was common knowledge that Brezhnev's people in Moscow and Rashydov's in Tashkent served up mutually agreed upon, falsely inflated figures about the cotton harvest. It was all about propaganda and money—the two mafias, or, actually, the one cotton mafia, pocketed huge sums for the fictitious hundreds of thousands of tons of cotton.

THE MAFIOSI got rich, but millions of their kinsmen, the miserable cotton pickers, went begging. For work with cotton is only seasonal, lasting at most a quarter of the year; what is one to do after that? There are neither orchards nor gardens left, neither goats nor sheep. Millions of people are walking around without employment and with no chance of getting any. Life has dimmed, reaching a fever pitch only during harvesttime, in the fall, and then sinking again into a heavy, hot, stifling tropical deadness.

A TYPICAL colonial situation: the colony supplies the raw material, the metropolis manufactures ready-made products out of it. At most ten percent of the cotton gathered in Uzbekistan is woven in the Republic. The rest is sent to textile mills in the central sections of the Imperium. If cotton ceased to be cultivated in Uzbekistan, the textile basins in Russia would come to a standstill.

BECAUSE THE ORDER from Moscow was (as it still is) "More and more cotton," the area under cultivation in Uzbekistan was constantly increased, as was the quantity of water poured out into the fields. Technology was out of the question—drains, pipes, canals, and all such inventions. Water was simply diverted from the rivers, and it spilled out over the fields. But before it reached the stands of cotton, a third of it was already lost, sinking uselessly into the sand.

IT IS A KNOWN fact that a dozen or so meters below the surface of every desert lie large deposits of concentrated salt. If water is conducted to it, the salt, together with the moisture, will begin to rise to the surface. And that is exactly what happened now in Uzbekistan. The concealed, crushed, deeply secreted salt started to move upward, to regain its liberty. The golden land of Uzbekistan, which was first cloaked in the white of cotton, was now glazed over with a lustrous crust of white salt.

BUT ONE DOESN'T have to study the ground. When the wind blows, one can taste the salt on one's lips, on one's tongue. It stings the eyes.

THE WATERS of the Syr Darya and the Amu Darya, instead of flowing into the Aral Sea, were, according to man's will, squandered along the way, spilled over fields, over unending deserts, along an immense distance of more than three thousand kilometers. For this reason, the calm and broad currents of both powerful rivers—the only source of life in this part of the world—instead of swelling and intensifying in the course of their journey (as is customary in nature), began to decline, to shrink, to get narrower and shallower, until, short of reaching the sea, they were transformed into salty, poisoned, and muddy pools, into spongy and foul-smelling ditches, into treacherous puddles of duckweed, finally sinking below ground and disappearing from view.

THIS SETTLEMENT is called Muynak, and until a few years ago it was a fishing port. It now stands in the middle of the desert; the sea is sixty to eighty kilometers from here. Near the settlement, where the port once was, rusting carcasses of trawlers, cutters, barges, and other boats lie in the sand. Despite the fact that the paint is peeling and falling off, one can still make out some of the names: *Estonia, Dagestan, Nahodka*. The place is deserted; there is no one around.

During the last twenty years, the Aral Sea, which one cannot even glimpse from Muynak, has lost a third of its surface area and two-thirds of its volume. Others calculate that only half of the surface of the sea remains. Over this period, the water level has fallen by thirteen meters. The desert, into which its former bottom has been transformed, is already nearing three million square hectars. Every year, seventy-five million tons of salt and poisons from artificial fertilizers, deposited here earlier by the rivers, are thrown up from these deserts into the atmosphere by the winds and sandstorms.

IT IS A SAD settlement—Muynak. It once lay in the spot where the beautiful, life-giving Amu Darya flowed into the Aral Sea, an extraordinary sea in the heart of a great desert. Today, there is neither river nor sea. In the town the vegetation has withered; the dogs have died. Half the residents have left, and those who stayed have nowhere else to go. They do not work, for they are fishermen, and there are no fish. Of the Aral Sea's 178 species of fish and *frutti di mare*, only 38 remain. Besides, the sea is far away; how is one to get there across the desert? If there is no strong wind, people sit on little benches, leaning against the shabby and crumbling walls of their decrepit houses. It is impossible to ascertain how they make a living; it is difficult to communicate with them about anything. They are Karakalpaks—they barely speak any Russian, and the children no longer speak Russian at all. If one smiles at the people sitting against the walls, they become even more gloomy, and the women veil their faces. Indeed, a smile does look false here, and laughter would sound like the screech of a rusty nail against glass.

Children play in the sand with a plastic bucket that's missing a handle. Ragged, skinny, sad. I did not visit the nearest hospital, which is on the other side of the sea, but in Tashkent I was shown a film made in that hospital. For every one thousand children born, one hundred die immediately. And those that survive? The doctor picks up in his hands little white skeletons, still alive, although it is difficult to tell.

HALF THE PEOPLE here have jaundice. Those who have jaundice and then contract dysentery die at once. But how can one maintain even a modicum of cleanliness here? One can secure with ration coupons only a single piece of soap per month per person, and—although one doesn't need coupons for this—only a single bucket of water a day.

THE ARAL SEA and its tributaries provided sustenance for three million people. But the fate of this sea and of its two rivers also impinges on the situation of all the inhabitants of this region, of whom there are thirty-two million.

THE SOVIET AUTHORITIES have long worried about how to reverse the disaster—the destruction of the Aral Sea, the ruination of half of Central Asia. It is after all well known that the unprecedented increase in cotton cultivation has led to a tragic shortage of water, a shortage that is destroying a large part of the world (a fact which to this day continues to be concealed). Water must therefore be found, thousands of cubic kilometers of water, for otherwise the Uzbeks will die of thirst, sand will bury the cotton fields, the textile basins of Russia will come to a standstill, and on and on. But where can one get so much water? The first idea was to blow up the Pamir and Tien Shan mountains (where the two rivers have their sources). As a result of the gigantic explosions, avalanches of snow would start to move down these mountains and, descending into the warmer regions of the planet, would change into water as plentiful as the waters of the Nile and the Amazon, the water would flow into the desiccated rivers, the rivers would reach the sea, and everything would be as it once was—meaning good, meaning normal.

But this plan had two weak points. First, mountains as immense as the Pamirs and Tien Shan could be blown up only with nuclear bombs, and the tremendous explosions and earthquakes that would ensue could be badly received by the rest of the world. But there is a more important reason why the idea was finally abandoned: while blowing up the massifs of the Pamirs and Tien Shan would indeed release the great volume of water frozen in the glaciers, it would release it only once, and then in such quantities that there would be a serious risk of drowning a significant portion of the former USSR. Still, the search for a solution continued.

IN TASHKENT I was received by Victor Duhovy, the general director of the Sanira conglomerate. Sanira is one of the numerous arms of the former USSR's Ministry of Water Administration, which takes care of the Aral Sea as well as the Syr Darya and the Amu Darya. We can now see how it takes care of them. One has to understand what a ministry means in the Imperium. The ministry in question employs two million people. Every morning, two million people get out of bed, walk to work, sit down at their desks, take out paper and pencils, and have to start doing something. The lucky ones are those who have fieldwork. They pull out all sorts of measuring instruments, magnifying glasses and sextants, slide rules and scales, and precisely measure and count everything. But even if one accepts that there are that many things in the world to measure and count, it is still not easy to find work for these two million people. That is why masses of experts and officials work here on each and every idea—even utterly fantastic ones.

DIRECTOR DUHOVY WALKED up to a large map hanging on the wall in his office. It was a map of the former USSR and the Eurasian continent. Duhovy: a likable, energetic gentleman with a pleasant manner.

"There is a solution," he said to me, "please, look." He ran his hand over the map from top to bottom. "One must simply," he explained the movement of his hand, "redirect the course of the great Siberian rivers from the north to the south. Then the water will flow to us."

I LATER CHECKED the distance to these rivers. To reach the nearest one, one would have to dig a canal 2,500 kilometers long.

WRITING THIS BOOK, I telephoned Anvar, an engineer from the conglomerate that Duhovy administers.

"What's new?" I asked.

"Nothing special," he answered, "we're working."

"On what?" I asked.

"How to redirect the waters of the Siberian rivers in our direction."

# Pomona of the Little Town of Drohobych

IN DONETSK I saw a woman selling cow's hooves. It was on one of the main streets—University Street. She stood there in the bitter cold, rubbing her hands together for warmth, and on the table before her lay several pairs of worn-down cow's hooves. I walked up and asked her what they were good for. "You can make soup out of them," she answered, "there is fat in hooves."

NOT FAR FROM THERE stands the White Swan department store. In this part of the world, an inflamed and determined crowd fulfills the same function as that performed in the West by colorful advertising—it attracts customers. A throng of people is rushing to a counter on the ground floor, shoving, storming. A shipment of shoes has arrived. I go take a closer look. They are selling shoes one pair per person. It does not matter what pair, it does not matter to whom; the saleswomen do not even look to see what is inside the boxes. Everyone just grabs a box, forces his way out of the crowd, and stands on the side, where a point of exchange has immediately formed. Gradually, through a chain of transactions, discussions, and compromises, people work their way toward the ideal, which is for each to obtain the kind of shoes he or she needs.

GALINA GOBIERNA, a professor of economics, told me what the division of profits looks like in a Donetsk factory or mine: Moscow takes fifty-four percent, Kiev takes thirty percent, the Donetsk authorities take eleven percent, and five percent is left over for the particular establishment itself.

I ASKED A GIRL standing at a bus stop which way I should walk to get to the train station. "I will show you," she proposed. Despite the fact that this was downtown, we waded up to our ankles in mud. It was overcast; a sharp wind was blowing.

Donetsk is the center of the Ukrainian coal basin; in certain neighborhoods, piles of coal and slag lie directly in the streets. Black dust settles on walls; and on the facades of so many identical buildings that stretch for kilometers, one after the other, it creates dark streaks, gray water stains, brown rusty-looking lichens.

"Do you like Donetsk?" the girl asked timidly. People are sensitive on such matters, feel hurt if one says something critical. I began to search feverishly and diligently for something positive to say about the city, but my voice apparently lacked sincerity, for when I fell silent she responded with determination, even proudly: "But in the summer roses bloom in our city. A million roses. Can you imagine? A million roses!"

I SPEND HALF the night at the Donetsk station, waiting for the train. In the evening, everything is already closed here: the only bar, in which they sell tea with sugar, the newsstand, the ticket booths. In the large, poorly lit hall, people are asleep on the wooden benches, sitting tightly side by side or lying down. Tired from traveling and waiting, they assume in sleep the most unusual, catatonic poses. Wrapped in shawls and kerchiefs, hidden inside coats and hats with earmuffs, they look from a distance like motionless, bulgy bundles, packs, packages, arranged in rows.

Silence, stuffiness, and darkness.

Then, suddenly, in one corner of the hall, from inside the invisible depths of one of these bundles, a cry arises. A woman springs up, circles round the hall, thrashes about helplessly. "*Vory! Vory!*" she shouts with despair. ("Thieves! Thieves!") She probably awoke and sensed she no longer had her purse. For a time she runs between the benches, wonders out loud why, why her purse. She calls on God for help. But no one stirs, so she roams around a bit more, disheveled, sleepy, then finally returns to her place, sits down, rolls herself back up into a bundle, and falls silent.

A moment later, however, again—in some other place, another voice, equally fearful, terrified: "*Vory! Vory!*" And another woman runs among us, showing us that her hands are empty. But no one sees this; everyone is curled up, hidden, huddled over.

Only the granny sitting next to me opens her eye for a moment, and says, perhaps to me, perhaps to herself, "*Zyt' strashno*" ("life is terrible"), clutches her oilcloth bag even more tightly, and sinks again into her shallow, vigilant sleep.

A WOMAN IN our compartment was traveling to Odessa for her son's wedding. She lived somewhere in Siberia, on the Lena River. Usually, two, four, or six people travel in a single compartment. Men and women together. The customs are rigid. First, women make up their beds and change, then men. Once, pajamas were the popular evening-nighttime outfit; now, more and more frequently, it is sweat suits. One passes time in a railroad compartment pleasantly. Everyone offers everyone else something; they share whatever they have—pierogi, baked chicken, bread with cheese. I once found myself traveling with a lady who had soup as well as bowls and spoons with her—just so she could offer some to others. You will almost always find a bottle of vodka or cognac in a compartment—invariably someone will have thought to bring it along for the road. Sometimes I had nothing to eat, and right away others gave me whatever they had. At one time, people were afraid of one another and there was silence in the compartment, but now there is *glasnost* and everyone is talking at once. When the dams finally burst and whatever remaining mutual distrust disappears, the storytelling begins in earnest, the confessions, the exchange of opinions.

Siberia is called the largest prison on earth. The czar deported hundreds of thousands of his subjects here; here the Bolsheviks imprisoned millions of innocent people. But our Siberian, Claudia Mironova, considers Siberia a place of sanctuary, an island of liberty. The immeasurable distances, the enormous taiga, and the lack of roads facilitated isolation, provided refuge, enabled one to vanish from view. Entire communities of dissenters, says Claudia Mironova, were able to survive here. They survived the czar and the Bolsheviks—no one knew where they were. A man in a boat reached them once, she recounts. He carried with him paper and paints, pencils and crayons. He sailed down the Lena, stopping at villages and farms, and from small school or passport photographs he painted for women likenesses of their sons who had died in the war. That was how he made his living, not dependent on anyone. And she herself, Claudia Mironova? When they were herding everyone into the kolkhoz, one night she and her husband, taking with them a cow and two pigs, fled deep into the taiga. They settled there, built a shed, and later even a little house with an enclosure. During the entire Stalinist era, she says with pride, they did not see a single stranger. She posits as the key to their survival her knack for canning lard. Lard—therein lies the secret of life. The secret of life and the prerequisite for liberty. If you do not have lard—meaning, if you do not possess this basic, elementary wealth—you will not be free. That is what Claudia Mironova says, sharing with us the most important lesson of her life. Later, she explains how one should scald the cans and jars so as to preserve the lard well. What herbs, which can be gathered on the taiga, should be used. She gives the proportions and the recipe for the decoction. She explains how to disembowel the pig and how to cut it up.

Through the window I see abandoned artillery pieces—guns of medium caliber—half-buried in what passes for a road, running parallel to the tracks. A dozen or so new-looking barrels and shields stick up out of the mud; the rest have already sunk into the bog and the water. Then several minutes later, perhaps twenty armored cars—also half-buried. Not a living soul anywhere, just emptiness and more emptiness, the flat Ukrainian plain.

All the way to Odessa we eat the lard that Claudia Mironova cuts with a sharp jackknife from a large slab, placing its nutritious, fragrant slices on pieces of bread for us.

THE SUBURBAN TRAIN that runs from Odessa to Kishinev is a dilapidated piece of junk, hammered together with nails and sheets of tin, patched over with wooden planks and plywood riddled with holes. Traces of destruction everywhere. How many times already has each car been demolished, smashed, broken, and ripped? Inside, a typically suburban gang: chums, hooligans, tarts, bad boys. This train is theirs, this platform, this world. They shove, roar with laughter, but not cheerfully; this is an aggressive, cautionary roar that is meant to provoke you. There is no doubt in my mind, because we are standing closely pressed together, that it is only a matter of time before I will feel the prick of a knife under my ribs or glimpse a razor blade near my eye. It is like this until Tiraspol. The gang gets out, and only Romanian peasants are left on the train, meek, silent, staring fixedly into the twilight gathering outside the windows.

> We spent the entire morning taking in all the sights of Kishinev. In everything there was the strangest mixture and assortment; the names on street signs are in French, Polish, Russian, German, Armenian. The prevailing language, the language of the street, is Moldavian, i.e., Romanian, and it is in this language that the peddlers advertise their merchandise, rolls (*franzoli*), pears, watermelons and other fruit (all sold by weight). At the inn where we were staying, one of the signs was in Polish; there was a broker, a Jew, as is usually the case in our country, and the hired coachman turned out to be born in Vilnius. The owner had an Italian name. There was a similar mixture in everything. It is no wonder that Kishinev exemplifies the characteristic feature of the population of Bessarabia: a gathering of people of the most diverse

> provenance. Next to survivors from the East, an elegant personage slinks by in a dress coat imported from Vienna and yellow kid gloves, while next to an Armenian barber's shop a hand organ plays the arias of Donizetti and Bellini, the waltzes of Straus. . . . (Józef Ignacy Kraszewski, *Memoirs of Odessa, Jassy, and Budzak*, 1843)

WHAT IS LEFT of that Kishinev? Today it is two cities. One built in the most recent decades—neighborhoods of tall apartment towers covered in pale limestone slabs. This city of anthills arranged in rows is rapidly displacing and destroying old Kishinev—the enchanting, southeastern little town spread out over green hills, of which a few sleepy nooks still remain, a few small streets crossing one another on the perpendicular. One could walk endlessly on these streets. While the sun is shining, they are shaded by old, spreading elm, ash, and chestnut trees. Both sides of every street are thick with lilacs and jasmine, barberry and forsythia. Strolling here, one can glimpse, in the depths of a courtyard, gardens, bowers, and verandas, flowering, warm, inviting.

IN THE EVENING, we drove along a winding and steep road to the cemetery. It was drizzling. Near the main gate, barely visible in the darkness, stood a cottage where the cemetery superintendent lived. Father Antoni Anglonietis, a young, Polish-speaking Lithuanian who has been serving in Kishinev for several years, also has a room in the cottage. He took me to the old, ruined cemetery chapel nearby, and when we had finished looking at it he opened a hidden door and we walked down the stairs to the catacombs, where there is another chapel, spacious and well lit. The local faithful—Germans—had covertly built the catacombs and the chapel as a secret place of prayer. They built it over the course of many years, working nights and holidays, in great secrecy, so that the authorities would not find them out. They scattered the excavated earth over the hills surrounding the cemetery, for a fresh mound of soil could arouse suspicion.

Later, the priest, a tall, thin blond with energetic, vigorous movements, drove me in his dilapidated Moskvich to the church in the center of old Kishinev. He opened the massive gates and switched on the light. The authorities had only just given back the church, which had been used as some sort of warehouse, but the faithful had already managed to set up a simple altar and whitewash the walls.

It was bright, quiet, and deserted.

Our footsteps echoed loudly as we walked. We stopped in front of the chancel.

"I have been left alone," the priest said. "All of my parishioners, fifteen hundred Germans, have just left Kishinev."

I WAS TAKEN to a house where Leonid Niedov worked in a large dark concrete cellar. Niedov served seven years in the camps on account of saying, "During the time of the Romanians there was more kielbasa." When he was released in 1964, Solzhenitsyn sent him a telegram from Ryazan: "*Vsie dushoy pozdravlayem, raduyemsia.*" ("I greet you with all my heart, we rejoice.") Just at that time Khrushchev was removed and Brezhnev assumed power in the Kremlin. Having gotten out of the camp, the hungry and unemployed Niedov deliberated about how he could make a living. Because he had a measure of artistic talent (let us say, a certain artistic adroitness), he decided to cast figures of Party leaders out of lead and then sell them to institutions and to people in the marketplace. It wasn't a bad idea—in those times, anyone who refused to purchase such devotional items could be accused of being an enemy of the Soviet authorities. He began with Lenin, but because he had little lead and lacked experience, the likenesses of Vladimir Ilyich turned out small, the size of tin soldiers. Niedov became frightened because he immediately imagined that he would wind up in the camps again over this.

Lenin is great, the interrogating officer would say, and you have made him no bigger than a tin soldier.

"I was so terrified," Niedov continued, "that one night I threw the entire supply of Lenin figures into the furnace and melted them down." All right, but whose likeness should he work on now? Stalin, no, because he was discredited; Khrushchev, no, because he was discredited. So it had to be Brezhnev. But this time Niedov was careful—he made sure he had an adequate supply of lead, and he also made a large-enough cast. In this way, thanks to Brezhnev, whom he cast in various ways—heads, busts, and trunk and head—he lived for twenty years. When I descended into the dark, virtually pitch-black cellar, Niedov stood near the blazing furnace like a robust and industrious Hephaestus amid the choking, poisonous fumes emitted by the hot lead, barely visible beneath the clouds of smoke. This was a new epoch, and Niedov was melting down the Brezhnevs to create figures of St. George and the local patron, St. Stefan.

AT NIGHT from Kishinev to Kiev. I am not sleeping, but waiting for the train to pull into Vinnitsa. It is three o'clock in the morning. Profound darkness; a few weak lanterns barely illuminate the old station. Some motionless human figures on the platform. It is drizzling; the drops trickle down the windowpanes. One can see nothing else. But it is all there, behind the station building, in the depths of the night. Vinnitsa is the site of a mass murder, another Katyń, in the territory of the Ukraine. In 1937 and 1938, the NKVD shot to death thousands upon thousands of people here. Exactly how many no one knows. In 1943 they dug up the remains of 9,432 victims and then suspended further exhumation—to this day. Mostly Ukrainians and Poles lie in the graves. In one place, in the city itself, near a clump of old chestnut trees, they dug up thirteen mass graves. There were 1,383 murdered people in them. As soon as the 1,383 victims, all shot in the back of the head, had been buried, the Park of Culture and Recreation was set up on top of the graves. When the executions were finished, bandstands for dancing were erected over several of the graves, and, on one of them, a Ministry of Laughter.

IN KIEV I stay near the Boulevard of the Friendship of Nations, in the home of an elderly woman, M.Z. I have my own room, small and warm and full of books, including books in Spanish, for my hostess is a translator from that language. The tiny toilet, like most in this country, is filled from floor to ceiling with rolls of toilet paper and bags of laundry detergent. The kindhearted M.Z. takes good care of me, and, even when I return very late, warms up some soup for me, in which there is always a piece of meat on a bone. As I eat the soup, she tells me the story of how she miraculously managed to obtain this morsel, because, of course, it is indeed the most authentic of miracles—M.Z. and I both know this well.

I mention M.Z. because recently I had to explain to a group of people what drama is—the drama of fate, the drama of life—and also to give an example. To me, M.Z.'s life is such an example. Ten years ago, her husband emigrated to New York. He had a difficult time of it at first, until the Jewish community helped him, and then M.Z.'s husband, whom she now refers to as her former husband, got up on his own two feet. The only remaining person close to her is her fifteen-year-old granddaughter. Already M.Z. is very sick; she weighs too much and has difficulty walking. I return one day to find her holding a letter in her hand and visibly agitated. It is a letter from her husband, her former husband, who writes: Send me our granddaughter, I will educate her here, I will help her to develop, I will give her everything. Her husband, her former husband, is right; M.Z. understands this very well. What sort of future awaits her granddaughter in Kiev? And the child is so talented! But if she goes, M.Z. will be left alone, utterly alone, and—need one even say it?—one must take into account the dreadful laws of old age, one must look life squarely in the face. On the other hand, however, how can one deprive one's grandchild of such a golden opportunity? Why, she could become a doctor there, and play the violin, and meet a rich man.

"And what do you think of all this, sir?" M.Z. asks me, despairing. I see how her entire body is trembling, how over and over again she reads, sentence after sentence, that joyful-ominous letter (whose contents she conceals all day from her granddaughter), and I feel that I have stepped into the center of a human drama. I remain silent, and then beg M.Z.'s pardon. "Please forgive me," I say, "please do not be angry, but I really do not know how to answer."

POLITICS so dominates everything here now that I instinctively wanted to begin this report with a summary of some resolution just adopted by the Parliament of the Ukraine, or with some conversation with one of the local activists, but then I thought, No, I will start with something else, I will praise the city of Kiev. It is the only large city of the former USSR whose streets serve not merely for hurrying home but for walking, for strolling. Perhaps only Petersburg shares this quality, but there the climate is an obstacle—much colder, windy, rainy, or frosty. Whereas Kiev is warm, quiet, bathed in sun. In the afternoon, in the downtown area, one can see crowds of people, and these are not political crowds, not debating crowds, but simply thousands of passersby, who have left their airless, cramped offices and apartments to get some fresh air. In addition, traces of the old cafés have survived in Kiev. One can—after, of course, having stood in line for the requisite amount of time—buy a glass of tea and a pastry there, something inconceivable in Moscow, for example.

The city lies on hills, and some of the streets are winding and very steep. From the summits of the hills one can see the Dnieper Valley and the Dnieper itself—a river as wide as the Amazon, as the Nile, calm, slow, with an endless number of tributaries, bays, and islands. When the Ukrainians become rich, these waters will teem with sailboats and yachts—but for now all is still silent and rather empty.

The architecture of Kiev is a subject for a separate story. One can see all epochs and styles here—from miraculously preserved medieval cloisters and Orthodox churches to dreadful examples of Stalinist social realism. And in between those two, baroque and neoclassical and, above all, an exuberant, extremely ornate art nouveau. What a beautiful city this must once have been! The devastation of this architectural gem began in 1917 and still continues today. One day I purchased an extraordinary document published by the lovers of Old Kiev—a map of the city and a list of purposefully demolished buildings, churches, palaces, cemeteries. The list names 254 structures leveled by the Bolsheviks in order to erase the traces of Kiev's culture. Two hundred and fifty-four structures—why, that is an entire city! Fortunately, the incompetence and inefficiency of the system worked here to the advantage of art. The regime was unable to destroy everything, and many beautiful churches and buildings survived.

ONE SHOULD NOT be misled by this enduring external charm of the city, however. In many buildings, in entire housing complexes, people live very badly. The stairwells are filthy, the windowpanes broken, the outbuildings and courtyards dark because the lightbulbs have either been stolen or smashed. In many houses there is either no cold water or no hot water, or no water at all. Cockroaches and all other kinds of stubborn vermin are a universal plague. I stayed in some of these apartment buildings and visited acquaintances in others; I know what things look like. The so-called Soviet man is first and foremost an utterly exhausted man, and one shouldn't be surprised if he doesn't have the strength to rejoice in his newly won freedom. He is a long-distance runner who reached the finish line and collapsed, dead tired, incapable even of raising his arm in a gesture of victory.

I mention these trials and nightmares of daily existence because in the torrent of information flowing out into the world about events in the former USSR, there are no portraits of the lives of ordinary people, those millions upon millions of worn-out, destroyed, and impoverished citizens searching for food, clothing, and often simply for a roof over their heads. There is little that can still give them pleasure, make them joyful and enthusiastic.

KIEV'S KRESHCHATIK is something like a local Champs-Élysées. Once there were several well-stocked bookstores there, but now they are empty: the classics of Marxism-Leninism are no longer printed or sold, and there is as yet no new literature. Simply—a transitional period. Everything is now explained with that one key phrase: "transitional period." Communism collapsed, and what will happen next still remains to be seen. Everyone projects his own vision onto the future—there are as many expectations, hopes, and dreams as there are people. But there are also thousands, perhaps even millions, who have no illusions. They are the ones who night and day besiege the consulates of other countries. (In Moscow I even saw a line outside the consulate of the Congo! The Congo? Let it be the Congo! Just as long as it's far from this . . . and here follows a rude, quite unpatriotic word.) The Soviet people are remembering that they are not citizens of the USSR but simply Greeks, Germans, Jews, Hindus, Spaniards, Englishmen, Frenchmen, and so on, and so they want to return to their countries, to their symbolic homes, to the lands of their ancestors. Do they want to leave and abandon all the property they have acquired over a lifetime? What property? they respond, astounded. In this country, no one ever acquired anything. Well, perhaps several years in the camps, perhaps a dark corner in a communal apartment, perhaps a retirement pension of three dollars a month.

HALFWAY ALONG Kreshchatik lies a square (once it was called the October Revolution Square; now it is Independence Square) where today (it is August 31, 1991) a statue of Lenin still stands. But as of this morning workers have been erecting a crane here—they will be removing the statue. The operation is being observed by a crowd of onlookers as well as by several Western television crews who are colossally bored in Kiev and now, at last, will have something to do. Everything else aside, the statue must be removed because slogans decidedly unflattering to the Father of the Revolution have sprouted on the stone figure: EXECUTIONER, SS, or, the mildest of them, LUCIFER. There is no shortage of Lenin statues in the Ukraine—five thousand, it is said. Where did they get that figure? It's simple. They just added up all factories, schools, hospitals, kolkhozes, army units, ports, train stations, universities, villages, towns, cities, larger squares, bridges, parks, et cetera, et cetera, knowing that there had to be a statue of Lenin at each location, and arrived at the figure of five thousand.

Erecting the statues of Lenin, incidentally, posed no less a problem than that now entailed in their removal. In nearby Moldavia I met a man who spent ten years in a camp as a result of trying to install a heavy bust of Lenin in a second-floor common room. The doors were too narrow, so this unfortunate decided to hoist the bust up over the balcony, first coiling a thick rope around the neck of the author of *Marxism and Empirical Criticism.* He didn't even have time to untie the noose before he was arrested.

IF WE PASS the statue and keep going, we will reach a small, quiet street called Ordzonikidze, where (symbolically) the recent Ukrainian revolution took place in its entirety. At the entrance stands an unprepossessing and rather run-down little palace—the seat of the Ukrainian Writers' Union, the headquarters of the revolution. Nearby, almost directly opposite, rises a powerful, gigantic, oppressive edifice: the Central Committee of the Ukrainian Communist Party, the place of business for all those who were the terror of the Republic—Kaganovich, Shcherbici, Ivashko. Two buildings—an architectural David and Goliath—with a history of frequent battles between them and, this time, a favorable outcome: David defeated Goliath.

I HAD VISITED the little palace on Ordzonikidze a year ago because I was told that I would be able to meet the poet Ivan Drach there, leader of the Popular Movement for Reconstruction of the Ukraine (RUCH). The organization came into being relatively late, in September 1989, and included various independent and opposition groups that for years had been persecuted and suppressed, the main one being the Ukrainian Helsinki Group. It is not surprising that the Ukrainian Language Society was among those groups attacked and oppressed. The revolution in the Ukraine, like everywhere else, was waged at least partly over language. Half of the fifty-two million inhabitants of the Ukraine either do not speak Ukrainian, or they speak it poorly. Three hundred and fifty years of Russification have inevitably produced such a result. The ban against printing books in Ukrainian was in force for decades. As early as 1876, Alexander II ordered that instruction in Ukrainian schools take place only in Russian. Several months ago I visited the third-largest city in the Ukraine—Donetsk. The battle to open at least one elementary school teaching Ukrainian was by then already in its second year. Teachers assembled children in the park and there instructed them in Ukrainian. Teaching Ukrainian? Why, that was counterrevolution, an imperialist conspiracy!

Also in Donetsk, during a demonstration, a young RUCH activist was brave enough to remove from inside his jacket the yellow-and-blue Ukrainian flag and hold it aloft. People gaped, astonished, bewildered. "Let them get used to it," he said to me knowingly.

Simplifying greatly, one can say that there are two Ukraines: the western and the eastern. The western (the former Galicia, territories that belonged to Poland before the war) is more "Ukrainian" than the eastern. Its inhabitants speak Ukrainian, feel themselves to be one hundred percent Ukrainian, and are proud of this. It is here that the soul of the nation survived, its personality, its culture.

Things look different in the eastern Ukraine, which covers a territory larger than the western. Thirteen million native Russians live here and at least as many half Russians; here Russification was more intense and brutal; here Stalin murdered almost the entire intelligentsia. In 1932 and 1933, he had several million Ukrainian peasants starved to death and ordered tens of thousands of Ukrainian intellectuals shot. Only those who fled abroad were saved. Ukrainian culture was better preserved in Toronto and Vancouver than in Donetsk or Kharkov.

The differences between the western Ukraine (called the Ukrainian Piedmont) and the eastern were still in evidence at the time of my visit too, during the months of the struggle for independence. The monthly *Friendship of Nations* (number 4, 1990), published in Moscow, states: "In Kiev, which has a population of three million, forty thousand will come to a proindependence demonstration, and in Lvov [the capital of the western Ukraine], which has a population of one million, three hundred thousand will come. In Donetsk, which is larger than Lvov, five thousand will come."

• • •

I RETURN to Ordzonikidze Street, to the Writers' Union palace. It is difficult to get in to see Ivan Drach. Dozens of people besiege his office. They have arrived here from all over the Ukraine; they want to tell him about their troubles; they are seeking advice and assistance. I can see that there is no chance of a conversation. Late that evening I call him at home from my hotel. "Let's try tomorrow," he says in a weary voice.

Drach is an excellent poet, with a significant body of work, but now he has no time for writing. "One must put poetry aside," he says, "and save the Ukraine, save its culture." Russification is so advanced that in a few years' time there will be no one left who can read new Ukrainian literature. Besides, one must first restore the existing literature to its reader. The average Ukrainian doesn't even know the names of that literature's greatest twentieth-century writers—Mikol Chvilovy and Vladimir Vinnichenko. These were names that the regime wanted to condemn to oblivion. And how many inhabitants of the Ukraine have had access to the poems of Vasili Stusa, Aleksei Ticheg, Yurii Litvin—Ukrainian poets murdered in recent years by the KGB?

Books in Ukrainian constitute only twenty percent of those published here. Most of the rest are in Russian. As far back as 1863, Moscow prohibited the publication of any books whatsoever in Ukrainian, with the exception of works of belles lettres.

ONE OF MY many trips to Kiev took place in January 1990. The people I met were extremely moved by what they were talking about. And they were all talking about one thing—the fact that on January 21, on the anniversary of the proclamation of the short-lived Ukrainian independence of 1918, hundreds of thousands had joined hands and formed a chain stretching more than five hundred kilometers between Kiev, Lvov, and Ivano-Frankovsk. Today, in light of what later happened in August 1991, in light of the structural collapse of a vast expanse of the world (and, for many people, of the whole world), a gesture such as the creation of a chain of human hands, even one five hundred kilometers long, can seem trivial, but to those I spoke with it was a shock, a miracle, a revolution. For several reasons. For one, this was the first time a large campaign had been carried out, not on the orders of the Central Committee, but owing to the initiative of a young, independent organization—RUCH. Yes, it turned out that the so-called "leading role of the Party" had become a fiction, that the leading role would now in fact be taken over by grass-roots organizations which the society itself had called into being, and that the society would listen only to them. Second, it became clear that Ukrainians had kept alive the memory of their first independence, a memory that bolshevism had tried to erase for seventy years. This chain, then, had enormous psychological significance. It tightened round the neck of the greatest nightmare of Sovietism, which is the feeling of having no alternatives, of hopelessness.

From that moment, history speeds up in the Ukraine. Still in January, Pope John Paul II ratifies the structure of the Ukrainian Catholic Church. (The story of the relations between the four Christian communities in the Ukraine—the Ukrainian Catholic Church, the Roman Catholic Church, the Orthodox Church, and the Ukrainian Autocephalous Orthodox Church—is a separate chapter in contemporary Ukrainian history, a chapter full of tensions, emotions, and pain.) In March, elections are held throughout the Republic to fill seats on councils at all levels. In three districts (again, this is in the western Ukraine), the democratic opposition comes to power. (How my favorite Ukrainian writer, Vinnichenko, the creator of the idea of a democratic Ukraine, would have rejoiced!) Finally, June 16 arrives—the Parliament passes a declaration of the sovereignty of the Ukrainian Soviet Socialist Republic. The declaration proclaims the primacy of the laws of the Republic over those of the USSR and also the right of the Republic to possess its own army and to mint its own currency. The declaration states that the Ukraine will be a neutral and nonatomic state. (This has great importance, since enormous stocks of the weapons of mass destruction are located in the territories of the Republic.) Yet for all its historical significance and eloquence, the declaration of June 16 is at that moment still more a statement of intent than a document describing facts.

Therefore the battle continues. Student and miner strikes erupt in the fall. Students occupy the center of Kiev and demand the resignations of the Republic's Soviet leaders. In the course of that same year, around twenty political parties come into being, with increasing influence wielded by, among others, the Ukrainian Republican Party and the Ukrainian Green Party. (Chernobyl lies a mere eighty kilometers north of Kiev.)

August 19, 1991, arrives.

The coup d'état attempt in Moscow. In the Ukraine everything is calm; the Ukraine waits. But several days later the Supreme Council of the Ukraine convenes in Kiev and on August 24 proclaims the "creation of the independent Ukrainian state—Ukraine." The proclamation adds that "the territory of the Ukraine is indivisible and inviolable." In the rush of these events, which at the time are rolling across the world with the speed and strength of a powerful avalanche, the fact that Europe has suddenly grown by one large state (large by the standards of the European continent) does not make a tremendous impression. Our Western imagination (this principle was once described by Walter Lippmann) lags behind events, needs time to plumb their meaning and grasp their dimension.

But Russians grasp immediately what has happened. I am in Moscow watching a session of the Supreme Council of the USSR. The moment is dramatic because Lukianov is speaking—formerly the leader of this council and Gorbachev's right hand, now accused of being the ideological mastermind of the conspiracy against him. Complete silence reigns in this usually noisy hall.

Suddenly, Laptin, the deputy chairing the session, interrupts the proceedings and announces in a nervous voice: "Comrades, there have been developments in Kiev. A delegation of the Supreme Council of the USSR must fly there at once!" Rudzkoy, Yeltsin's deputy, and Sobchak, the mayor of Petersburg, depart at the head of the delegation. Both had played leading roles in the defeat of the neo-Stalinist putsch, but both are Russians and thus they understand what Russia is without the Ukraine. "Without the Ukraine," the Polish historian J. Waswicz wrote back in the thirties, "Moscow is relegated to a northern wilderness."

• • •

THE FUTURE OF Ukraine will develop in two directions: in terms of its relations with Russia, and in terms of its relations with Europe and the rest of the world. If these relationships unfold propitiously, Ukraine's chances are excellent. For it is a country of fertile soil and precious natural resources, blessed with a warm, hospitable climate. And it is a large nation of more than fifty million—strong, resilient, and ambitious.

In the fall of 1990, Aleksandr Solzhenitsyn published his plan for the kind of state that he believed should arise in place of the USSR. In the publication—entitled *How to Build Russia?*—he proposes that the future state comprise Russia, Belorussia, Ukraine, and northern Kazakhstan. Let us give back the rest, Solzhenitsyn advises, because "we do not have the strength for the peripheries."

The Ukrainians rejected this plan and others like it. "The only solution to the Ukrainian problem," Leonid Plushch, the Ukrainian dissident, recently wrote, "is the creation of our own state, which will marshall the defensive mechanisms and the appropriate means for cultural development." The Ukrainian intellectuals, who once feared Russian Communists, are now vigilantly observing the attitudes of Russian democrats. Nikolai Riabchuk, one of several excellent Ukrainian essayists, expresses the anxieties that have led to this vigilance when, writing about the program of the Russian Movement for Democratic Reforms, he asks: "Impero-democrats instead of Impero-communists?" Sakharov's widow, Elena Bonner, voiced similar sentiments in early September. "I fear," she said, that which dwells within Russians, their "spirit of expansion and domination."

And the relations of Ukraine with the rest of the world? Until 1917—and in certain parts of the country this was true as recently as 1939—the Ukraine was one of the world's most variegated tapestries of cultures, religions, and languages, an extremely rich, colorful garden in which Westerners immersed themselves with wonder and fascination. How many Polish, Russian, Jewish, Hungarian, Italian, Austrian, German, Romanian traces still remain here, despite the devastation and destruction? In September I visited the Polish cemetery in Żytomierz (150 kilometers from Kiev along the road to Lvov): the grave of the son of Moniuszka, of the wife of Kraszewski, of the sister of Paderewski, of the family of Conrad. The family vault of General Dąbrowski, which served until recently as an occasional brothel.

The strength of Ukraine vis-à-vis the rest of the world is its emigration. A large portion of Canadian wheat grows on the fields of Ukrainian farmers in Alberta and Ontario. The Ukrainians form influential, economically and culturally strong communities in Detroit, New York, and Los Angeles, as well as in Western Europe. These emigrants are strongly attached to Ukraine. Ukrainian patriotism has a peasant quality: it is firmly rooted in the native soil. In Kiev today there are already many Ukrainians from Canada and the United States. They want to establish banks and businesses, to trade, to start up publishing houses. Soon Ukraine will have its own airlines, its own seagoing fleet, its own currency and army.

Questioned about the future Ukraine, one of its leaders, Mihailo Horyn, told me in Kiev: "We want Ukraine to be an enlightened, good, democratic, and humane state."

Enlightened, good, democratic, and humane. Amen.

LVOV. One evening, Father Ludwik Kamielowski takes me to his home. He lives with his mother and wants me to meet her.

Mrs. Bronisława Kamielowska is an elderly woman with a warm, kindly face. Bent over, carrying an invisible burden, she speaks calmly, in an even-tempered voice, as though her concern about that which she is describing belongs to her in some former incarnation, an incarnation with which she, the Bronisława Kamielowska who sits before me, now has very little in common. Thinking about her later, I remembered a sentence Paul Claudel wrote in his old age: "I look at my earlier life as on an island receding in the distance." The frantic acceleration and mutability of history, which are the essence of the times we live in, dictate that many of us are inhabited by several personas, practically indifferent to one another, even mutually contradictory.

Mrs. Kamielowska gave birth to ten children. Six of them died of hunger before her eyes. She is the female embodiment of Job, Job of the epoch of the Great Famine. That she, a woman, survived that cataclysm only confirms the fact that the Great Famine claimed most of its victims among children and men. Women turned out to be, relatively, the strongest, the most resilient. "How good is God," Mrs. Kamielowska says at one point, "that he gave me so much strength!"

Here, in this tiny apartment, I observe scenes of the Great Famine through the eyes of the mother of Father Ludwik. (The priest is her youngest child.) I do not ask her for the names of the deceased, or whether their graves exist somewhere, because I feel that I shouldn't ask about anything at all and should only listen to what will be confided to me.

First, briefly, about the history of the Great Famine. At the start of 1929, the sixteenth Conference of the All Soviet Communist Party/Bolsheviks ratifies the program for universal collectivization. Stalin decides that by the fall of 1930 the entire peasantry of his country (which at that time means three-quarters of the population, more than one hundred million people) must be in kolkhozes. But the peasants do not want to join kolkhozes. Stalin proceeds to snuff out their resistance by two methods. He sends hundreds of thousands of them to the camps or deports and resettles them in Siberia, and the rest he undertakes to starve into obedience.

The main blow falls on the Ukraine, on this land where in the village of Butryn, county Szepietowka, Mrs. Kamielowska lives with her husband, Joseph, and her children.

Officially, the matter presented itself as follows: Moscow had determined the size of the quota each village was obliged to deliver to the state—how much grain, potatoes, meat, and so on, but the quotas were significantly greater than what the land could realistically be expected to yield. Understandably, the peasants were unable to fulfill the plan imposed upon them. So then, by force—usually by military force—the authorities started confiscating everything edible in the villages. The peasants had nothing to eat and nothing to sow. A massive and deadly famine began in 1930, lasting seven years and reaping its grimmest harvest in

1933. The majority of demographers and historians today agree that in those years Stalin starved to death around ten million people.

> The forms of hunger are terrible and varied. Hunger became the norm of life. In the entire country, only certain individuals had adequate amounts of nourishment. They were the highest officials and the cannibals. But both these categories constituted a negligible portion of society. Millions of the hungry were prepared to do anything just for a piece of bread. . . . Hunger divided people. Many of them lost the ability to feel compassion, the desire to help others. . . . In photographs from that period we see people passing indifferently next to a child lying in a gutter, we see women conversing calmly next to corpses strewn in the road, we see coachmen sitting comfortably on wagons from which protrude lifeless arms and legs. . . . Six-year-old Tania Pokidko picked a clove of garlic from the garden of a neighbor, Gavril Turko. He beat her so severely that after she had dragged herself home she died. Her father, Stiepan, was a Red guerrilla. He took four of his children, already swollen from hunger, and went to the county authorities to ask for help. When he was refused, he said to Polonski, the secretary of the county council: "It would be better if you ate them than for me to have to see how they suffer." And he hanged himself on a tree in front of the council building. A peasant woman, Fiedorchuk, took pity on a neighbor's children—six-year-old Nicholas and two-year-old Ola—and promised their parents that she would give them each a cup of milk a day. But the children did not receive the milk, because their father said to his wife: "All our neighbors' children have died long ago, why should we feed ours? We have to save ourselves before it is too late." A seven-year-old boy steals a fish in the market. The enraged crowd pursues him, catches him, stomps on him, and disperses only when the child's body lies lifeless. The peasant Vasil Luchko lived with his wife,

Oksana, an eleven-year-old daughter, and two sons—six and four years old. His wife, an energetic woman, would travel to Poltava to look for food. One day, a neighbor came by Vasil's house and saw that the older boy was hanging in the door frame.

"What have you done, Vasil?"

"I hung the boy."

"And where is the other one?"

"In the closet. I hung him yesterday."

"Why did you do it?"

"There is nothing to eat. When Oksana brings back bread, she gives everything to the children. And now, when she arrives, she will also give me something to eat."

Tragedies occurred when those who traveled to other regions to obtain food found no one left alive upon their return. Death ruled the countryside. Mass graves with room for several dozen corpses at a time were dug in advance—no one doubted that they would be filled within several days and that new ones would have to be dug . . . wagons transporting bodies to these graves became a common sight throughout the countryside . . . representatives of the regime walked from house to house asking if anyone had died, and if someone had, they helped drive the body to a communal pit. . . . What did people eat? Acorns were deemed a delicacy. Besides that, bran, chaff, beet leaves, tree leaves, shavings, sawdust, cats, dogs, crows, earthworms, frogs. In the spring, when grass appeared, dysentery and diarrhea mowed down more than even hunger did. In the mid-thirties, the situation in the countryside became so ghastly, that whoever happened to be thrown into prison considered himself one of fate's chosen—at least he would get a piece of bread there. (Sergei Maksudov, *Zvenia*, Moscow, 1991)

To crush the peasant opposition, the authorities closed village shops, schools, and medical clinics. Peasants were not allowed to leave their villages, were prevented from entering the towns. Signs were placed along the roads near the entrances to villages considered mutinous: STOPPING HERE IS FORBIDDEN, SPEAKING WITH ANYONE IS FORBIDDEN! In villages lying along railroad lines, peasants would rush toward the tracks whenever a train was approaching. They would fall to their knees, raise their arms in supplication, cry out: "Bread! Bread!" The train crews were instructed to shut the windows, draw the curtains.

Entire families died—later, entire villages.

> Seeing that death was nearing, the village started to howl. In the entire village peasants were howling—it was not the voice of reason or of the soul; it was like the noise leaves make in the wind, or the rustle of straw. I would get angry then: Why are they howling so plaintively? They are no longer human, and yet they cry so. I went out into the fields sometimes and listened: they are howling. I walked farther: it seems to have stopped. But I take several more steps and hear it again—it is the neighboring village howling. And it seems that the whole earth is howling together with the people. There is no God, so who will hear it? (Vasily Grossman, *Everything Flows*, Warsaw, 1990)

MRS. KAMIELOWSKA says that the worst of it began in the summer of 1932. A law was then passed that the peasants called the Law of the Blade of Grain. Stalin invented it and wrote it himself. It had to do with the protection of kolkhoz property. According to it, one could be sentenced to several years in the camps, or even shot, if one stole as much as a blade of grain or a carrot or a beet. Similar punishment awaited the tractor driver whose tractor broke down, or the kolkhoz member who lost a hoe or a shovel.

The law was promulgated in the beginning of August, when the grain was still high in the fields. In many places where wheat or rye grew, watchtowers were built. NKVD men were posted on them, with rifles ready to shoot—they were to drive away anyone who would dare pick so much as a single blade. The edges of the fields and the roads were likewise patrolled by mounted NKVD men, also guarding the harvest. Even the Pioneers were sent in to help, but were later pulled out, for these were children, and children died in the greatest numbers—not only from hunger, but also because cannibals carried them off.

So people saw the wheat, saw the swaying blades. Whoever had any strength left walked out of his cottage to look at the growing crops. But the peasants had to stand at a long distance from the fields. They knew that if they came closer, a shot would ring out. And the summers happened to be hot then, sunny. From the cottage window one could see, far away, black spots on the horizon—these were human skeletons, dressed in rags, consumed by fever and typhus. Some of them did not return to the village, but stayed there, looking, forever.

It sometimes happened, Mrs. Kamielowska reminisces, that a horse would drop dead right under one of the NKVD men, for their animals were also skinny and weak. One would see above a stand of grain the silhouette of an NKVD man on horseback. He would sit, look around, and then suddenly vanish. The horse had simply collapsed under him. A rare moment of hope would ensue, because there would be confusion among the NKVD and one could take advantage of these few seconds to get to the grain and pick a few blades. This was something at least, enough only for a day, perhaps for two, but, nevertheless, something.

Death came from hunger, but it also came from eating. A brigade of agitators would sometimes arrive from town and bring bread. People threw themselves upon it, ate, ate, and then started to cry, to contort from pain. Some died instantly.

The worst thing was the house searches. The government people would pull up the floorboards, rake up every square inch of the garden, dig in the field. They were making sure there wasn't any food hidden anywhere. If they did find any, they would take it all away and throw the owner into prison. They took Mrs. Kamielowska's husband—whom she calls Józik—six times. She would go to the district's administrative office, kneel, cry. She was a fortunate woman, for somehow they would always let him go. And the reason she was fortunate, she maintains, is that she believed in God. God will never abandon man, she tells me with conviction. She herself is the best proof of this. Because later they deported her to Kazakhstan and took her husband to the war. In Kazakhstan things were as difficult as in the Ukraine, and on top of that the climate was worse. She walked eight kilometers through ice and wind to the kolkhoz to labor. She was certain that her husband had been killed in Germany. And then, look! Here he is, back from the war! It was from that reunion that Father Ludvik was born, who is sitting here with us and smiling.

What the Bolsheviks were up to, words cannot describe. One time, someone brought a newspaper from town. Inside, a photograph—grain growing high in the fields. And the accompanying text said that the cities were going hungry, that there were lines for bread night and day because the peasants were lazy, they didn't want to harvest the crops, and everything was rotting in the field. The hatred toward the peasants was great, and yet it was after all the peasants themselves who were dying of hunger! When they put them on the train bound for Kazakhstan, they would pass through deserted villages. The windows boarded up, the doors ajar, swinging and squeaking in the wind. No people at all, maybe only an NKVD man. No livestock of any kind—the livestock had either died or been slaughtered. There wasn't even a dog barking—the dogs had been eaten long ago.

MAKSUDOV believes that this genocide in the Ukraine called the Great Famine—although it was officially known as the collectivization of agriculture and the building of the kolkhoz system—brought such a terrible curse that this agricultural land has not recovered to this day. "But the life of the victors in this cruel war," he writes,

> turned out to be not so wonderful after all. For theirs was a Pyrrhic victory. Grain production, which had almost doubled between 1923 and 1928, remained after collectivization at the same level for twenty-five years, although the region's population, naturally, was increasing. Cattle raising never got over the blow that was the slaughter or

> starvation of more than one hundred million horses, cows, bulls, sheep, and pigs. It is beyond any doubt that the ongoing agricultural crisis in the USSR has its roots in those distant years, in that "victory" that turned out to be a defeat. The land and the peasants retaliated the only way they were able to against those who had conquered them. The earth stopped giving birth, and the peasants lost their love of working the land. It was a terrible, but a just, revenge.

HISTORIANS EXPLAIN the genocide in the Ukraine (and in the northern Caucasus) in various ways. Russian historians see it as an instrument of the destruction of traditional society and the construction, in its place, of a formless, docile, half-enslaved mass of *Homo sovieticus*. Ukrainian historians (among them Valentin Moroz) believe that Stalin's goal was to save the Imperium: the Imperium cannot exist without the Ukraine. Yet the twenties witness a renascence of Ukrainian nationalistic ambition, which develops under the slogan "Far from Moscow!" The main repository of the Ukrainian spirit is the peasantry. To break that spirit, Stalin must destroy the peasantry. At the time, there were around thirty million Ukrainian peasants. Technically, one could have annihilated a significant portion of them by building a network of gas chambers. But that is an error Stalin did not commit. He who builds gas chambers bears all the blame, brings the disgrace of being a murderer down upon himself. Instead, Stalin saddled the victims of the crime with all the guilt for it: You are dying of hunger because you do not want to work, because you do not see the advantages of the kolkhoz. Furthermore, he complained, because of you the inhabitants of the cities are going hungry, women cannot nurse because they have no milk, children cannot go to school because they are too weak.

The Ukrainian countryside died in silence, isolated from the world, gnawing on the bark of trees and on the leather laces of its own shoes, looked upon with contempt by people from the cities, who stood in the streets in unending lines for bread.

• • •

I RISE in Lvov near dawn. It is still dark when I walk out into the street. I see a little light swaying in the distance: the day's first streetcar is approaching. I take it to the train station and buy a ticket to Drohobych, on the suburban line. It is bright daylight by the time I arrive, and a pale sun appears between the thinning clouds. (It is February.) Leszek Gałas and Alfred Szrejer are waiting for me on the platform. Mr. Gałas must hurry to work, but Mr. Szrejer is retired and can spend the day with me.

Pilgrimages are made to Drohobych because this is where the writer Bruno Schulz lived, created, and died. Mr. Szrejer was a pupil of Schulz's who, in addition to writing and painting, taught crafts and drawing in the Władysław Jagiełło Secondary School. "When we didn't feel like doing anything in class, we asked him to tell us a story. He would stop the lesson and recite a tale. He liked to do this very much."

Schulz lived in a one-story house at 12 Floriańska Street, from which he had a very short walk to the school on Zielona Street, maybe several hundred meters. All he had to do was cross two small streets and a beautiful old square. There is a church nearby, and then another square. Behind that church, at the edge of the square, stands a bakery today. It was there, in 1942, on the street, that Karl Gunter, a Gestapo agent, shot Bruno Schulz. Gunter had a small woman's pistol.

Bruno Schulz's life thus ran its course in this little town, and, finally, within that even smaller triangle between Floriańska Street, Zielona Street, and the square near the bakery. Today people can walk this route in several minutes, reflecting upon the mystery of Schulz's extraordinary imagination. But it is doubtful that they would reach any clear and insightful conclusions. Only once did this beautiful little town yield its extraordinary secrets. Only once, and only to Bruno Schulz, who was a vigilant and sensitive particle of it, its discreet, silently passing spirit.

That is why my question is utterly absurd: "Mr. Szrejer, where are the cinnamon shops?"

Szrejer stops, and there is a mixture of surprise, irony, and even reprimand in his gaze. "Where are the cinnamon shops?" he echoes. "Why, they were in Schulz's imagination! It is there that they shone. It is there that they emitted such a unique fragrance!"

Mr. Szrejer wants to show me his properties, or, more precisely, that which once belonged to his family. This pharmacy belonged to his grandfather, and this house to his father, who got his Ph.D. in chemistry in Zurich and was the director of an oil-refinery laboratory in Jassy.

His family perished in the ghetto, and the few survivors emigrated to Argentina.

For sixteen years after the war, Mr. Szrejer played the violin and sang in a movie-house orchestra, first at the Kirov (formerly Wanda), and then at the Komsomolec (formerly Sztuka). Later, he taught in a school of music.

"And here," says Mr. Szrejer, when we had already been walking a long time around the town, "here was a synagogue—now it's a furniture warehouse. Those dry sticks you see there? Countless weeds grow here in the summer." Could that idiot girl, Tluya, have had her bed here? Maybe she could have.

Everything is so unclear, so unfathomable. Schulz wrote *The Cinnamon Shops* during the most terrible year of the Great Famine in the Ukraine, not far from Drohobych. Schulz most certainly knew nothing of this great tragedy, hidden as it was from the world. Yet what forces could have been at work here, what mysterious currents, associations, connections, and oppositions, that would lead him to begin his book with a magnificent, stupefying vision of satiety?

> On those luminous mornings Adela returned from the market, like Pomona emerging from the flames of day, spilling from her basket the colorful beauty of the sun—the shiny pink cherries full of juice under their transparent skins, the mysterious black morellos that smelled so much better than they tasted; apricots in whose golden pulp lay the core of long afternoons. And next to that pure poetry of fruit, she unloaded sides of meat with their keyboard

of ribs swollen with energy and strength, and seaweeds of vegetables like dead octopuses and squids—the raw material of meals with a yet undefined taste, the vegetative and terrestrial ingredients of dinner, exuding a wild and rustic smell.

# Return to My Hometown

FOR THE FIRST TIME in Petersburg. It is August, but it is nevertheless cold and drizzling. Dostoyevsky saw the cloudy, Scandinavian weather as a feature of this city: "At last the damp autumn day, muggy and dirty, peeped into the room through the dingy window pane with such a hostile, sour grimace that Mr. Golyadkin could not possibly doubt that he was not in the land of Nod but in the city of Petersburg" (Fyodor Dostoyevsky, "The Double").

The author of *Notes from the Underground* often suggested that the irritations, angers, and melancholias of his heroes were related to the climate and atmosphere of the city: "From early morning I had been oppressed by a strange despondency. It suddenly seemed to me that I was lonely, that everyone was forsaking me and going away from me. Of course, anyone is entitled to ask who 'everyone' was. For though I had been living almost eight years in Petersburg I had hardly an acquaintance" (Fyodor Dostoyevsky, *White Nights*).

I was walking from the station (I had arrived on the overnight train from Moscow) thinking about Mr. Golyadkin and his extraordinary adventures. But not only about him. Petersburg has figured in so many novels, poems, and legends that it seems to be not so much a real city as an invented one; and because of the talents of Pushkin, Gogol, and Dostoyevsky, at moments their heroes seem to us more real than the people whom we are just now passing in the street.

The street is called Nevsky Prospekt and cuts across old Petersburg from the east to the west. The closer it gets to the Neva River, the larger and more ornate become the apartment buildings and other edifices that stand on either side of it. The architecture alone, as it becomes increasingly grand and dignified, announces that we are approaching a place of special, momentous, highest importance. And in fact, at the end of Nevsky Prospekt, on the right, suddenly, as if someone had raised the curtains, appears the vast panorama of the Palace Square.

An imposing view!

On the left side of the square, along its entire length, stretches the mass of the Winter Palace—green, azure, and white, decorated with artful latticework and pilasters—the seat of the czars.

Opposite, on the other side of the square, stands the long, monumental edifice of the General Staff, painted a light ocher.

And between these splendid structures lies the broad, flat, and empty expanse—so enormous that I am tempted to call it immeasurable—of the Palace Square. Something glimmers at one end of it, somewhere a vehicle will pass, a human figure will scurry by, but all this only underscores the immensity of this place, its imperturbable immobility.

The panorama of this square, its conception, plan, and composition, possesses a profound symbolism that says more about this country than dozens of dissertations and handbooks could. For this square exemplifies the character and structure of power. Its highest form is represented by the Winter Palace—the seat of the ruler. Whereas its right arm, its only and most important one, is neither spiritual power (no church is visible here) nor legislative power (there is no Parliament building in sight), but the military, troops, and weapons housed in the building of the General Staff.

The monarch and his army—is that why the Russian eagle, the coat of arms and the symbol of the state, has two heads, and not one?

One can walk endlessly around the streets of old Petersburg. There is so much interesting architecture here, so many canals, so many squares, so many nooks and crannies. From here Pushkin left for his fatal duel (at the corner of Nevsky Prospekt and Moyka); here Akhmatova wrote her shocking "Requiem"; this way passed the coach of Apollon Apollonovich, hero of the novel *Petersburg* by Andrei Bely, who said: "After Petersburg, there is nothing." When I wander thus along streets lined with thousands of solid, bourgeois apartment buildings, one question keeps arising in my mind: How, in such a fortress of capital, private property, and wealth, could the Bolsheviks have triumphed? These buildings, after all, were the repository of an enormous social force, of major interests, of financial and organizational might! Where were all these people, what were they thinking, what were they doing, when Lenin was reaching for power?

The American historian Richard Pipes (*The Russian Revolution*, 1990) answers in this way:

> Curzio Malaparte describes the bewilderment of the English novelist, Israel Zangwill, who happened to be visiting Italy as the Fascists were taking power. Struck by the absence of "barricades, street fighting and corpses on the pavement," Zangwill refused to believe that he was witnessing a revolution. But, according to Malaparte, the characteristic quality of modern revolutions is precisely the bloodless, almost silent seizure of strategic points by small detachments of trained shock troops. The assault is carried out with such surgical precision that the public at large has no inkling of what is happening.
>
> This description fits the October coup in Russia (which Malaparte had studied and used as one of his models). In October, the Bolsheviks gave up on massive armed demonstrations and street skirmishes, which they had employed, on Lenin's insistence, in April and July,

> because the crowds had proven difficult to control and provoked a backlash. They relied instead on small, disciplined units of soldiers and workers under the command of their Military Organization, disguised as the Military-Revolutionary Committee, to occupy Petrograd's principal communication and transport centers, utilities and printing plants—the nerve centers of the modern metropolis. Merely by severing the telephone lines connecting the government with its Military Staff they made it impossible to organize a counterattack. The entire operation was carried out so smoothly and efficiently that even as it was in progress the cafés and restaurants along with the opera, theaters, and cinemas were open for business and thronged with crowds in search of amusement.

What comes to mind immediately is the astonishment of Alexis de Tocqueville describing the mood on the eve of the French Revolution: "This may help to explain the singular fact that at the very moment when the Revolution was knocking at the door so few apprehensions of any kind were felt by members of the upper and the middle classes, and why they went on blithely discoursing on the virtues of the people, their loyalty, their innocent pleasures, and so forth. Such was the blindness, at once grotesque and tragic, of these men who would not see!" (*The Old Regime and the French Revolution*).

The other side of Europe, 125 years later, and yet there are similarities. In both instances, the same factor brings victory to the attackers—the factor of surprise.

THE GOAL of my journey was not Petersburg but Novgorod, 150 kilometers to the south, and Professor Aleksander Grekov, who lived there.

Novgorod was a famous city in the Middle Ages, something along the lines of a Florence or an Amsterdam of the north—a dynamic concentration of commerce and craftsmanship, a long-flowering center of various arts, especially of sacred architecture and icon painting. A unique political system existed here. For hundreds of years (from the eleventh to the fifteenth century) Novgorod was a kind of independent, self-governing feudal republic in which the highest authority rested with a council composed of different elements of the city's population and the neighboring free peasantry. The people elected a prince who ruled in their name and could be recalled at any moment. For those times and in that part of the world, these were unheard-of practices. The symbol of the freedom and independence of this city-state was a great bell with which the residents were summoned to the council. Thus, when Ivan II of Moscow finally conquered Novgorod in 1478 and ordered the bell removed, that act alone signified that the city had lost its independence. There are historians who believe that this was one of those critical moments that determined the direction in which Moscow, and all of Russia, would go. Novgorod was a democratic city, open to the world, maintaining contacts with all of Europe. Moscow was expansionist, permeated with Mongol influences, hostile toward Europe, already slowly entering the dark epoch of Ivan the Terrible. Therefore, if Russia had gone the way of Novgorod, it might have become a state different from the one at whose head Moscow came to stand. But things turned out otherwise.

VOLODIA P. makes a living taking souvenir photographs under the bulgy, dark bronze monument to Russia's millennium for tour groups that come to Novgorod to see the collected masterpieces of old architecture and painting—the local kremlin. (A kremlin is a type of ecclesiastical citadel, a gathering of churches, cloisters, and service buildings surrounded by walls and, once, the seat of princely power.) Because the lower section of the monument consists of statues of 129 great Russians, Volodia can take your picture against whatever group of celebrities and heroes you choose. If a tour group of military men arrives, Volodia will position them against Aleksander Nevsky, Dimitry Donsky, Aleksander Suvorov, Mikhail Kutuzov, and Ivan Paskievich. If it is a group from some Writers' Union, they will have Mikhail Lomonsov, Ivan Krylov, Aleksander Griboyedov, and Mikhail Lermontov in the background. Teachers will find themselves in the company of Cyril and Methodius, Maxim the Greek and Tichon Zadonsky. Volodia will place a tour group of government workers and economists between Mikhail Romanov—the founder of the dynasty—the slender, gracefully sitting Catherine II, the pensive Peter I, and the proudly upright Nicholas I.

Volodia's occupation must be quite profitable, for when he takes me to his home, the first thing I see in his bachelor's apartment is countless shiny, dark metal boxes, columns, and towers—all sorts of Panasonics, JVCs, and Sonys, which my host immediately switches on. There is also a pretty girl with a good figure, who, after only a moment's conversation, asks me in all seriousness if I would intercede on her behalf and persuade Volodia to get married. "Because he refuses to marry me!" she explains, worried and slightly offended.

We go back to the kremlin, to the monument. A school excursion group, waiting for Volodia, who has promised them a photograph (he is the only photographer here) stands in the drizzling rain, bent over a table on which Anna Adreyevna displays souvenir postcards for sale. When the children go to have their picture taken, I start picking out some postcards for myself. I do not know what brought it on, but suddenly Anna Andreyevna, a woman of maybe forty, maybe sixty, years of age, stretches out her hands to me from the overly short sleeves of her coat.

"Look," she says, enraged and despairing, "look, they made my hands like a man's!"

She shows me her veinous, rough, massive palms and repeats: "They made my hands like a man's!"

On her lips, this sounds like the most terrible of accusations, like horror, like a curse.

"From the time I was a young girl," she explains, shouting and bursting into tears, "I had to work as a locksmith. My whole life—as a locksmith."

"And today, look," she tells me with a mixture of pain and dread in her voice, "today I have hands like a man's!"

And although she has kept company with them since childhood, although she sees them every day, she looks at them now with shame and terror.

Slender, slight Anna Andreyevna, a woman with graying hair and a pale, ill-looking face, threatens the air with the steel fists of a strong, overworked locksmith.

And yet in the end she discovers in this accursed fate of hers a bright spark, a crumb of some sort of human comfort, for a moment later she adds: "They made my hands like a man's, they made me a Stalinist, but they never made me a Communist!"

Slowly she calms down, and when I am leaving she says to me in a voice already quiet, gentle, and resigned: "If they would only let me live normally for a while now."

TO REACH the large old building in whose basement work Professor Grekov and his wife, Valentina Borisova, one must pass the great Sofia Cathedral (an eleventh-century masterpiece) and walk deep into the kremlin, crossing various squares and courtyards. It is a spacious room—actually several connected cellars—furnished with rows of long, wide tables on which are arranged piles of small wall fragments. Lights are on everywhere; otherwise it would be dark in here, even pitch black. Two or three people are seated at each table, picking up fragments of masonry and examining them closely. Total, vigilant, and concentrated silence reigns, only rarely—and this is an important moment—interrupted by an exclamation:

"I have Elias's eye!"

"I have the sky-blue color! These are probably the martyrs of Paraskieva!"

And a discussion begins, consultations, comparisons.

This is what is happening here:

Many smaller churches and monasteries had stood in the vicinity of the Novgorod kremlin. Among them was the Church of the Lord's Transfiguration, built in the fourteenth century on a small hill three kilometers away. In 1380, a group of anonymous painters (probably Serbs) decorated the interior of the church with magnificent frescoes. Their surface area totaled around 350 square meters. During the Second World War, Russians turned the church into a bunker and an artillery observation point (it is on the only elevated land on an otherwise flat, meadow-covered, treeless plain), at which the Germans constantly took aim with cannons and mortars. Because they fired at the church for more than two and a half years, after the war all that remained on the hill was a mountain of rubble more than five meters high. For the next twenty years, the mountain was overgrown with grasses, weeds, and bushes, until, in 1965, someone started to poke around in the rubble and discover small, colorful fragments of frescoes. Over the next several years, three hundred cubic meters of debris were carefully dug through and ten cubic meters of colored bits were sifted out of it, then transported to the Novgorod kremlin, to the building where for the last twenty years Professor Grekov, his wife, and a group of enthusiasts have been attempting to piece together again from these little stones, morsels, and particles, thoroughly shattered and ground up by artillery fire, the old, fourteenth-century frescoes, in which anonymous painters (probably Serbs) conveyed their vision of the Lord's Transfiguration.

Wooden frames line the walls of the entire workroom in which lie the already recovered fragments of Christ's head, or the aureole of St. Yefrem, or the garments of a young martyr.

The greatest difficulty, says the professor, is that the frescoes had never been adequately photographed, that there is no documentation, and that consequently one sometimes has to rely on the shaky and misleading testimony of eyewitnesses.

Talking with Aleksander Pietrovich Grekov, I am aware of being in the presence of a man of unique, extraordinary imagination. It must be an imagination replete with thousands of question marks, of dilemmas. This piece of wall, on which the trace of a flame remains: Is it a fragment of the fire in which God appears, or, on the contrary, is it part of the infernal fire into which the Almighty will cast the hardened and incorrigible sinners? And this tiny sliver on which the clear image of a tear has been preserved. Is it the tear of the mother, who lays her son, Man, into his grave, or the tear of joy on the face of one of the women who hear that Christ is risen?

"Six days later, Jesus took with him Peter and James and his brother John and led them up a high mountain where they could be alone. There in their presence he was transfigured: his face shone like the sun and his clothes became as white as the snow" (Matthew 17:1–2).

Which of these golden rays, scattered on one of the tables, are part of this sun? Which of these white particles, lying on one of the chests, are fragments of the clothes that became white as the snow?

"But anyone who is an obstacle to bring down one of these little ones who have faith in me would be better drowned in the depths of the sea with a great millstone round his neck" (Matthew 18:6).

Do these chips of waves, which someone here is just now carefully inspecting under a light, symbolize these dangerous depths of the sea, or, rather, are they part of the painting of the sea upon which Christ is walking with dry feet toward his disciples?

"Tell me. Suppose a man has a hundred sheep and one of them strays; will he not leave the ninety-nine on the hillside and go in search of the stray?" (Matthew 18:13).

Does this lock of wool, the drawing of which has been preserved on this bit of plaster, belong to one of the ninety-nine well-behaved and obedient sheep, or is it a remnant of the reckless and unruly sheep, for whom the patient Shepherd searches over the hillsides?

And thus observing how from thousands of particles, bits, and crumbs, from dust, molecules, and pebbles, the professor and his students have been for years piecing together portraits of saints, sinners, and legends, I feel as though I were a witness, in this cold and dusty underground, to the birth of the sky and of the earth, of all the colors and shapes, angels and kings, light and darkness, good and evil.

FROM NOVGOROD to Minsk, for the congress of the National Front of Belorussia. Their great writer, Vasili Bykau, took me there. Bykau is a big, tall man, taciturn, even largely silent, but silent in a kind, amicable way. The hero of one of his novels Agieyev, in appearance and behavior very much resembles Vasili himself. Agieyev visits his hometown, searching for remnants of the past:

> He looked around. The square had changed so much as to become unrecognizable, but the church remained, and that is what helped him get his bearings. One had to turn into the alley now and follow the street downward. Trying to control his anxiety, Agieyev set off at a rapid pace toward the outskirts of town, first toward Zielona, a street well known to him, lined with typical wooden houses with tiny orchards and gardens that stretched toward a deep ravine with a stream along its bottom and old trees along the sides. (Vasili Bykau, *The Quarry*)

Belorussia is a level country, flat as a tranquil sea—in the summer green and sapphire from bluebottles, in the winter white and black from snow and crows—where there are countless little towns such as the one Agieyev visits. Belorussia is an agricultural country, a peasant country, and it is in the villages that the Belorussian language was preserved. This is evident too during the sessions of the congress. Many delegates from the towns say a few sentences in Belorussian, then apologize and switch to Russian—it is easier for them to speak in Russian. Delegates from the villages do not have these difficulties. Belorussia's strategically important location led the czars and the Bolsheviks to conduct a methodical, brutal, and bitter campaign of Russification there. In the thirties, almost the entire Belorussian intelligentsia was either shot or deported. The massacres were organized by Beria's confidant and friend Canava, who was a Georgian. Those who were being executed were accused of being Polish agents. Moscow was anxious that Belorussia be inhabited by a Russian-speaking population—not even necessarily ethnic Russians, just Russian speakers.

At the congress there is much discussion of the consequences of the catastrophe at Chernobyl. The wave of radioactivity from the electrical plant struck Belorussia first and foremost. The monthly *Neman*, published in Minsk, ran a photograph of a

Belorussian boy born after the Chernobyl explosion. He is white as porcelain, has enormous, sad, black eyes, and, instead of hair, a pale down all over his head.

I am all ears as one of the delegates ponders: Which domination is more dangerous for Belorussia—the Russian or the Polish? And he concludes that it is the Polish, because Poland is more attractive.

ALL DAY by bus from Minsk to my hometown, Pińsk. The same landscape from morning to night, as if one were standing still. In some ports only the shallow and winding bed of the Neman River. In some ports the straight line of the Oginski Canal.

Pińsk. I feel like Agieyev:

> Trying to control his anxiety, Agieyev set off at a rapid pace toward the outskirts of town, first toward Zielona, a street well known to him, lined with typical, wooden houses with tiny orchards and gardens that stretched toward a deep ravine with a stream along its bottom and old trees along the sides.

At noon I went to the church. After the mass, as people were dispersing, I walked up to them and asked if anyone remembered my parents, who had taught in the school here. And I told them my name. It turned out that those leaving the church were my mother's and father's students, older now by fifty years.

I had returned to my childhood home.

# The Sequel Continues
## (1992–1993)

# The Sequel Continues

RUSSIA OPENED its twentieth-century history with the Revolution of 1905 and is closing it with the revolution that resulted in the breakup of the USSR in 1991.

HISTORY IN this country is an active volcano, continually churning, and there is no sign of its wanting to calm down, to be dormant.

THE RUSSIAN WRITER Yurii Boriev compared the history of the USSR to a train in motion:

> The train is speeding into a luminous future. Lenin is at the controls. Suddenly—stop, the tracks come to an end. Lenin calls on the people for additional, Saturday work, tracks are laid down, and the train moves on. Now Stalin is driving it. Again the tracks end. Stalin orders half the conductors and passengers shot, and the rest he forces to lay down new tracks. The train starts again. Khrush-

chev replaces Stalin, and when the tracks come to an end, he orders that the ones over which the train has already passed be dismantled and laid down before the locomotive. Brezhnev takes Khrushchev's place. When the tracks end again, Brezhnev decides to pull down the window blinds and rock the cars in such a way that the passengers will think the train is still moving forward. (Yurii Boriev, *Staliniad*, 1990)

And thus we come to the Epoch of the Three Funerals (Brezhnev's, Andropov's, Chernenko's), during which the passengers of the train do not even have the illusion that they are going anywhere. But then, in April 1985, the train starts to move again. This is its last journey, however. It will last six and a half years. This time Gorbachev is the engineer, and the slogan GLASNOST—PERESTROIKA is painted on the locomotive.

THE MORE ABSTRACT a meaning one gives to the appellation "Russia," the easier it is to speak about it. "Russia seeks a path," "Russia says—no," "Russia goes to the right," and so on. At such a high level of generality, many problems lose their significance, cease being relevant, vanish. The ideological and national macroscale marginalizes and invalidates the difficult, vexing microscale of everyday life. Will Russia remain a superpower? When juxtaposed against such a monumental question, of what import is the one that so perturbs Anna Andreyevna from Novgorod—when will they let her live normally for a while? The language of the ubiquitous political discourse forces out, from the mass media and, what is worse, from our memory, the vocabulary with which one can express his private problems, personal drama, individual pain. They do not have a roof over their heads? This is no longer of concern to us; it is a matter for the Salvation Army or the Red Cross.

And yet it is impossible to avoid this abstract approach. One can present the enormous scale of the unfolding events only through language and concepts that are general, synthesizing—

yes, abstract—all the while remaining aware that time and time again one will fall into the trap of simplifications and statements easily undermined.

THERE ARE writers who imbue the notion of "Russia" with a mystical meaning, ascribing to it the mysterious, unfathomable qualities of a holy thing. The poet Fiodor Tiutchev writes that "One cannot comprehend Russia with one's reason . . . one can only have faith in Russia." Dostoyevsky believes that Russia is for Europe something enigmatic and incomprehensible: "For Europe, Russia is one of the riddles of the Sphinx. The West will sooner discover the *perpetuum mobile* or the elixir of life than plumb the essence of Russianness, the soul of Russia, its character and disposition."

The faith in Russia sometimes assumes a religious coloring. I saw a demonstration in Moscow during which a large crowd was delivering a litany to Russia with as much devotion as pilgrims to Jasna Góra recite prayers to the Mother of God.

OTHER RUSSIAN writers stress that Russia is unlike any other country, that one should treat it as something exceptional, as a distinct and unique phenomenon. "When one speaks of Russia," writes Piotr Chaadayev, "one often regards it as a state like any other; this is not at all the case. Russia is a whole separate world." Constantine Aksov claims the same thing. "Russia," he writes, "is a country utterly without precedent, not even slightly similar to European states and countries."

AT FIRST, I didn't envisage a great journey. I wanted only to travel to the Caucasus, where I had been two decades earlier, at the end of the sixties. That small area, conquered by Russia and then forcibly incorporated into the USSR, interested me truly, for I am most fascinated by the mental and political decolonization of the world, and there, beyond the Caucasus, just such a process was unfolding. The twentieth century is not only the century of totalitarianisms and world wars, but also history's greatest epoch of decolonization: more than a hundred new states have appeared on the map of the world, entire continents have won—at least formal—independence. The Third World was born and a great demographic explosion began—the population of poorly developed countries began to increase at a rate three times greater than that of wealthy countries. A dozen problems result from this, which will be the worry of the twenty-first century.

The same process of Third World expansion that led to the breakup of the colonial empires of England, France, and Portugal could also be felt within the last colonial empire on earth—the USSR. By the end of the eighties, the country's non-Russian inhabitants constituted nearly half of its population, whereas the governing elite was ninety-five percent Russian or composed of the Russified representatives of the national minorities. It was only a matter of time before awareness of this fact would move these minorities toward acts of emancipation.

SO INITIALLY I planned to travel, as I had done earlier, from Moscow to Georgia, then to Armenia and Azerbaijan. But I was told that this was impossible. The border between Armenia and Azerbaijan is closed; there is a war over which no one has any influence.

This was a shock to me.

How could someone here declare that there is something happening in the USSR over which Moscow has no influence? It was this—the acknowledgment on the part of the imperial powers of some impossibility—that was for me the real revolution! I remember twenty years ago, in Azerbaijan, wanting to visit the Svierdlov kolkhoz rather than the Kirov kolkhoz, but being told that this was impossible: Moscow has given us such and such a program, we cannot change anything. The telephone calls began, the questions, the explanations. Finally, a reply: Agreed, let it be Svierdlov. And all this was over a trifle, an absurdity. But the system depended on that kind of punctiliousness, on a psychotic control of every detail, an obsessive desire to rule over everything. Yurii Boriev writes about some of the matters with which Stalin occupied himself. He issued orders of this kind: "Transfer the sewing machine belonging to tailor's shop number 1 to factory number 7. J. Stalin."

And here we have a major event—two republics close their borders and are conducting a war—and Moscow can do nothing about it!

I experienced a second shock a day later, upon arriving in Yerevan. I went for a walk and suddenly encountered, in the streets, groups of armed, bearded men. I saw that they were not Red Army. Passersby said that they were divisions of the independent Armenian liberation army. It was incomprehensible to me that there could be troops in the Imperium that were not part of the Red Army or of the KGB. Knowing the country and the system from earlier years, I was awaiting the moment when Russian troop divisions would move on the capital of Armenia, massacre the young men, and as punishment resettle thousands of the city's inhabitants in Siberia. But nothing of the sort happened.

The third surprise, on the evening of that same day, was a scene I witnessed on the television screen, during a report from a session of the Supreme Council. One of the deputies was quarreling with the secretary-general of the Central Committee—with Gorbachev. I stiffened. Quarreling with the secretary-general? Once, this meant execution. Later—the irreparable destruction of one's career. And now—the deputy left the podium to general applause.

Summing all this up, I thought: This is the end of the Soviets! For me, the Imperium fell apart then, in the fall of 1989, on the route from Moscow to Yerevan. Everything that happened later was merely the tossing of additional debris onto an already-existing pile of rubble.

I BELIEVE that only those for whom Stalinism-Brezhnevism is part of their life experience can perceive and comprehend the depth, extraordinariness, and immensity of the transformation and revolution that took place in the USSR between 1985 and 1991. I met young fellow reporters in the course of my travels.

What they were seeing they deemed interesting, but part of the normal run of things. For me, everything was unprecedented and astonishing; I could not believe my own eyes.

A FEW WORDS about 1985.

The crisis of the Communist system—and concomitantly of the USSR—becomes at this time increasingly profound, clear, sharp:

- The Third World national liberation movements linked with Moscow wither away and die.
- Communist parties in Western countries collapse and lose their meaning.
- Poland's Solidarity, despite the repressive power of martial law, creates a permanent and widening breach within an actual Socialist system.
- Moscow increasingly falls behind in the arms race with the West, lags more and more visibly with its outdated technology and low labor productivity, loses position after position in the game to control the world.

As the superpower is sapped of its strength and sinks into twilight, a whole generation of leaders departs with it. In the several years preceding the historic 1985, Kulakov, Rashidov, Suslov, Brezhnev, Kosygin, Ustinov, and Andropov die one after the other. The last of this group, Chernenko, dies on March 11, 1985. Others, like Gromyko and Grishin, are increasingly infirm, wallow in alcoholism or, like Aliyev, in monstrous corruption.

Public opinion does exist in this country, although in the preperestroika years it was expressed differently than in democratic states. People made their views known through silence, not speech. The way in which they were silent was significant and said volumes. The way in which they looked at something or at someone had its eloquence. Where they appeared and where they were absent. The way (slowly) in which they gathered for a forced meeting and the way (instantaneously) in which they then dispersed. Despite the government's contempt and arrogance vis-à-vis society, it nevertheless paid attention to the kind of silence that prevailed in that society. I met a student in Petersburg who, during a Komsomol congress in that city (during Brezhnev's time), was "responsible for the atmosphere in the hall." Public opinion in 1985 is best expressed by the title of a film made at the end of the eighties by the Russian director Stanislav Govoruhin—*Tak zyt' nielzia* (One Cannot Live Like This).

And all those crises in which the Imperium is at this time immersed internationally and domestically occur under conditions of universal, everyday human misery, ubiquitous material want and hopelessness. For one must remember that that which was called the privilege of the governing elite was only a relative privilege, existing against a background of penury. The resident of a wealthy country could often laugh at such privileges. For instance, scandal broke out somewhere in the Ukraine because the trunk of the car of some Party official sprang open as he was driving and passersby noticed that there was kielbasa inside. I was myself a witness to another scandal in Ufa—rotten apples were being sold in the market, while workers of the apparat could buy apples that were admittedly worm-eaten, but not rotten! How many times, as I entered various apartments, did my hosts greet me at the door with the words: "*Rishard, izvini nashu sovietskuyu nishchetu*!" ("Forgive us our Soviet misery!") Sometimes the subject of evening conversation was the standard and quality of life in wealthy countries. At the end of my accounts, the Russians would smile and say with a certain resignation in their voice: "*Eto nie dla nas. . . .*" ("That is not for us. . . .")

IN SUCH A SITUATION, in March 1985, on Andrey Gromyko's recommendation, Mikhail Gorbachev is chosen secretary-general of the Central Committee of the Communist Party of the Soviet Union. A month later, during the Party's April plenum, he delivers the speech that ushers in the era of perestroika and *glasnost.*

In some sense perestroika and glasnost are the artificial lungs hooked up to the increasingly enfeebled, dying organism of the USSR. Thanks to them, the USSR will survive for another six and a half years. I mention this because Gorbachev's enemies claim that he assumed the leadership of a flourishing USSR and brought about its breakup. It was just the opposite—the USSR was disintegrating for a long time, and Gorbachev extended its life for as long as it was possible to do so. I mention it also because (this is one of the world's great paradoxes), just before the breakup of the USSR, the view of that country as a model of the most stable and durable system in the world had gained wide acceptance among Western Sovietologists, and especially among a group of American political scientists. The main proponent of this way of thinking was Jerry F. Hough, a professor at Duke University. As Theodore Draper notes (*New York Review of Books*, June 11, 1992), there was not one American political scientist who predicted the collapse of the USSR.

That is why, when the USSR ceased to exist at the end of 1991, one could hear exclamations of surprise and consternation around the world. How is that possible? So stable, and yet it fell? So indivisible, and yet it crumbled? From one day to the next? But this "from one day to the next" applied only to the final act. In reality, the process of disintegration began much earlier.

FOR ME, perestroika was the combination of two great processes to which the society of the Imperium was subjected:

- A mass detoxication to cure fear
- A collective journey into the universe of information

Someone who wasn't brought up in an atmosphere of general, animal fear, and in a world without information, will have difficulty understanding what this was all about.

The foundation of the Soviet Imperium is terror and its inseparable, gnawing offshoot—fear. Because the Kremlin abandons the politics of mass terror with the deaths of Stalin and Beria, one can say that their departure is the beginning of the end of the Imperium. The thaw under Khrushchev and then the years of stagnation alleviate somewhat the frightful nightmare of Stalin's epoch, but nevertheless do not radically eliminate it. The persecutions of dissidents continue; people still lose their jobs if they think otherwise than they are supposed to; censorship rages on, et cetera. Only perestroika and *glasnost* introduce a significant change. For the first time people begin to express their opinions publicly, to have views—to criticize and postulate. They overdo this, of course, get drunk on it, which in the long run becomes extremely tiring, because everyone, everywhere, is endlessly talking, talking, and talking. Or writing, writing, and writing. A deluge of words, billions of words—in assembly halls; on all the airways; on tons, hundreds of tons, of pieces of paper. This overabundance of speech, this agitated stream of words, is abetted by the Russian language itself, with its broad phrasing, expansive, unending, like the Russian land. No Cartesian discipline here, no aphoristic asceticism. One must wade through the torrent of some lecture or struggle through countless pages of text before one arrives at a sentence of value. How one must toil to attain this gem!

Not only can one talk now, but there is also something to talk about. For, simultaneously, the voyage into the universe of information began. To generalize and simplify, one of the fundamental differences between the first half of our century and the second half (especially the most recent years) is the radically different access to information that characterized each of these epochs. In this regard, a man living in the first half of the century, especially in the USSR, was closer to the caveman than to the man who today sits before a computer and who, just by pressing the keys, can immediately obtain all the information he wants. Lev Kopieliev, a Russian dissident writer, draws attention to this difference in his book *The Idols of My Youth*, writing that insofar as information is concerned, even adults were children then, whereas today even children are adults. During the first half of the century in the USSR, people really knew very little. Access to information was one of the real privileges. The archives of the KGB were more closely guarded than the arsenals of the weapons of mass destruction. One Russian journalist (I do not remember his name) recalls that when he asked Brezhnev, after the Soviet invasion of Czechoslovakia, to whom one was allowed to write concerning the situation in that country, Brezhnev replied: "Write everything, but only in a single copy, and send it only to me."

And now there are suddenly references to Katyń, to Kuropaty, to Solovki. . . .

AFTER FIVE YEARS of great effort and tension, Gorbachev is increasingly fatigued, disoriented, and nervous. He is visibly losing his initiative and dynamism, and his politics, until now so creative and, given Russian circumstances, so innovative and extraordinary, are becoming routine, indecisive, concessionary. In December 1990, his minister of international affairs and a tried-and-true ally, Eduard Shevardnadze, warns publicly that the country's conservative forces are preparing a coup d'état and offers his resignation. Gorbachev doesn't react. His entourage now consists of people he himself appointed to the highest positions and who will soon betray him. They are all Party bureaucrats, agents of neo-Stalinist reaction.

The critical year 1991 arrives. It begins with bloody events in Vilno and Riga. Troops from the KBG attack an unarmed demonstration in Vilno with tanks—more than a dozen people die; dozens more are wounded. The Lithuanians encircle their Parliament building with concrete barricades. The interior, when I enter it, calls to mind a fortified castle under siege. Sandbags in the windows, everywhere young armed volunteers keeping guard—they are expecting an attack at any moment. President Landsbergis, tense but composed, is among them, giving them courage. In Riga and in Tallinn, as in Vilno, concrete barricades protect the buildings of the newly declared national parliaments. The most imposing barricades are in Tallinn. To reach the Parliament, one must walk through corridors built to resemble the labyrinth of Minos.

Who is responsible for the blood spilled in Vilno and in Riga? ask the democrats in Moscow as they point to Kriuchkov, the chief of the KGB, and Pugo, the minister of internal affairs. But Gorbachev doesn't dismiss them. Does he lack the strength? Does he not know what to do?

In the summer he goes with his family on vacation to the Crimea.

His entire entourage, with Vice-president Yanayev at the forefront, moves to attack. On August 19, a three-day coup begins. Tanks surround the so-called White House—the seat of the government and of the Parliament of the Russian Federation, as well as the office of its president, Boris Yeltsin. Yeltsin condemns the conspirators and organizes a defense of the White House.

The coup is suppressed and its leaders are imprisoned. It is revealed later that the tank corps sent out to battle for control over the nuclear superpower had been given nothing to eat for two days. Many of them did not have boots—they were wearing sneakers. The women helping to defend the White House took pity on them, went off to their homes, and brought them back something to eat. The fortified tank corps assured the compassionate ladies that they would not fire—and they kept their promise. Several days later, the Moscow press reported that when the coup was beginning, the mother of its leader, Yanayev, was lying in the Kremlin hospital. At the news of the revolt, which would give power to her son, the hospital's patients dragged themselves out of their beds and went to the old woman to give her their most heartfelt congratulations. When the revolt failed and Yanayev was arrested, these same patients again dragged themselves out of their beds, but this time they went to the director of the hospital, categorically demanding the expulsion of the old woman.

Gorbachev returns from the Crimea. On Sunday, August 25, the funeral of the three Russian victims of the latest events takes place. A million people converge on the Kremlin, where the procession begins, to pay their respects. I hear someone's faraway voice, reaching me from a loudspeaker. People in the crowd are talking; no one is paying any attention.

"Who is that speaking?" I ask.

"Gorbachev," someone answers, and keeps on talking.

No one is listening to Gorbachev any longer; he has ceased to interest people.

• • •

HISTORY IS MADE before our eyes, at every moment, every hour. I am witness during this funeral to the birth of a new class. As we are standing on Kalinin Prospekt waiting for the front of the funeral procession, a tall young man in a shabby oilcloth coat walks up to the crowd and cries: "Defenders of the White House, step forward!"

Silence. No one moves. But after several more requests, a student—judging by his appearance—emerges from the crowd. A moment later, someone else. Before long, a large group of these defenders has gathered. The man in the oilcloth coat soon realizes that the volunteers are starting to form a crowd of their own, so he stops the recruiting. He begins to write down the last names of those who have stepped forth and tells them to come to a meeting on the following Tuesday. They will form an organization, or the movement of the Defenders of the White House. They will receive badges and identification cards. Some years from now they will become ministers, generals, ambassadors.

AFTER THE AUGUST coup Gorbachev resigns as secretary-general of the CPSU. Soon thereafter, Yeltsin dissolves and illegalizes the Communist Party. I am in Kiev at the time. The massive building of the Ukrainian CP is glaringly deserted. Two policemen stand in front of the main entrance, replying to every question with silence and a shrug of the shoulders. And where is the support of the system, the Party apparat? They have already managed to assume new administrative positions in government and commerce or are heading up joint ventures—outposts of the nascent capitalism.

Gorbachev must feel increasingly alone. He is still enormously popular in the West. The West would like to live in harmony with the rulers of the Kremlin, but it has one condition—that they be likable, that they smile, that they be well dressed, relaxed, cheerful, humorous, courteous. And now, after six hundred years of hopeless waiting, such a man appears: Gorbachev! London and Paris, Washington and Bonn, all open wide their arms, rejoice. What a discovery! What a relief!

Elderly American ladies set off in droves to visit Russia.

"Let's go to Moscow! Let's have lunch with Gorbi!"

Russians observe all this wide-eyed.

The Russian peers of the American lady tourists, standing in line for hours for a piece of meat or cheese, regard the secretary-general with somewhat less enthusiasm.

He must of course be aware of this. He must feel the emptiness all around him growing. One of the pillars of the system is the so-called *telefonnoye pravo* (law of the telephone), by which the more highly situated official telephones the one below him and issues instructions. Dismiss Smirnov. Execute Korsakov. The more lowly situated functionary must perform as told without asking any questions. If he refuses, he himself will be dismissed or executed. Such a system of communication ensures that later there will be no paper trail, no proof of decision making. Responsibility vanishes into thin air. *Telefonnoye pravo* also works in the opposite direction. Before the more lowly situated official makes any decision, he calls the higher one and asks for his approval. Thus, among other things, it is the number of telephone calls from below, their kind and significance, that allow the higher official to ascertain whether he is still important. Many former Party bosses have written in their memoirs that they concluded that their fall was being prepared from the fact that the telephones on their desks rang with decreasing frequency, then fell silent altogether. This signaled the end of one's career, demotion, dismissal, and—once—death.

At the end of 1991, the telephones on Gorbachev's desk ring less and less frequently. The center of power has moved elsewhere: as of June 12, the president of the Russian Federation is Boris Yeltsin, who gradually seizes the reins of government over the greater part of the territories of the Imperium.

It is Yeltsin who in November suspends and illegalizes the ruling Communist Party. (At that point it has close to twenty million members.) It is on his initiative, without Gorbachev's knowledge (or at least without his consent), that the leaders of the Russian Federation, as well as of the Belorussian and Ukrainian republics, meet at the beginning of December in the Białowieża forest and resolve to create a new union—the Commonwealth of Independent States. Two weeks later, the leaders of the five Central Asian republics join this initiative. The shape of the new Imperium starts to emerge.

Gorbachev remains alone.

On December 25 he resigns as president of the USSR. The red flag with the hammer and sickle is removed from the Kremlin.

The USSR ceases to exist.

I FOLLOWED the fate of perestroika and the process of the downfall of the Imperium on two screens simultaneously:

- on the screen of a television set (or, rather, on the screens of dozens of television sets, because I was constantly changing cities, train stations, hotels, and apartments), as well as
- on the screen of the country's ordinary, daily reality, which surrounded me during my travels.

It was an unusual collision of two theaters:

- the theater of high politics (the television transmitted for hours on end the deliberations of the Supreme Council, of various congresses and conferences), as well as
- the theater of pedestrian existence—lines on a dark and freezing morning, nights in cold Siberian apartments, joy at the news that a mess hall had been opened and that one would be able to get a bowl of warm soup.

This schizophrenic perception in two different dimensions directed my attention toward the fundamental, even unbridgeable, gap that exists in our epoch between the time of material culture (or everyday life) and the time of political events. In the Middle Ages, both these times had a more or less convergent, compatible rhythm: cities were built over centuries and dynasties lasted centuries.

Today it is different: cities are still built over decades, but rulers often change every few years or even every few months. The political stage revolves many times faster than the stage of our daily existence. Regimes change, governing parties and their leaders change, but man lives just as he previously had—he still does not have an apartment or a job; the houses are still shabby, and there are potholes in the roads; the arduous task of making ends meet still goes on from dawn to dusk.

Perhaps that is why many people turn away from politics: it is for them an alien world, animated by a rhythm different from the one that punctuates the life of the average human being.

Television contributed greatly to the collapse of the Imperium. Merely by showing political leaders as normal people, by allowing everyone to look at them from up close—to see how they quarrel and become nervous, how they make mistakes and how they perspire, how they win, but also how they lose—by this lifting of the curtain and thus admitting the people to the highest and most exclusive salons, the salutary and liberating demystification of power took place.

Belief in the mystical nature of power had been one of the tenets of Russian political culture. As late as the middle of the nineteenth century, portraits of the czar—as saint—hung in the churches. The Bolsheviks adopted this tradition readily and with alacrity. The lives of the leaders were enveloped in the deepest mystery. The leader resembled a pharaoh/mummy. He walked stiffly, did not smile, and remained silent, his gaze fixed on an indeterminate point in space. Staffs of Sovietologists extrapolated the structure of power in the Kremlin by analyzing the sequence in which names appeared in various communiqués. And they were right to do so, because detailed and rigid instructions governed the sequence, the number of times, the exact page of the newspaper, and the size of type in which the name of a given leader could be printed. Functionaries responsible for Party protocol watched over this obsessively. Look, Mikoyan stepped onto the platform ahead of Ustinov, there's something to this! And all of Moscow would be abuzz with gossip and conjectures.

The growing role of television in politics has led all coup

plotters to change their tactics: formerly, they would assault presidential palaces, governmental and parliamentary seats; now they try first and foremost to gain control of the television-station building. Recent battles in Vilno and Tbilisi, in Bucharest and in Lima, were waged over television stations, not the president's palace. The screenplay of the latest film about a coup d'état: tanks roll out at dawn to capture the television station while the president sleeps peacefully, the Parliament building is dark; there isn't a soul around. The plotters are headed for where the real power lies.

EACH GREAT transformation, change of regime, social revolution, is divided into three stages:

- The period of the destruction of the old system
- The period of transition
- The period of the construction of the new order

The former Soviet Imperium finds itself currently in the period of transition in which elements of the old system mingle with the forerunners of the new order. The notion of the transitional period is today the answer to everything. Things aren't going well? Too bad, it's a transitional period. Supplies are inadequate? That's understandable; it's a transitional period. The old bosses are still ruling? Don't worry; it's only a transitional period.

Taking into consideration the immensity of the country, as well as the fact that profound historical processes take long stretches of time, one can assume that this transitional period will last quite a number of years.

The main task, content, and idea of the transitional period are implementing large-scale economic and political reform, changing the regime, and creating a new quality of life.

Two historians—the Russian Natan Eydelman and the American Richard Pipes—define the two fundamental perspectives on all reforms in Russia.

Eydelman: Reform in Russia always came from above. The call always had to originate at the very summit of power, gradually trickle down, and there be realized. This feature was responsible for the limited character of the reforms. At a certain moment the impetus for reform weakened, the reform got stuck, stood still.

Pipes: Reforms in Russia are dictated by external circumstances and events. One such circumstance might be a Russian setback in the international arena, the country's undue marginalization in the game to control the world. Russia's shrinking international role is an argument for the reform camp, which persuades conservatives and other opponents that the country should be rendered efficient and modernized so that it can regain its global standing.

That is how it was until now. How it will be in the future—time will tell.

As I mentioned, Sovietologists did not foresee the sudden collapse of the USSR. But even those who believed and prophesied that this superpower would one day fall expressed fears that before the Bolsheviks would surrender power and depart, they would set the country afire and drown it in a sea of blood.

Nothing of the kind happened.

The fall of communism in this state occurred relatively bloodlessly, and in ethnic Russia, completely bloodlessly. The great Ukraine announced its independence without a single shot being fired. Likewise Belorussia.

We are witnessing in the contemporary world the growing phenomenon of velvet revolutions, bloodless revolutions, or—as Isaac Deutscher expressed it—unfinished revolutions.

Characteristically in these revolutions, although the old forces are departing, they are not departing completely, and the battle of the new with the old is simultaneously accompanied by various adaptive processes, taking place on both sides of the barricade. The operative principle is the avoidance of aggressive, bloodthirsty confrontations.

It is interesting that today blood flows only where blind nationalism enters the fray, or zoological racism, or religious fundamentalism—in other words, the three black clouds that can darken the sky of the twenty-first century. In places where it is a matter of the transformation of the social structure and the various forms of class struggle that accompany this, the process takes place much more gently and, yes, bloodlessly.

GOING BACK TO RUSSIA: What remains today, in 1994, of the old system, of the former USSR? There remains:

- The old nomenclature. It is still in power. It is the governmental, economic, military, and police bureaucracy. All told, as Russian sociologists compute, around eighteen million people. There is no alternative to this nomenclature for now. The opposition never did exist as an organized force. Dissidents were always few in number, and the majority of them left the country anyway. Some time has to pass before a new political class will arise. It is a process that always takes years.
- Two enormous armies: the Russian army (formerly the Red), as well as domestic troops. There are the border troops and the railroad troops. The air force and the navy. All told—several million people.
- The powerful KGB and the militia.
- All of middle and heavy industry, still in the hands of the state, including the highly built-up military-industrial complex, an enormous armaments machine employing some sixteen million people in production and in research institutes. The captains of this industry play an important and active role in political life.
- The state as landowner. In agriculture, kolkhozes and sovkhozes predominate.
- The whole sphere of old habits of thought, of social behavior, and of benighted views that had been inculcated into people for decades.
- The old legal system.

In addition to these institutions of the old regime, there is also another large and tragic legacy of communism—the awareness of the terror and repression, of the persecutions that began in 1917 and that lasted for decades, assuming in certain years the character of mass extermination. The historians and demographers who occupy themselves with this matter differ significantly in their estimates of the scale of the perpetrated murder. The minimum estimate was calculated by the demographer Siergei Maksundov. According to him, between 1918 and 1953, 54 million citizens of the USSR perished of unnatural causes (including the victims of the First and Second World Wars). The maximum estimate is given by Professor I. Kurganov, who computed that between 1918 and 1958, in the camps, in prisons, and on the fronts of both world wars, 110.7 million citizens of the USSR lost their lives (*Znamia*, January 1990).

Another kind of legacy of the totalitarian system is the universal poverty of this society. The poverty of apartments, the poverty of the kitchen, the poverty of life.

The third legacy is the staggering demoralization of significant portions of society—the growth of all types of gangs, the terror exercised by armed bands, the criminal power of the rackets. In addition, the ubiquitous presence of the most diverse mafias, reaching as far as the highest rungs of power. The active and impudent black market in weapons, including missiles. The defiant and terrifying thievery. Epidemic corruption. Alcoholism, rape, cynicism, as well as omnipresent, common churlishness.

The fourth and final legacy is the ecological depredations—smoky cities, the universal lack of ventilation in places of work, poisoned rivers and lakes, nuclear-waste dumps. And above all, fifty-six antiquated and overburdened nuclear power plants—fifty-six potential Chernobyls, which nevertheless cannot be closed down because they illuminate large cities and supply energy to many factories.

THE PERIOD of transition in which the Imperium now finds itself, and in which it will remain for years, actually began in 1991. In its course, the gap between the time of material culture and the time of political events might become even more pronounced. There will certainly be many political developments; in material progress—significantly fewer.

What is happening on the political stage? A fierce battle for power is being waged by various groups. Anti-Yeltsin forces want to overthrow the president and his government. It is difficult to determine clearly which of these groups standing on either side of the barricade are progressive and which conservative, difficult to say whether in general such criteria have any meaning or application here. Officially, it is said that Yeltsin's group wants reform and the opposition groups (active mainly in the Parliament) do not. But is it really this way? The need for reform is today an objective necessity dictated by the time and the situation, and any team that attains power must somehow reform and change the disintegrating economy, because otherwise the country will perish, and that very team with it.

Of course there is the question of the tempo of reform. But how can one measure and define this? Experts maintain that in 1992 Russia took a step forward, but that this step could have been larger—and even, significantly larger. In other words, while the country has apparently taken a step forward, has it really just stayed in place? As a result, the society is tired and disenchanted. Perhaps it is disenchanted because Yeltsin and the many Western experts advising him estimated the chances of reform too optimistically, forgetting that reform will mean the transformation of a reality that is a granite boulder shaped over seventy years by blood and iron. How much time, strength, and money one must have to crumble this boulder! It seems to me, the backwardness of this country, its indigence, neglect, and ruination, are so great that a year seems too short a period during which to expect clear progress. Let us wait ten, twenty, years.

And yet this year of disenchantments has been sufficient to put a chill on the political atmosphere of the country.

Everyone has forgotten about perestroika and glasnost.

The democratic camp, so active during the struggle against communism, has been pushed to the margins of the political stage and finds itself either in disarray or simply forgotten. In general, democracy is spoken about less and less in Russia.

A mood of waiting and apathy prevails throughout society; people are largely apolitical.

Forces calling for the consolidation of power (especially of central power) and a strong, mighty nation are gaining the upper hand. It is a climate that encourages authoritarian methods of government, favorable to various forms of dictatorship.

AND THE FUTURE?

A difficult question. Almost no prognoses about the contemporary world come true. Futurology is in crisis; it has lost its prestige. The human imagination, shaped for thousands of years by a small, simple, and static world, today cannot grasp, is no match for, the reality that surrounds it, which is augmenting at a rapid rate (especially due to the advances in electronics and the accretion of information), in which there is increasingly more of everything, in which millions of particles, elements, units, and beings are in continual motion, in battle, in new configurations, arrangements, and assemblages, all of which it is no longer possible to seize, to stop, or to describe.

Despite these difficulties, one can assume that three processes will come to predominate in Russian life.

The first is the battle between the forces of integration and disintegration. Nationalism. Russians will want to maintain a large and strong state, an imperial superpower, whereas various non-Russian minorities will pursue more and more explicitly their own, autonomous goals. These minorities now constitute only twenty percent of the population of the Russian Federation (eighty percent, or 120 million, are Russians), but the non-Russian population is growing at a rate five times greater than the Russian, which means that the percentage of Russians is decreasing rapidly. The dominance of the Russian language is likewise shrinking. Fewer and fewer people in the territories of the former USSR speak Russian, and it is being studied less and less. In the course of my journey, I had difficulty communicating in Russian in several places, especially when speaking with young people. Older people know Russian best, the young know it less well, and small children almost not at all.

(About Russians still: twenty-six million of them live beyond the borders of the Russian Federation, chiefly in the Ukraine and in Kazakhstan. Their future is uncertain.)

The process of the "Asiatization" of the Russian Federation caused by the rapid increase of the non-Russian population is accelerated by the emigration of Germans and especially the large emigration of Jews. The latter feel threatened by the growing anti-Semitism, the specter of new persecutions and pogroms.

This battle between the forces of integration and disintegration might also take place among the republics over the question of borders. The question concerning the borders of the territories of what was once the USSR is a potential time bomb. Between 1921 and 1980, the then republics of the union underwent more than ninety territorial changes and border revisions. In 1990, there were more than fifty border conflicts among them, and today that number is even higher. Many of these borders, as in Africa, cut across lands inhabited by the same people. (Such is the case with the border between Tajikistan and Uzbekistan.)

The confrontation between Christianity and Islam might become another source of this border conflict. Islam is undergoing a violent rebirth, is the religion of people speaking Turkic languages, and there are around sixty million of these people in the territories of the former USSR.

Besides the battle between forces of integration and disintegration, a second process will be the progressive polarization of society according to the material conditions of life. At one pole the rich will congregate (and grow richer), at the other the poor (and grow poorer). As in every society with a low standard of living, the contrasts in Russia will be especially sharp, striking, provocative. This will be capitalism, or pseudocapitalism, in its most primeval, ruthless, aggressive form.

The third process will be development itself. I define the nature of this development with an awkward term—enclave development. In a highly developed European country, in Holland, for example, or Switzerland, the entire material world around us is developed at more or less the same level: the houses are neatly painted, there are panes in all the windows, the asphalt on the roads is smooth and the traffic lines well demarcated, the stores everywhere are well stocked, the restaurants are warm and clean, the streetlamps are lit, and the lawns are evenly mowed. In a country with enclave development, however, the landscape looks different. An elegant bank stands amid shabby apartment buildings; a luxurious hotel is surrounded by slums; from a brightly illuminated airport one plunges into the darkness of a grim, squalid city; beside the glittering display window of a Dior boutique, the dirty, empty, and unlit windows of local shops; next to impressive cars, old, stinking, crowded city buses. Capital (largely foreign) has constructed its fragrant and shining sanctuaries, these excellent enclaves, but it has neither the means to nor any intention of developing the rest of the country.

RUSSIANS ARE debating—what should be done? Some say: Return to the roots, to old Russia. Solzhenitsyn maintains that czarist Russia was a splendid country, "rich and flowering" (Aleksandr Solzhenitsyn, *How to Rebuild Russia?*). Then, unfortunately, the Bolsheviks came and ruined everything. And yet witnesses of that earlier epoch paint a less idyllic picture of Russia:

> And once again after years I traverse your roads,
> And once again I find you, the same, unchanged!
> Your deadness, immobility, and senselessness.
> Your fallow lands
> And thatchless cottages and rotten walls.
> Your squalor, foul air, boredom, the same dirt as
> earlier,
> And the same servile gaze, now impudent, now
> dejected.
> And although you were freed from slavery,
> You do not know what to do with freedom—
> you, the people . . .
> And everything is as it once was.
>
> (Ivan Turgenev, "The Dream")

And Anton Chekhov wrote in 1890:

> . . . we have let *millions* of people rot in prison, destroying them carelessly, thoughtlessly, barbarously; we drove

> people in chains through the cold across thousands of miles, infected them with syphilis, depraved them, multiplied criminals, and placed the blame for all this on red-nosed prison wardens. All civilized Europe knows now that it is not the wardens who are to blame, but all of us, yet this is no concern of ours, we are not interested. (*Letters*, volume 1)

Return to the old culture? But Russian culture was either aristocratic or peasant—whereas now there is no aristocracy or peasantry. The middle class, the bourgeoisie, was never numerous here—and was, frequently, foreign.

THE PROBLEMS, dilemmas, that face this society, and above all the intelligentsia, the democrats.

For instance, society and the state. How can one involve society in governing the country? How is the state to be democratized?

The Russian land, its characteristics and resources, favor the power of the state. The soil of native Russia is poor, the climate cold, the day, for the greater part of the year, short. Under such natural conditions, the earth yields meager harvests, there is recurrent famine, the peasant is poor, too poor to become independent. The master or the state has always had enormous power over him. The peasant, drowning in debts, has nothing to eat, is a slave.

Simultaneously, it is a land rich in natural resources—in oil, in gas, in iron ore. But these are natural resources whose exploitation and profits are easy to monopolize, particularly by a strong bureaucratic-authoritarian state. In this way both the soil's poverty and its riches undermine the people and bolster the regime. It is one of the great paradoxes of Russia.

AND YET this country's future can be seen optimistically. Large societies have great internal strength. They have sufficient vital energy and inexhaustible supplies of all kinds of power so as to be able to raise themselves up from the most grievous setbacks and emerge from the most serious crises.

China was able to lift itself up from the depths of humiliation and hunger and to begin to develop independently and successfully. Likewise India. Likewise Brazil and Indonesia. The large populations of these countries, their complex cultures, their ability to endure and their ambition to create, have produced, even under difficult circumstances, astonishing results. This general law of human evolution certainly applies to Russia as well.

And one more thing: the West, whom Russia fascinates but also fills with fear, is always ready to come to its aid, if only in the interests of its own peace. The West will refuse others, but it will always help Russia.

OVER THE FIELDS of Russia, in the winter, Nicholas from Leo Tolstoy's *War and Peace* drives his troika:

> Again checking his horses, Nicholas looked around him. They were still surrounded by the magic plain bathed in moonlight and spangled with stars.
>
> "Zakhár is shouting that I should turn to the left, but why to the left?" thought Nicholas. "Are we getting to the Melyukóvs'? Is this Melyukóvka? Heaven only knows where we are going, and heaven knows what is happening to us—"

## A NOTE ABOUT THE AUTHOR

*Ryszard Kapuściński was born in eastern Poland in 1932. After studying Polish history at Warsaw University, he began work as a domestic reporter. Later, as a foreign correspondent for the Polish Press Agency (until 1981), he gained critical and popular praise for his coverage of civil wars, revolutions, and social conditions in the Third World. In Latin America, Africa, and the Middle East, he ventured into the "bush"—the word that has become his trademark—to search out hidden stories. In addition to his books on the Third World, Kapuściński has written about the Polish provinces and the Asian and Caucasian republics of the Soviet Union. His other books include* Another Day of Life, Shah of Shahs, The Emperor *and* The Soccer War. *He lives in Warsaw.*

## A NOTE ON THE TYPE

*The text of this book was set in Sabon, a typeface designed by Jan Tschichold (1902–1974), the well-known German typographer. Because it was designed in Frankfurt, Sabon was named for the famous Frankfurt typefounder Jacques Sabon, who died in 1580 while manager of the Egenolff foundry.*

*Based loosely on the original designs of Claude Garamond (c. 1480–1561), Sabon is unique in that it was explicitly designed for hot-metal composition on both the Monotype and Linotype machines as well as for film composition.*

*Composed by Crane Typesetting Service, Inc.*
*West Barnstable, Massachusetts*

*Printed and bound by The Haddon Craftsmen,*
*Scranton, Pennsylvania*

*Designed by Iris Weinstein*